T THRU DANE COUNTY-1832

ce Records - February 20, 1943
LN, Land Office Clerk,
UBBERT.

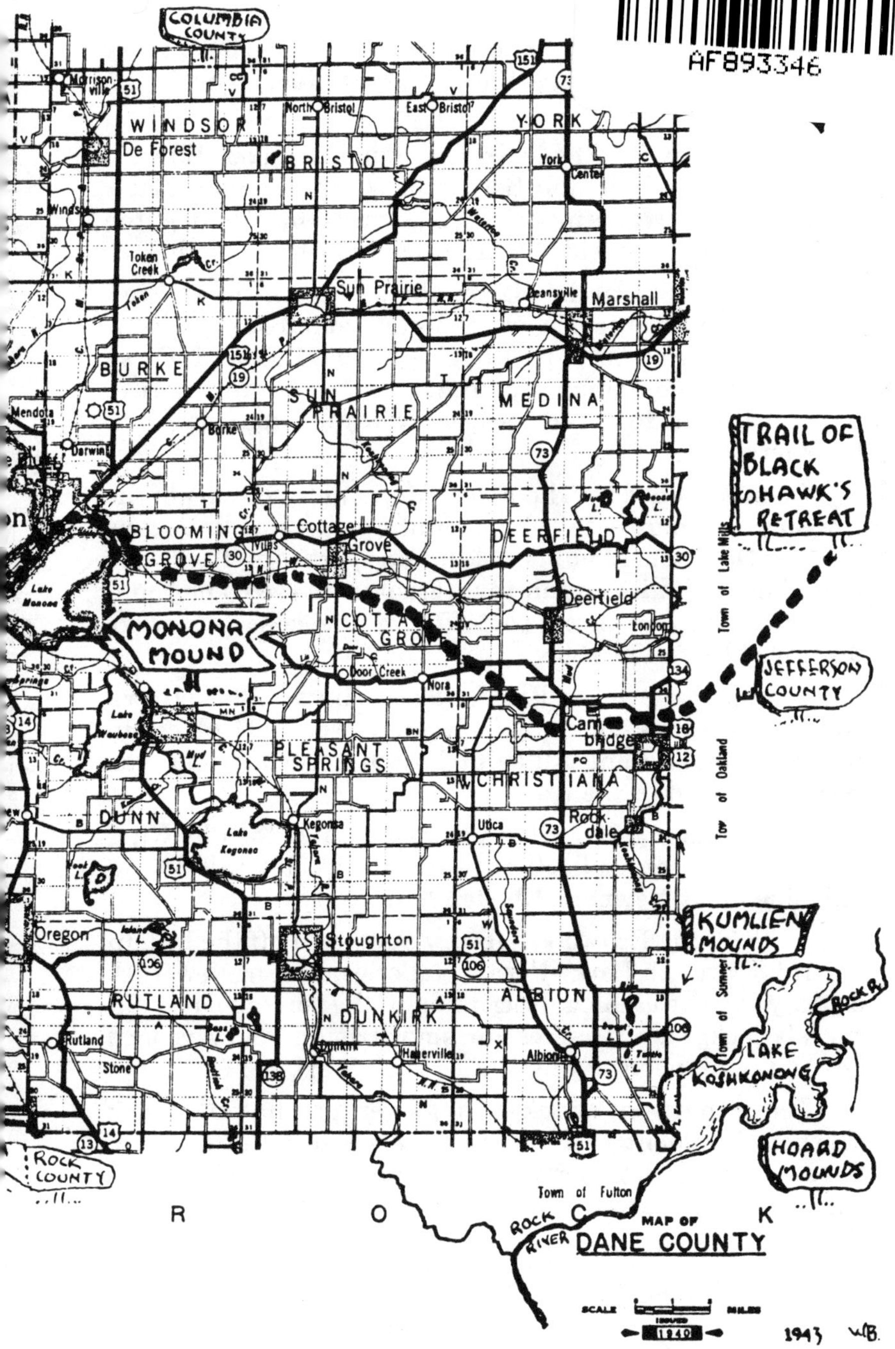

FRONT COVER

Makataimeshekiakiak [Black Sparrow Hawk, 1767-1838], Sac, 1833, oil on panel 29″ x 10¾″ by Charles Bird King (1785-1862) is reproduced by courtesy of The Warner Collection of Gulf States Paper Corporation, Tuscaloosa, Alabama.

King, born in Rhode Island, studied under Edward Savage in New York and Benjamin West in London. Later he settled in Washington, D.C., where he became the principal artist-in-residence from 1816 until his death.

Between 1821 and 1842 (in the pre-camera era), King painted the portraits of more than one hundred prominent Indians leaders who were brought to Washington, D.C., as guests of the government as part of an elaborate effort to influence them to accept peaceably white expansion into their territories.

Commissioned by Thomas L. McKenney, founder of the Bureau of Indian Affairs, the paintings became known as the War Department gallery of Indians portraits. They were placed in the Smithsonian Institution in 1858 as a national treasure. All but three portraits in the collection were destroyed by fire in 1865.

Strangely, however, King's 1833 portrait of Black Hawk was NOT commissioned by McKenney, was NOT placed in the War Department galley of Indian portraits, and was NOT destroyed in the fire.

It was among 21 Indian portraits bequeathed by King from his personal collection to the Redwood Library and Athenaeum of Newport, Rhode Island.

In 1970, the Redwood Library auctioned off the Indian portraits through Parke-Bernet Galleries, Inc., in New York on May 21. The catalog description of the portrait says, "In the left background, flames and smoke rising from a wooded island (an allusion to the Black Hawk War)."

Ten of the twenty-one paintings were purchased by Jack Warner, President of the Gulf States Paper Corporation. Seven more Indian portraits by Charles Bird King have since been added to the Warner Collection.

The Indian portraits quickly became one of the main attractions of the company's corporate headquarters in Tuscaloosa, Alabama. Public tours are conducted daily (after working hours on week days).

The Battle of
WISCONSIN HEIGHTS

Best wishes to
TOM STEWART
from
C. B. Thayer

5/10/83
from Mom & Dad

The Battle of
WISCONSIN HEIGHTS

An Eye-Witness Account of the Black Hawk War of 1832

Compiled and Edited
by
Crawford Beecher Thayer

The Battle of Wisconsin Heights

FIRST EDITION

This volume is number 140 of a limited printing of 3000 Sesquicentennial First Edition copies published in commemoration of the 150th Anniversary of the Black Hawk war.

C. B. Thayer

ISBN 0-9611000-1-X

Printed in the United States of America by Banta.

BLACK HAWK: Watercolor and pencil "Sketch from the life by J. [James] R. Lambdin Louisville 1834". Reproduced by courtesy of the Edward E. Ayer Collection, The Newberry Library, Chicago, Illinois. Lambdin was director of the Pennsylvania Academy of Fine Arts from 1845 to 1864.

DEDICATION

to

LYMAN C. DRAPER

(1815 - 1891)

GENTLE SCHOLAR & EDITOR
COMPULSIVE COLLECTOR
and
CO-FOUNDER - SECRETARY
of Wisconsin's
STATE HISTORICAL SOCIETY
"His Chiefest Monument"

Whose Vast Draper Collection
of Pre-Territorial Wisconsin
and Trans-Alleghany
Historical Manuscripts and Papers
Constitutes a Priceless Legacy
of Primary Source Material
for a Nation Seeking Its Roots
in the Pioneer Life of the American Frontier.

TABLE OF CONTENTS

Acknowledgements: Photos on pp. L, LII, 23, 25, 27, 32, 62, 130, 132, 230, and 244 were reproduced by arrangement with the State Historical Society of Wisconsin. Ne-a-pope (p. 165) was provided by the National Museum of American Art, Smithsonian Institution, gift of Mrs. Joseph Harrison, Jr. Madison at night (p. 119) by Nevin Vivian is a black-and-white print from his famous color photograph. Historical markers at Lake Mills (p. 105), Bascom Hill (p. 121), and at Highway 12 near Sauk City (p. 257) are C.B.Thayer photos. Historical marker at Hustisford (pp. 91 and 95) were provided by Herbert Neuenschwander. The Fort Atkinson, Wisconsin, Historical Society provided Atkinson (p. LIX), Fort Atkinson (p. 11), Black Hawk (p. 254), Troop Positions (p. 137) and Dodge (p. 48). The map (inside front cover) is from *The Wisconsin Archeologist,* December, 1943. War theater map (p. LVII) is by the *La Crosse Tribune.* Survey maps (pp. 150, 153) and field notebook pages (p. 267) were provided by the Board of Commissioners of Public Lands, Madison. Photos of the Editor are by Jim Jewell (p. 342), *Daily Jefferson County Union* staff (p. 345), Tom Kohl (p. 347), and Ted Ninman (p. 349), *Janesville Gazette* staff photographer. Except for pictures of Black Hawk credited elsewhere, all other photos were provided by the Illinois State Historical Library, Springfield, Illinois.

ILLUSTRATIONS

THE BATTLE OF WISCONSIN HEIGHTS

APPENDIX A: Eye-Witness Reports

APPENDIX B: Black Hawk's Trail

PROFILE OF THE EDITOR

ACKNOWLEDGMENTS

Of Chris Blumer, *Daily Jefferson County Union,* Fort Atkinson, Wisconsin.

Of Bob Brown, *The Janesville Gazette,* Fort Atkinson, Wisconsin.

Of Marshall Cook, *Directions,* Edgerton, Wisconsin.

Of Monroe H. Fabian, Associate Curator, The National Portrait Gallery, Smithsonian Institution, Washington, D. C.

Of Doris Fletcher, Arts Project Manager, The Warner Collection, Gulf States Paper Corporation, Tuscaloosa, Alabama.

Of Hugh Highsmith, The Highsmith Company, Inc., Fort Atkinson, Wisconsin.

Of Jim Jewell, Free-Lance Writer and Photographer, Linden, Wisconsin.

Of Judy Kellers, Administrative Assistant, Board of Commissioners of Public Lands, Madison, Wisconsin.

Of Helmut Knies, Hoard Museum, Fort Atkinson, Wisconsin.

Of Tom Kohl, Opportunities, Inc., Fort Atkinson, Wisconsin.

Of Mary Michals, Curator of Prints and Photographs, Illinois State Historical Library, Springfield, Illinois.

Of Bob Mullen, Free-Lance Writer and Photographer, Eastman, Wisconsin.

Of Herbert E. Neuenschwander, "Mr. History" of Hustisford, Wisconsin.

Of Lonni Nidy, *The Sauk Prairie Star,* Sauk City, Wisconsin.

Of Pat Peckham, *The Sauk Prairie Star,* Sauk City, Wisconsin.

Of Howie Stiff, artist, Fort Atkinson, Wisconsin, who did all keyline paste-ups for this book.

Of Hannah Swart, Curator, Hoard Museum, Fort Atkinson, Wisconsin.

Of Chris Wanie, *Daily Jefferson County Union,* Fort Atkinson, Wisconsin.

Of Evelyn A. Weiskircher, Shullsburg, Wisconsin, who provided the John Ryan manuscript.

Of Ellen M. Whitney, Compiler and Editor of the Black Hawk War Collections of the Illinois State Historical Library, Springfield, Illinois.

Of Myrna Williamson, Reference Assistant, Iconographic Collections, State Historical Society of Wisconsin, Madison, Wisconsin.

Of Ione Winkelman, Johnson Creek, Wisconsin, who set all of the type for this book.

Of the staffs of the following institutions, for innumerable courtesies: Fort Atkinson (Wisconsin) Historical Society and Hoard Museum, Illinois State Historical Library (Springfield), the National Portrait Gallery of the Smithsonian Institution (Washington, D. C.), National Archives and Records Service (Washington, D. C.),

The Newberry Library (Chicago), Tulane University Library (New Orleans), and the University of Wisconsin-Platteville Area Research Center.

PREFACE

" 'Wisconsin Heights' fairly promised to prove a watchword, before which 'Tippecanoe,' &c., might hang its head."

—Lt. Philip St. George Cooke,
6th Infantry Regiment, U.S. Army

T*he Battle of Wisconsin Heights* is an eye-witness account of the Black Hawk war as it moved through today's Dane and Dodge counties of Wisconsin in July, 1832.

It details the movements of the Illinois and Michigan Territory (Wisconsin) mounted militia volunteers under the commands of James D. Henry and Henry Dodge as they "disobey" the orders of Brigadier General Henry Atkinson and so "win" the encounter with Black Hawk and his starving band of some 1,200 men, women, and children, including about 500 warriors.

Chronologically, the events described in *The Battle of Wisconsin Heights* follow those of *Hunting A Shadow: The Search for Black Hawk* and preceed the action described in *Massacre at Bad Axe,* other volumes in the Black Hawk War Eye-Witness Series.

These volumes are published in recognition of the Sesquicentennial of the Black Hawk war of 1832, the last Indian war in the Northwest Territory and the next-to-last

Indian war East of the Mississippi river. (The long Seminole war in Florida finally petered out in 1841.)

Two people have been particularly instrumental in making this eye-witness series possible: Ellen M. Whitney of the Illinois State Historical Library and Lyman C. Draper of the State Historical Society of Wisconsin.

Ellen M. Whitney organized, edited, and published the Illinois library's vast holdings of the original source material. Her monumental, four-volume work, *The Black Hawk War 1831-1832,* brings to light for the first time a missing segment of our heritage after its being buried in the original handwriting for nearly 150 years.

Lyman C. Draper, long-time Recording Secretary of the Wisconsin organization, exerted great effort to obtain reminiscences from early settlers of Wisconsin. He also personally interviewed Wisconsin Indians so their stories could be recorded for posterity.

Their primary source material and much more raw material (in the National Archives in Washington, D.C., for example) now cries out to be woven into a chronological narrative.

My purpose in developing the Black Hawk War Eye-Witness Series was (1) to locate as many primary source references to the Black Hawk war as possible, (2) to group these individual pieces of information by subject matter, and then (3) to place them in the proper chronological sequence to create for the first time ever a definitive and coherent narrative of the events of the war.

In *The Battle of Wisconsin Heights,* the story of the Black Hawk war of 1832 is told only in the exact words of actual participants. That is why this book is printed almost entirely in quotation marks.

The tiny superscript numbers throughout the text refer to the notes at the end of the book, notes which indicate the source for each eye-witness quotation.

If there is no closing quotation mark at the end of a paragraph, it simply indicates that the quotation continues into subsequent paragraphs until the quotation is closed by quotation marks and the superscript is added to direct you to the source of the paragraphs.

This book, you see, was written by eye-witnesses to history. I have simply compiled all of their material (that I could find) and fit it together in chronological order, from July 9 to July 25, 1832, limiting the scope of this book to the activities of the troops with Brigadier General James D. Henry and Colonel Henry Dodge, activities which include the battle of Wisconsin Heights on July 21, 1832. I have put into the text each and every reference I was able to find on each and every subject. Because of these multiple references to the same event, you get the benefit of many different points of view. This provides a richer picture of what actually happened than if I had given you only one flat statement about each event, or—worse—if I had told the story in my own words rather than (as I have) in the exact words of those who were actually there and participated in the action.

Modified Myths

Eye-witness reports of the Black Hawk war, when put together into a chronological sequence, provide strong evidence that some well-accepted myths about the war simply are not true.

The most outrageous myth of the entire Black Hawk war, perhaps, is the myth that Jefferson Davis was an active participant, an idea created by Davis himself when he was interviewed in later years by Charles Aldrich for an article, "Jefferson Davis and Black Hawk", in *The Midland Monthly* magazine.

Davis described an engagement that sounds as if it were the battle of Wisconsin Heights: "We were one day pursuing the Indians," Davis said, "when we came close to the Wisconsin River. Reaching the river bank the Indians made so determined a stand and fought with such desperation that they held us in check. During this time the squaws tore bark

2d Lieutenant Jefferson A. Davis
Company B, 1st Infantry Regiment,
U.S. Army

from the trees and made little shallops, in which they floated their papooses and other impedimenta . . . across to an island; also swimming over their ponies. As soon as this was accomplished, half of the warriors plunged in and swam across, each holding his gun in one hand, and swimming with the other. As soon as they reached the opposite bank, they opened fire upon us under cover of which the other half slipped down the bank and swam in like manner. This was the most brilliant exhibition of military tactics that I ever witnessed, a feat of the most consummate management and bravery, in the face of an enemy of greatly superior numbers. . . . I have never read of anything that could compare with it. Had it been performed by white men, it would have been immortalized as one of the most splended achievements in military history."

The precision swimming routine of the Indians as imagined by Davis seems more like a water ballet in an aquatic show for tourists than like what actually happened at the battle of Wisconsin Heights.

Two facts need to be recalled at this point:

First, that Jefferson Davis was not there. He was home on leave in Woodville, Mississippi, as late at July 9, and did not rejoin his Company B, 1st Infantry Regiment, (stationed at Fort Crawford, Prairie du Chien) until August 18, 1832, still in plenty of time to take Black Hawk to prison in Jefferson Barracks, Missouri, which he did.

Second, that even if Jefferson Davis *had* been with his unit (which he wasn't) during the Black Hawk war, he would not have participated in the battle of Wisconsin Heights. From July 11 to July 17, the U.S. Army Infantry regulars under the command of Colonel Zachary Taylor were constructing the stockade at today's Fort Atkinson. Then they marched toward today's Palmyra, Wisconsin, in a second futile attempt to get across Bark river in order to find Black Hawk's hide-away island in a huge swamp. The troops with Brigadier General Henry Atkinson learned on July 20 that Black Hawk's trail had been found by the troops sent to Fort Winnebago for food, and on July 21 (the day of the battle of Wisconsin Heights) Jefferson Davis's Company marched with the others towards Blue Mound. They camped on the west bank of Rock river just below its outlet from Lake Koshkonong at about the same time the battle of Wisconsin Heights was taking place many miles away.

But, for all of this (especially since the historical marker about the Battle of Wisconsin Heights quotes Jefferson Davis's remarks), it may be as difficult to convince the casual reader that Jefferson Davis was NOT in the Black Hawk war as it is to convince the casual tourist that the concrete statue of the Indian near Oregon, Illinois, is NOT Black Hawk, even in spite of the statue's long hair and the sculptor's avowed intention of capturing the spirit of Indianness.

Black Hawk's Trail

The map of Black Hawk's escape route through Dane county (inside the front cover) was developed by A. O. Barton, one-time Dane County Register of Deeds.

He used the map to illustrate an article he wrote for *The Wisconsin Archeologist* quarterly, Volume 24, Number 4, December, 1943. His article, entitled "Black Hawk Retreat in Dane County", explains the map in detail and is reprinted near the end of this book.

Barton's map shows Black Hawk's trail as entering Dane county at Cambridge, Wisconsin. However, Hagan thinks the trail may have entered Dane county a few miles north of Cambridge, along the line of old highway 30.

Who is Hagan?

In 1945, the Wisconsin legislature (in Chapter 478, Laws of 1945) requested a report on the route through Wisconsin followed by Black Hawk's forces in 1832. William Thomas Hagan wrote the report, *Black Hawk's Route Through Wisconsin,* published in 1949 by The State Historical Society of Wisconsin.

Hagan's investigation concludes that the troops may

have discovered Black Hawk's trail within the boundaries of present-day Watertown, and that the trail went through Aztalan, Lakes Mills, north of Cottage Grove, and on to Lake Monona. From this point, Black Hawk's trail is authenticated by notations made by John Mullet, U.S. government surveyor, in his field notes in 1833.

Readin' and Writin'

Some early settlers on the frontier weren't the world's greatest spellers. That's why one of the more difficult tasks I had in editing this book was to make sure that I mispelled words correctly so they matched the spelling in the original source. Even so, the reference to the "untied states", for example, is still perfectly understandable.

But I *have* taken two liberties with original source material.

First, I separated much original material into individual action units so I could place each word, phrase, clause, sentence, or paragraph in the correct chronological position. For example, between "we marched early in the morning" and "we camped late at night" (which might very well have been just one sentence in the original source), I took the liberty of placing all of the other activities of the day.

Because of this editorial technique, several somewhat extended eye-witness reports of the battle of Wisconsin Heights were chewed up into small snippets, and the full flavor of the original was lost. For this reason I have published these reports as complete units at the end of this book. Although the battle reports of General James D. Henry and Colonel Henry Dodge appear in the main text as complete units, I have printed them again in full so the Appendix contains all known eye-witness accounts of extended length. Indeed, the reports of Cooke, Wakefield, and Black Hawk are taken from their respective published books, detailed in the Bibliography.

The second liberty I have taken with original material (for clarity and easier reading) was to create paragraphs now and then where they may not have existed in the original.

Weather Reports

A weather report, including three temperature readings, heads each chapter in this book.

These reports were kept daily by the United State Army Hospital Department at each fort. Reports used in this book were kept in a bound "Diary of the Weather" by the hospital staff at Fort Winnebago (Portage, Wisconsin).

The diary today is in the Manuscript Archives of the State Historical Society of Wisconsin in Madison, and is filed as follows: "Wis., MSS, 3 CL, Fort Winnebago".

In some instances, I have included additional weather information, taken from the body of the text itself. Because my remarks here explain the source of the weather reports, I have not given them superscript numbers (to refer to their source) in the text.

The most crucial impact of weather upon the Black Hawk war was this: It put an early end to the July 21 battle of Wisconsin Heights. Rain dampened the high grass so much that, if the troops had followed the fleeing Indians into the brush, their flintlock guns would not have fired. Thus Black Hawk and his people escaped—for a while—thanks to a rainy afternoon in 1832.

Jig Saw Puzzle

Creating these books is like locating and fitting together the scattered pieces of a giant jig-saw puzzle. Although some pieces of this historical event are still missing (perhaps in Illinois attics?) and others may be destroyed and lost forever, enough pieces have been found and do fit together to give us a glimpse into our past and to help us recapture a part of our lost heritage.

Material long since buried continues to come to light. More will appear in the future, especially as this book is read by those who have Black Hawk war letters and papers in their possession. Indeed, if you have pertinent information about any detail of the Black Hawk war, please send a photocopy of it to the Fort Atkinson Historical Society, 407 Merchants Avenue, Fort Atkinson, Wisconsin 53538, for inclusion in any subsequent revision of this Sesquicentennial Edition.

Availability

The books in this Black Hawk war eye-witness series are published privately as a labor of love and are not, therefore, readily available in most commercial outlets.

To obtain your copy of this or other volumes in this series, simple contact the Fort Atkinson Historical Society, 407 Merchants Avenue, Fort Atkinson, Wisconsin 53538.

Profile of the Editor

Some of my offspring and in-laws expressed disappointment that I had not included anything about myself in the first book I published in this series. With the help of many newspaper reporters and photographers, I have corrected this hitherto intentional omission...for whatever good it will do.

Crawford Beecher Thayer
Fort Atkinson, Wisconsin
August 27, 1982

Brigadier General Henry Atkinson,
Commander of the Right Wing
of the Western Department, U.S. Army

INTRODUCTION

*A Summary Statement of Operations Against the Sack Enemy During the Black Hawk War by Brigadier General Henry Atkinson for Colonel Roger Jones, Adjutant General, U.S. Army**

"Head Qurs. Right Wing Westn. Dept. Jefferson Barracks

"November 19, 1832

"Sir, Understanding that an impression existed or perhaps exists at this time, at Washington that I had it in my power last spring to have prevented Black Hawk from crossing the Mississippi to the East side with his [British] Band [on April 5, 1832], I claim the privilege of making a statement of facts which will, I am sure, when read exculpate me from any blame or want of decision touching the subject. To which I beg leave to add a summary statement of my operations against the Sack [Sauk] enemy during the recent campaign.

---

* EDITOR'S NOTE: The bold face type in this report indicates those events of the Black Hawk war which are developed in detail in this book.

Major General Alexander Macomb,
Commanding General of the Army

"A reference to the files of the Dept. of War will show that an order was issued on the 17th. March, by the General in Chief [Alexander Macomb] requiring me to proceed with the troops at this post [Jefferson Barracks below St. Louis] to Rock Island, and demand from the Sack and Fox tribes of Indians the principal persons concerned in the attack upon, and murder of a number of Menominie Indians near Prairie du Chien in August 1831--and further to [take] such steps as might be necessary to prevent a combi[ned attack on*] the Sacks and Foxes which it was unde[r]stood the Sioux and Menom[inies] were preparing to make.

"This order was received on the 1st of April, and in [pur]suance thereof I embarked at this place on the 8th of April (as [early as] transports could be provided,) with six companies** of the 6th Regt. on board of Steam Boats for Rock Island. Arrived at the lower rapids*** on the 10th at 2 O.C. P.M. where I received information that Black Hawk, joined by about a hundred Kickapoos, and a few Pottowattimies had, on the 5th of April crossed the Mississippi with his Band at the Yellow Banks****, a point

---

* I prefer this reading to the reading given in the published Black Hawk war papers of the Illinois State Historical Library, which is as follows: "...to prevent a combi[nation of] the Sacks and Foxes...."[1]

** Company C of Captain Henry Smith, Company E of Lieutenant Asa Richardson, and Company K of Captain Thomas Noel embarked on the steamboat Chieftain under the immediate command of Brevet Major Bennet Riley.

Company G of Captain George C. Hutter, Company D of Captain Jason Rogers, and Company I of Captain Zalmon C. Palmer embarked on the steamboat Enterprise under the immediate command of Capt Zalmon C. Palmer.[2]

*** Extending 12 miles upstream from today's Keokuk, Iowa.

**** Actually Lower Yellow Banks, today's Oquawka, Illinois.

70 miles below Rock Island, the whole force amounting to 500 well appointed horsemen besides men and boys employed in navigating their canoes, capable of bearing arms forming an efficient body of between six and seven hundred men. This was the first intimation I had of the disaffection of Black Hawk. A reference to dates will show that he crossed over three days before I set out to execute the order, at a point more than three hundred miles above me, and five days before I had any notice of his intentions to do so. On the morning of the 12th, we arrived at the Yellow Banks the place he crossed at, and whence six days before he had taken up his march for Rock River. These facts show that I had it not in my power by previous advice, or by the then existing state of things to prevent his crossing, or to arrest his march.

"At 12 O. C. on the night of the 12th. we reached Rock Island, and on the morning of the 13th. Black Hawk with his moun[ted] force were reported to be passing up on the east side of Rock [river] six miles distant from our position--some of his canoes were [also] seen passing up that river. At first I thought of attempting to ar[rest] his progress, but on viewing the whole ground I was convinced my [force] was too weak to encounter the Indian force that would be op[pose]d to me. Their canoes were in Rock river sheltered by numerous Islands that fill the first several miles of that stream. It was not possible to bring a Steam Boat to bear upon them, and there was a total absence of small craft. No practicable mode of attack was left, except taking a position at a narrow point on Rock river twelve miles above its mouth where it might be commanded with a field piece--A point the Indian force were assembling at. Under this aspect of things the question presented itself would it be prudent, indeed would it not be rash and unjustifiable to attempt to seize the pass with only two hundred men, the extent of our force, with a certainty of coming in contact with more than 600 well armed Indians ready for the conflict. I did not feel justified in making the attempt, because if unsuccessful it would give fresh confidence to the Indians, encourage the disaffected of other tribes to join them, and subject a long line of unsuspecting frontier to certain attack and massacre. Under these reflections I refrained from making an attack, and sent off at once by express, intelligence to the frontier of the danger that threatened its inhabitants--Also information to [John Reynolds] the Governor of the State of Illinois of the invasion of the State, and advising him to throw out a few companies of rangers upon the frontier, leaving to his own judgement what further steps were necessary to be taken under the existing state of things 'till the advice of the general government should be received upon the subject. I then proceeded to act in respect to obtaining a surrender from the friendly Sacks, and Foxes, the Menominie murderers, and took measures to guard against an attack upon these bands by the Sioux and Menominies as has been heretofore reported to the General in Chief.

"The Governor of Illinois without further notice ordered a large body of militia into the field and directed their march upon Rock Island. In the interim I drew from Fort Crawford [at Prairie du Chien] three companies* of the 1st Regt. of Infy., all the disposable force at that Post, desired the senior officer of militia at Galena, [Colonel James M. Strode, Commander, 27th Regiment, Illinois militia] and Genl [Henry] Dodge of Michigan [Territory] to organize the militia force under their respective commands and hold them in readiness for active service if required. At the same time ordered up supplies from St. Louis.

"On the 7th. May, Governor Reynolds arrived at a point four miles above the mouth of Rock river, with a Brigade of mounted volunteers under the immediate orders of Brigadier General [Samuel] Whiteside. Finding this force in the field, although I had not officially called for them, I deemed it advisable under all the circumstances connected with the posture of affairs to receive them into the service of the U. States, which was accordingly done on the 9th., distributed

---

* Lieutenant William L. Harris's Grenadier Company A, Captain Samuel MacRee's Light Infantry Company B, and Captain Thomas F. Smith's Battalion Company G, the entire detachment under the command of Captain Smith.[3]

provisions to them the same day, and the next morning directed their march upon Prophets Village*, forty miles above, with discretionary authority to make a stroke upon the enemy if it could be done with propriety. The regular troops moved by water the same day with supplies for the whole army for some thirty days.

"Governor Reynolds, and Genl. Whiteside on their arrival at Prophets Village availed themselves of the discretionary order they had received and proceeded to Dixons Ferry**, reaching that point on the 12th. where they were joined by [Isaiah] Stillmans Battalion of rangers. Upon the urgent appeal, I understand, of that officer and some other gentlemen who were present, Governor Reynolds ordered Major Stillman to proceed with his Battalion in pursuit of the Indians. On the evening of the 14th. he fell in with part of the Indian force near the mouth of Sycamore Creek, was defeated and put to flight. This information reached me on the 15th. thirty miles below Dixons Ferry. On the 17th. at 12 O.C. I arrived with the regular troops at this point, Dixons.

"A new state of things were now presented. My plan, which had been strongly inculcated of not striking a blow upon the Indians until it could be done with a certainty of success was destroyed by the precipitate movement of Stillmans Battalion. Nevertheless it was now necessary, as blood had been shed, to press our operation with increased energy, as it was thought the enemy could strike upon the frontier--provisions for several days were issued to the volunteers and on the morning of the 19th. the mounted force, accompanied by myself, marched upon Sycamore Creek. The regular [U.S. Army Infantry] troops under Col. [Zachary] Taylor moved by water for the same point. On the evening of this day an express from Ottowa overtook us with information that the Indians were burning houses on du Page river, on the next morning another express came up from the same point with intelligence that similar

* At todays Prophetstown, Illinois.

** At today's Dixon, Illinois.

John Reynolds, Governor of Illinois

devastations were being committed on Fox river. Col [James] Johnson who had now been put in command of Stillmans Battalion was ordered to proceed without delay to Ottowa, mouth of Fox river, to cover that frontier, his arrival was a few hours to[o] late to save the families massacred on Indian Creek. The regulars and volunteers continued their movement upon Sycamore Creek, as I was convinced that a successful stroke upon the main body of the enemy, would tend to destroy the branches also. On the 21st. Col. [William S.] Hamilton who had been sent out with five or six active men to ascertain if possible the position of the enemy met us five miles below Sycamore Creek, and reported that he had followed the trail of the Indians some fifteen miles up that stream, that they had scattered into small parties and from the direction of the various trails, they had most probably gone over to the *Big Woods* on Fox river.

"The enemy having now, as it was confidently believed, left Rock river, and their [there] being no means of transporting provisions or baggage by land for the regular troops, Gen. Whiteside, accompanied by Col. Taylor and Capt [William S.] Harney U.S. Army, was ordered to pursue with his mounted men, the trail of the enemy up Sycamore Creek, and scour the country across to Fox river, whilst the regular troops fell back to Dixons, to preserve our base of operations and the line of communication across from Peoria to Galena.

"Genl. Whiteside falling upon only detached trails continued his route across to Ottowa, urged on, no doubt, by the impatience of the volunteers to reach that point, with a view of being discharged, a privilege they already claimed upon the ground that they came out to serve but a month, and which was granted them by the Governor on the 27th. the day after the Brigade reached Ottowa. It immediately dispersed except about 250 men who volunteered to remain twenty days for the protection of the frontier. Letters from Governor Reynolds Genl. Whiteside and Col. Taylor, were brot to me at Dixons by express on the night of the 27th. detailing the failure of the mounted troops to find the enemy, and the unexpected, perplexing and embarassing information that the militia force were about to be

Captain William S. Harney,
Commander of Company K,
1st Infantry Regiment, U. S. Army

discharged. To remedy matters now as far as possible, I proceeded on the morning of the 28th. across the country with my Staff to Ottowa, a distance of fifty miles, arriving there after night, where I found the few volunteers* that had agreed to remain for the protection of the frontier unorganized and about to disperse. On the morning of the 29th. they were enrolled for twenty days, and formed into a Battalion under Col. [Jacob] Fry, an able and energetick officer,--proceeded on the 29th. to the foot of the Illinois rapids to confer with Governor Reynolds, who had the day previously gone down to embark in a Steam Boat for St. Louis. He had been advised of my arrival, by express, the night I reached Ottowa--called upon and arranged with him for a militia force to be assembled at Ottowa by the 12th. to the 15th. of the ensuing month--despatched Staff Officers for supplies of provisions, arms, ammunition, and a limited quantity of light camp equipage for the militia.

"Returned on the 31st [of May] to Ottowa, I now found myself left with only about 250 volunteers for the protection of the frontier, 'till the new levies should arrive, and although no offensive operations could be undertaken it was necessary for me to remain in person at the head of this force, to give confidence to the frontier settlers and prevent an entire breaking up, and falling back into the interior. The regular troops could not be withdrawn from Rock river without throwing open the whole country back to the Mississippi--indeed it would have been giving up control of the country to the enemy, and opening a direct and easy communication for them across the Mississippi.

"Hence the necessity of holding the command of Rock river 'till active operations could be renewed. Holding the position at Dixons and throwing out some of the regular troops, and some of the volunteers from Ottowa into the intermediate country, Galena and the mineral district were sustained, and the enemy measurably restrained and held in the upper country, an object for the moment of great importance. My situation was painful in the extreme, the

* Including Abraham Lincoln.

scalping knife was in active operation without my being able to arrest it, and public opinion was goading me on all hands for inactivity, without taking into consideration that I was stripped of all offensive means by the discharge of the Illinois militia, at a moment too, when the precipitate conduct of the Rangers under Stillman had lit up the whole frontier into a blaze. My situation was truly critical, and nothing but an unhesitating perseverance in maintaining my position, with a handful of raw militia in the very face of the enemy 'till the new levies arrived enable me finally to succeed.

"If my operations were considered slow the opinion was founded upon erroneous impressions, for, between the discharge of Whitesides Brigade over which disastrous event I had no control, and organizing and taking the field with a new force of 3000 men there did not elapse three weeks, although many of the volunteer corps were drawn from a distance of 500 miles, for whom, in the same time, an ample supply of provisions, arms, and munitions were provided, and in forty days more an arduous and fatiguing campaign closed, with entire success, by destroying and capturing the whole force of the enemy.

"Of the small force I had at Ottowa I kept constantly detached until I was ready to take the field, one or two companies in conjunction with part of the regular force in the country between Rock river and Galena, to restrain detached parties of the enemy that infested that neighborhood.

"On the 12th. of June the new levies began to assemble at the foot of the rapids of Illinois, 15 miles below Ottowa the head of Steam boat navigation, where some temporary Block houses had been thrown up for the protection of our supplies, whither I repaired, having determined to organize the new levies at this point. On the 15th. [Alexander] Posey's [First] Brigade of 1000 men was organized--On the 16th [Milton K.] Alexander's [Second] Brigade of about the same number, and on the 20th [James D.] Henry's [Third] Brigade of 1200 men. Posey's Brigade accompanied by two

Major John Dement,
Commander of Spy Battalion,
First Brigade, Illinois Militia

companies* of the 6th Regt. that had been drawn from Fort Leavenworth, now under Lieut. Col. Baker, were ordered on the 19th. to march to Dixons Ferry, and there receive the order of Genl. [Hugh] Brady who had some days before joined me and volunteered his services. This corps of volunteers were intended to cover Galena, and the mineral district, and were disposed accordingly. The Spy Battalion of the Brigade under Major [John] Dement, that was a days march in advance fell in with about 120 of the enemy near Kelloggs**, 35 miles from Dixon's and was driven back into the fortified buildings at that place with some loss--about sixty of his horses were shot down around him, when the enemy withdrew. Posey being on his march for the same point was met by a courier with information of the disastrous event.

"He hastened to the relief of Dement, the enemy were still in the neighborhood on his arrival, but night coming on he deferred a pursuit until the ensuing morning, when it was ascertained the Indian force had fled in the direction of the main body, on Koskonong Lake. A few days previous to these occurrences Captain [Adam W.] Snyder with his company of Ottowa volunteers who had been detached in the direction of Galena, had a skirmish with part of the same detachment of Indians near Kelloggs which resulted in the loss of a few lives on each side.

"Alexander's Brigade was put in march for Dixons on the 21st., and Henry's Brigade accompanied by me, on the 23rd., reached Dixon's on the 25th. Soon after my arrival there an express 'brot. information that (judging from the trail) a large body of Indians were moving in the direction of the mouth of Plum river on the Mississippi, with a view it was thought of crossing to the west of that river. Being determined not to be drawn from my plan of operations, I detached Alexander, with his Brigade, with orders to proceed in the direction of the Indian trail, as reported, and

---

* Company A under Lieutenant John Nichols and Light Company B under 2d Lieutenant Gustavus Door.[4]

** Near today's Kent, Illinois.

after intersecting it should its course be continued towards the Mississippi to pursue it with the greatest energy, if, on the contrary, its course had been changed towards the upper Lakes, as I strongly apprehended, he would join me at the mouth of Pekitolica on Rock river sixty miles above, having determined to march upon that point with the Regulars and Henry's Brigade. The regular troops amounting to about 440 men, under Col. [Zachary] Taylor, with one field piece, and Henry's Brigade consisting of about 900 (six companies having been left at Ottowa and Fort Wilborn* to cover that frontier and protect the public Stores at those points,) were put in march on the morning of the 28th. upon Lake Koskonong under the immediate orders of Brig. Genl. Brady, accompanied by myself and Staff. Capt. [Zalmon C.] Palmer with forty regulars, and Capt. [Henry L.] Webbs company of mounted men of Henry's Brigade, were left at Dixon's to hold that position and protect the public Stores.

"Our march was continued with energy up the left bank of Rock river and on the morning of the 3d of July reached the foot of Lake Koskenong, when we found the enemy had the day previously decamped and struck off in various trails on both sides of the Lake, up the country**.

"The 4th. and 5th. were consumed in ascertaining the route of the main body of the enemy, which was at length ascertained to have entered the great swamp some miles above Lake Koskenong. Genl. Alexander with his Brigade arrived on the evening of the 4th., Posey with part of his Brigade and Genl. [Henry] Dodge with a Battalion of Michigan [Territory] and Galena volunteers arrived on the right [west] bank of Lake Koskenong on the evening of the 5th.

---

* At today's LaSalle, Illinois.

** Atkinson's activities from July 1 through July 24 are detailed in *Hunting a Shadow: The Search for Black Hawk,* the volume in the Eye-Witness Series which preceeds this one chronologically.

Colonel Zachary Taylor,
Commander of U.S. Army Units,
Army of the Frontier

Brigadier General Hugh Brady
Commander of 2d Division,
Army of the Frontier

"On the morning of the 6th. Alexanders Brigade was ordered to cross Rock river at the foot of the lake, and join Dodge and march in the direction of the enemy up rock river, whilst the [U. S. Army Infantry] Regulars and Henry's Brigade marched up the east bank under Genl. Brady, Posey had been ordered to join this division of of the army with his detachment--encamped in the evening on White Water*.

"After advising Alexander and Dodge by express on the morning of the 7th. of my intention to make a stroke upon the enemy that morning if possible, He being reported to be but a few miles in advance, covered by the river and swamp that lay between us, requiring their co-operation, The troops were put in motion and moved up the river over a difficult and almost impassable route some fifteen miles where we encamped, and were joined by Alexander & Dodge.**

Finding here that we were deceived (as has since been ascertained intentionally) by our Winnebago guides as to the position of the enemy--The difficulties presented by the swamps and muddy creek, and two of the Brigades having consumed their provisions it became, by the advice of a council of war, necessary to halt for a further supply. **Henry, Alexander and Dodge were ordered to Fort Winnebago with instruction to draw twelve days rations,** and Posey to Fort Hamilton to occupy that point, Dodgeville and Kellogg's with his corps, and to intercept the march of the enemy should he break from the swamps and move in that direction. **Henry, Alexander and Dodge were instructed to pursue the enemy should they fall upon his trail in either going or returning from Fort Winnebago, and to inform me by express.***

* Actually Bark river at today's Cold Spring, Wisconsin, near Fort Atkinson.

** Punctuation in the published letter does not make sense, so I have changed the two periods after the words "possible" and "co-operation" to commas.

*** These instructions were NOT included in the original orders.

Captain Gideon Lowe
Commander of Company D,
5th Infantry Regiment, U.S. Army

"The regular troops [commanded by Colonel Zachary Taylor] in the absence of the volunteers threw up a stockade and temporary block houses* for the protection of supplies that were hourly expected, and for the accommodation of the sick who were accumulating on our hands. Genl. Brady became here, too much indisposed, of dysentary, to perform duty.

"On the 16th. a train of 36 wagons arrived with provisions by the way of the Blue Mounds from Dixons and Galena.

"It is but just to remark here, that but for the waste of provisions by the volunteers, and unavoidable losses in swimming rivers and the miring down of horses in creeks and swamps the supply would have been ample 'till the train of wagons arrived, although they were delayed, several days.

"Alexanders Brigade returned on the 17th.

"on the morning of the 19th. the regular troops, and Alexander's Brigade were put in motion and moved up Rock river [actually Bark river] to co-operate with **Henry and Dodge, who would strike Rock river some twenty miles above, on their return from Winnebago. An express from them fell upon the trail of the enemy who had broken up and left the swamps, in the direction of the Ouisconsin river, this information was promptly communicated to Henry and Dodge, and by them to me,** on the morning of the 20th. at dawn at our encampment 15 miles above Fort Koskenong**.

"They [troops of Dodge and Henry] moved in pursuit with 800 picked men, sending the lame and weak horses and dismounted men to Fort Koskenong.

"The regulars and Alexander's Brigade were marched back to Koskenong on the 20th. and on the morning of the 21st. moved in the direction of the Blue Mounds, to cooperate in pursuit of the enemy. Capt. [Gideon] Lowe of the 5th. [Regiment, U.S. Army Infantry] with his company, was left

---

* At today's Fort Atkinson, Wisconsin.

** Near today's Palmyra, Wisconsin.

in charge of the supplies and sick [at Fort Koshkonong]. After a forced march of four days **we reached the Blue Mounds on the 24th. where Henry had fallen back for supplies, and was encamped. Dodge had gone to Dodgeville to recruit the strength of his Battalion.**

"Marched on the 25th. with the regular troops and Henry's and Alexander's Brigades for a point on the Ouisconsin sixteen miles distant, encamped near Helena, and the next morning moved upon that place where some light rafts had been constructed by the Quarter Masters Department for crossing the [Wisconsin] river.

"The enemy after the Battle of the Ouisconsin having **crossed that river and entered the wilderness on the opposite side,** I deemed it advisable to divest myself of all baggage, and select a body of the most efficient men and horses for a final pursuit--accordingly all the volunteers whose horses were unfit for the march were sent back to Fort Hamilton* where there was a depot of provisions, and a detachment of regular troops with the sick and baggage left at Helena.

"On the morning of the 27th. the volunteers including Dodge, who had joined, began to cross the river, but the rafts that had been provided were so small and limeted in number, only a part got over, on the next morning the regular troops and residue of the volunteers passed across, and our line of march was taken up with a force now reduced to 400 regulars and 900 volunteers--at the distance of four or five miles we fell upon the trail of the enemy, and pusued it with great and unabated energy, over the most difficult country imaginable 'till the morning of the 2nd. August, when the enemy were overtaken in the bank of the Mississippi and subdued [in the massacre at Bad Axe river] as heretofore officially reported.

"The Battle ground was occupied by us the succeeding day after the affair of the 2d. to ascertain the route of the remnant of the enemy, and to await the return of the Steam Boat Warrior which had been sent down to Fort Crawford with the wounded, on the night of the 2nd.

---

* At today's Wiota, Wisconsin.

"The Boat having returned on the evening of the 3d., and having for reasons stated in my official report, declined a further pursuit of the enemy, the regular troops were embarked on the morning of the 4th. and descended the river to Fort Crawford, whilst the volunteers took up their line of march for the same point.

"On arriving at Fort Crawford on the 4th. General [Joseph M.] Street the Indian agent for the Ouisconsin Winnebagoes was requested to have the chiefs of his agency, who had previously been called in by him, to meet me in council. In this interview, those Indians were charged with various suspicious traits of misconduct, and admonished against further deception. They were told that Black Hawk and the Prophet, with their families and probably many other fugitives had fallen back, on reaching the Mississippi, into their country, that they, the Winnebagoes, would not be allowed to harbour them; that if they attempted it they would be confounded with the consequences of the war and treated as enemies. If on the contrary, they wished to show the friendship they had just professed, to do so by the apprehension of Black Hawk and the Prophet, for which I would reward them with a gift of twenty horses. They promised that if they were in their country they should be arrested and given up.

"On the morning after our arrival at Fort Crawford I despatched the Steam Boat Warrior for Fort Armstrong*, with instructions through the commanding officer and Indian agent there, to Keokuck informing him to arrest and deliver up all the fugitives of Black Hawk's band that had crossed the Mississippi.

"Whilst these things were in operation, Genl. [Winfield] Scott arrived on the morning of the 7th., when a report of events and the arrangements adopted and being carried into effect by me, were submitted to him, which he approved, and the result was the apprehension and delivery of Black Hawk,

* At Rock Island, Illinois.

the Prophet, and some fifty other prisoners, men, women and children by the Winnebagoes, and every fugitive of note, and many others who crossed the Mississippi, by Keokuck.

"I have been thus minute to show that not only the pursuit and subjection of the Sacks was effected under my orders, but all the arrangements for the apprehension of the fugitives was planned and adopted by me. Genl. Scott however, has, in his reports, done me ample justice on both these points, as well as in every thing else connected with the campaign.

"If it should be thought I called for too large a Militia force, I must remark, that I was then under the impression, which has been fully confirmed by subsequent events, that nothing but a show of a heavy body of troops in the heart of the country occupied by the enemy, would prevent his being joined by a large number of Winnebagoes and Pottowattimies, swelling his numbers to some 1800 or 2000, and probably more. It is a well established fact that the Pottowattimies were concerned in the murders on Indian Creek, three of whom, who had been in both battles, and subsequently made prisoners and brought over to this post, have confessed the fact, and have been turned over to the civil authority of Illinois for trial.

"The Winnebagoes of Rock river*, and of a village on the Ouisconsin committed several murders in the Mineral district**, and it is believed the massacre of [Felix] St. Vraine, the Sack agent, and his party. Two young Winnebago men, wounded in the action of the 2nd. August, were made prisoners and brought down with the Sack prisoners to this post, circumstances and facts concurring to sustain the impression I have uttered.

---

* These included, among others, villages at today's Beloit, Wisconsin, and at today's Freeport and Prophetstown, Illinois. Henry Gratiot was their Sub Agent for Indian Affairs.

** The lead mining area of southwest Wisconsin, a "driftless" region, never covered by the pre-historic glaciers.

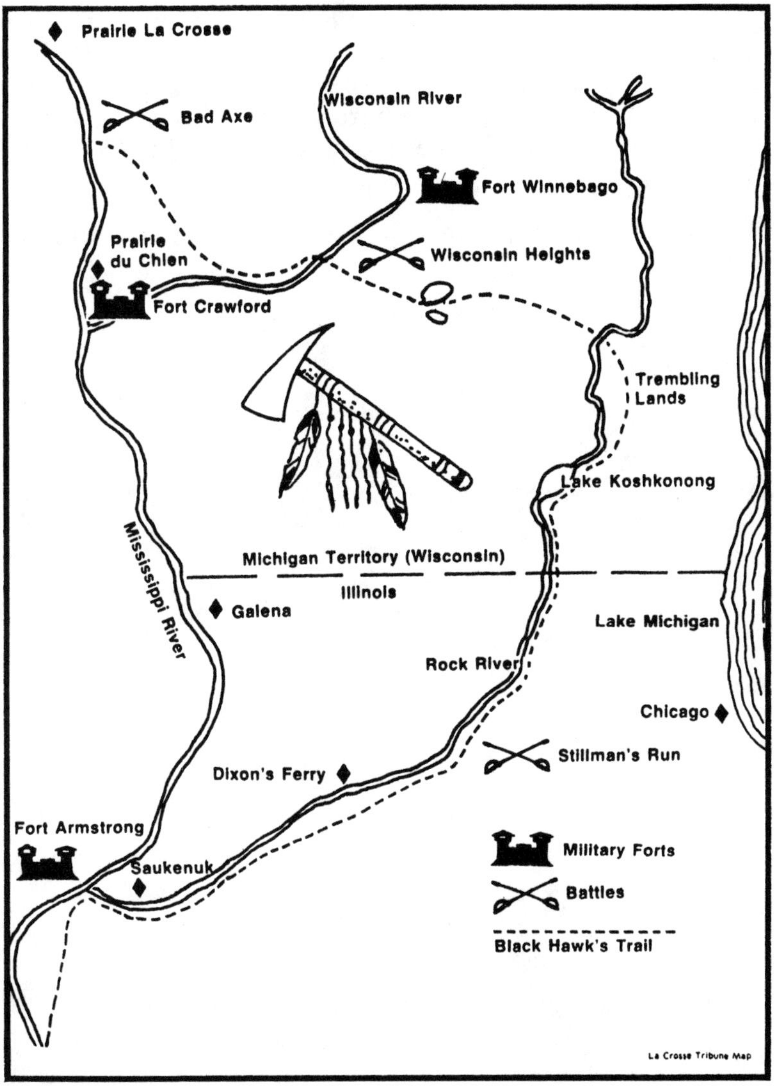
Prairie La Crosse
Bad Axe
Wisconsin River
Fort Winnebago
Wisconsin Heights
Prairie du Chien
Fort Crawford
Trembling Lands
Lake Koshkonong
Mississippi River
Michigan Territory (Wisconsin)
Illinois
Galena
Lake Michigan
Rock River
Chicago
Stillman's Run
Dixon's Ferry
Fort Armstrong
Saukenuk
Military Forts
Battles
Black Hawk's Trail
La Crosse Tribune Map

"In conclusion I beg leave to call your attention particularly to my exposition of the time, and circumstances of Black Hawk's crossing the Mississippi to the east bank with his Band--and to the embarassment I was subjected to, by the premature discharge of [Samuel] Whiteside's Brigade.

"H. Atkinson Br. Gn. u.S.army

"Col. R. [Roger] Jones adjt. Genl. u.S.army Washington City"[5]

Brigadier General Henry Atkinson

THE BATTLE OF WISCONSIN HEIGHTS

"It was generally reported, and not contradicted, that the volunteers had been improvident and wasteful to the degree of leaving in certain camps rations that had been issued by the barrel in unbroken bulk."[1]

— 2d Lt. Philip St. George Cooke, U.S. Army Infantry

MONDAY, JULY 9, 1832

clear, north wind

Thermometer: 7 A.M. - 64°
2 P.M. - 72°
9 P.M. - 65°

"The provisions of the army [in search of Black Hawk] were very nearly exhausted [by July 9, 1832], and the consequence was a temporary suspension of operations, until a further supply could be drawn from the nearest depot; this was Fort Winnebago*, distant about sixty miles.

"The division of mounted volunteers was ordered to march thither and draw fifteen days' rations, which they were to transport on their horses; whilst a convoy was to be despatched to our camp.

"I [Philip St. George Cooke] do not attempt to give more than a mere sketch of the actual operations of this campaign; for, not having been on the General's [Henry Atkinson's] staff**, I was not 'in the secrets of the cabinet:' I

---

* At todays's Portage, Wisconsin.

** Second Lieutenant Cooke was Acting Adjutant of the Black Hawk war detachment of the 6th Infantry Regiment, U.S. Army.

did not harass myself in seeking by cross questions, scraps of intelligence; or, in eternally discussing and criticising operations founded on intelligence and exigencies of which the critics were generally in profound ignorance; or, in volunteering advice to any of supposed influence who would listen, as some one or a few officers did, and seemed to suffer as much uneasiness as if they had borne a load of responsibility equal to that with which many adverse circumstances seemed to overload our commanding General.

"It was, however, impossible to mistake the causes of this delay, when a prudent General [Atkinson] and an able staff were evidently blameless.

"It was generally reported, and not contradicted, that the [Illinois mounted militia] volunteers had been improvident and wasteful to the degree of leaving in certain camps rations that had been issued by the barrel in unbroken bulk.

"And again, the militia convoys were incredibly timid and unmanageable, provision trains could not be got on; one was abandoned by guards and drivers, within two or three miles of our position here, in consequence of their having imagined that they had seen an Indian or two; thus were good plans thwarted in despite of the great exertions of the quarter-master department; which was indebted to the militia for an active and energetic head [Enoch March]."[1]

"The Volunteers having been for several days in great need of provisions, and not knowing when supplies would arrive, the Commanding General ordered [Brigadier General Milton K.] Alexander, & [Brigadier General James D.] Henry's Brigades & [Colonel Henry] Dodges battalion [of Iowa County, Michigan Territory, mounted volunteers] to march to Fort Winnebago & [Brigadier General Alexander] Posey to Fort Hamilton*, he directed Gen Posey to remain

* At today's Wiota, Wisconsin. Colonel William S. Hamilton of the Michigan Territory (Wisconsin) militia, youngest son of Alexander Hamilton, had a lead smelting operation there.

with his brigade at Fort Hamilton--Alexander, Henry & Dodge were to return to Fort Cosconong* as soon as provisions were procured, he gave verbal instructions to those officers to pursue the trail of the enemy if it was met with in going or returning--"[2]

"Posey Alexander & Dodge having lost their provisions in swimming the Pik-a-tol-i-ka and other streams, and the surplus on hand being nearly exhausted, and our train of wagons with provisions that were ordered from Galena and Dixon's not having been heard from, Gen. A. [Atkinson] deemed it advisable to detach Henry, Alexander & Dodge to Fort Winnebago, and a train of ~~baggage~~ pack horses under Capt. [Gideon] Lowe of the U. S. A. (which was supposed to be not more than 35 miles off) for 12 days supply."[3]

"Orders were issued this evening for Genl Henry & Gnl Alexanders Brigades to go to Fort Winebago for provisions Genl Poseys brigade to march to the Mineral district & remain at Fort Hamilton--"[4]

"Henry, Alexander and Dodge were ordered to Fort Winnebago with instructions to draw twelve days rations, and Posey to Fort Hamilton to occupy that point, Dodgeville and Kellogg's with his corps, and to intercept the march of the enemy should he break from the swamp** and move in that direction-- Henry, Alexander and Dodge were instructed to pursue the enemy should they fall upon his trail in either going or returning from Fort Winnebago, and to inform me by express-"[6]

The written orders were less permissive:

---

* At today's Fort Atkinson, Wisconsin.

** Somewhere in the area of today's Oconomowoc, Wisconsin. "The country they now occupy, abounds in lakes, thickets and marshes."[5]

2d Lt. Albert Sidney Johnston,
Acting Assistant Adjutant General
and Aide de Camp to Atkinson

"Head Qrs. of the Army of the Frontier

"Camp on Whitewater [Bark] river 9th July 1832

"Order No. 51

"Brig. Genl Alexanders [Second] & Brig. Genl Henry' [Third] Brigade of Illinois mounted Volunteers will march tomorrow morning to Fort Winnebago, & draw twelve days rations of Provisions (exclusive of the Subsistence of their respective commands during their stay at the Fort) & return to these Head Qrs. without delay.

"By order of Brig Genl. Atkinson

"(Signed) Alb. S. Johnston* A. D. C A.A.A Genl. [Aide de Camp & Acting Assistant Adjutant General]"[7]

* As a distinguished Confederate General in the Civil War, Johnston was killed at the battle of Shiloh.

"The soldiers was now becoming quite discontented (being the principal part of them) entierly without provisions and marching to a fort the name of which some of them had never before heard of and of the distance to which the most Inteligent of the officers and men had but and imperfect Idea"[8]

—Lieutenant James J. Justice,
Illinois Militia, Mounted Volunteers

TUESDAY, JULY 10, 1832

clear, north wind
Thermometer: 7 A.M. - 68°
2 P.M. - 72°
9 P.M. - 61°

"The provisions of the [militia] volunteers [in search of Black Hawk] being nearly exhausted, [Henry] Dodge's command, with [James D.] Henry's and [Milton K.] Alexander's brigades, were ordered to Fort Winnebago, about fifty miles distant*, for supplies."[1]

"Head Qrs. Army of the Frontier Camp on White water [Bark] river 10th. July 1832.

"Order No. 53

"The Comdg Officer of Fort Winnebago [Captain Joseph Plympton] will issue twelve days rations of Provisions to Brig Genl Alexanders & Henry' Brigades of Ill. mounted Volunteers & Genl Dodge' Michigan [Territory] Volunteers. While they are detained in receiving

---

* Actually about 65 miles distant.

them, their commands will be subsisted from the depot at that place. The Comdg. Officer will load the train of Waggons in charge of the Volunteers with provisions for this place taking care to leave a supply of fifty or sixty days for the post.

"By order of Brig Genl. [Henry] Atkinson

"(Signed) Alb S. Johnston A.D.C. A.A.A Genl."[2]

Later in the day Atkinson changed his mind about sending so many wagons:

"Liut. Albt. S. Johnston. To Capt. [Joseph] Plympton Comg Ft. Winebago

"Head Qrs: Army of the Frontier Mouth of White Water [Bark river] On Rock river 10th. July 1832

"Sir, The Commanding General has concluded to detain a portion of the Train of Waggons, Ordered to Fort Winnebago to receive provisions. instead thereof, he send ninety or one hundred Pack horses, for wheich, he desires that you will furnish a sufficient quantity of Provisions to load them.

"The General desires that you will send an extra quantity of Salt in the Waggons, say 8 or 10 Bushells.

"(signed) Albt. S. Johnston Aid De. Camp & A A A genl"[3]

Private John Ryan of Captain Benjamin W. Clark's Company of Iowa County (Michigan Territory) militia reported, "When we finally got to Atkinsons Comman [on the night of July 7 at today's Palmyra, Wisconsin], tired and hungrey (for our rations had all given out) instead of going to meet Blackhawk and his band Atkinson Ordered Dodge and his men to go to work at building fortifications. General Dodge told him that he did not come there to build forts, that he had come to fight Indians, and flatly refused to employ his men in building forts, much to the Indignation of

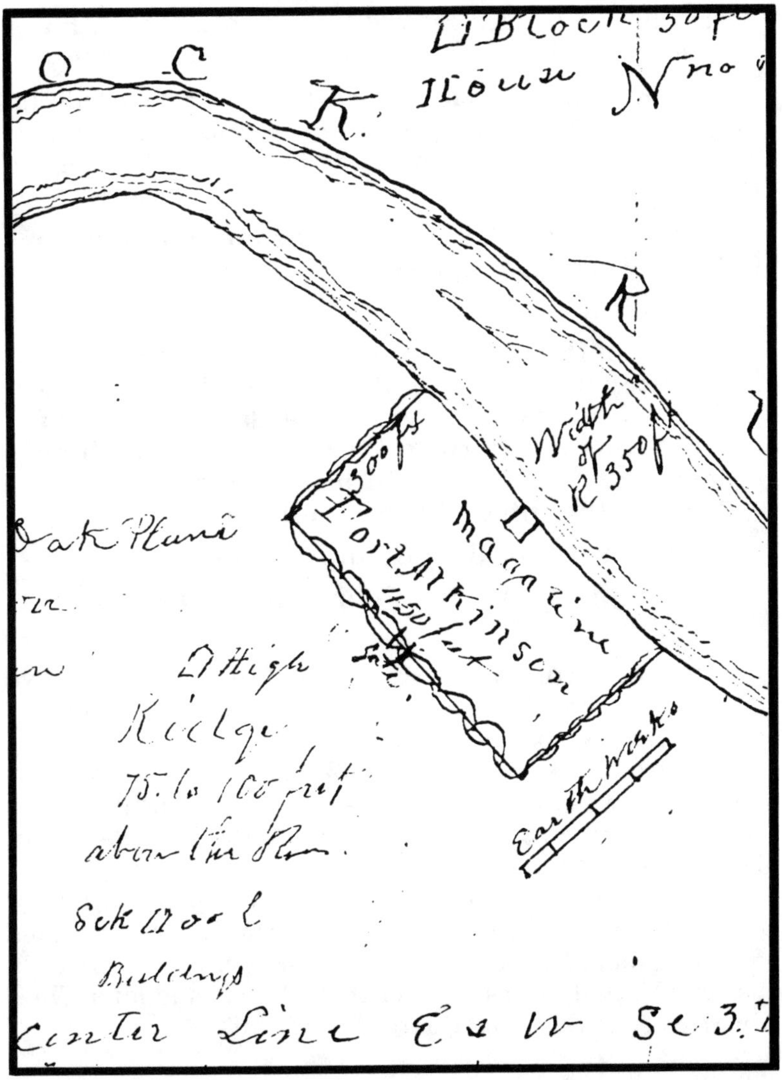

Milo Jones I wrote in later years, "The above is a Rough Sketch of old Ft. Atkinson as I saw It in 1835 — 3 years after evacuation.

"The Fort was simply a Stockade Built of Logs 10 to 12 feet Long Split in Halfs Set on end in a trench as you would set a Post and were Bullet proof to a point above a mans Head."

Atkinson who in turn refused to furnish Dodge with any provisions, a thing that looked to us almost inhuman"[4]

When Henry Dodge refused to build a stockade (at today's Fort Atkinson, Wisconsin), Atkinson sent Dodge and his troops to Fort Winnebago along with Alexander and Henry:

> **"Head Qrs Army of the Frontier Camp on White Water [Bark] river 10th July 1832**
>
> **"Order No. 55**
>
> **"Genl [Henry] Dodge' command of Michigan [Territory] & Galena Volunteers will proceed to Fort Winnebago, draw twelve days rations of provisions & return to these Head qrs. without delay. His command will be subsisted from the depot at that place during their stay**
>
> **"By order of Brig Genl. Atkinson**
>
> **"(Signed) A. S. Johnston A.D.C A.A.A. Genl."[5]**

"As we were out of provisions, Gen. Atkinson gave orders to Gen. Dodge and Gen. Henry's Brigade of volunteers to go back to Fort Winnebago to secure supplies. We started in obedience to these orders, and on our way got news that two of my [George Wallace Jones's] neighbors at Sinsinawa Mound had been killed by the Indians.* Gen. Dodge ordered me to go home and see to the safety of my family and friends. I returned home in company with Maj. [John] Dement, Mr. L. V. Bogy, afterwards United States Senator from Missouri, and Sidney Breese, who afterwards became United States Senator from Illinois and later Chief Justice of the Supreme Court of that State."**[7]

---

* "...on the Menominee a creek 9 or 10 miles from Galena at about 11 Oclock A.M. [on June 29] some Indians which lay concealed shot [James] Boxley and [John] Thompson dead"[6]

** George Wallace Jones's memory here causes some confusion. These men left the army on different days at different places.

George W. Jones, Aide de Camp
to Henry Dodge,
Michigan Territory Militia

"General [Alexander] Posey shaped his course for Dixons [actually Hamilton's fort] and [Milton K.] Allexander and [James D.] Henry took up their March through the willderness aiming for fort winebago The soldiers was now becoming quite discontented (being the principal part of them) entierly without provisions and marching to a fort the name of which some of them had never before heard of and of the distance to which the most Inteligent of the officers and men had but and [an] imperfect Idea We however pursued our Journey some of us with light hearts and all with light wallets which was the better for our poor horses which had not long since had to carry their owners with their arms and fifteen days Rations through the worst of swamps"[8]

Guided by the Winnebago orator White Crow,[9], Kaw-ray-kaw-saw-kaw, "Gen. Dodge, with his command of between two hundred and fifty and three hundred men, proceeded in advance of Henry and Alexander. This was a movement fraught with the greatest danger to him and his command; the march was directly toward the enemy, who were estimated at from 800 to 1,200 warriors. Had we encountered them being beyond supporting distance from the Illinois brigade, we must have been overpowered. Fortune, however, favored us...."[10]

Dodge covered half of the 65 mile distance to Fort Winnebago in one day. The Illinois militia under Henry and Alexander, "passing over some Verry bad road"[11], "Started for Fort Winnebago for Provision went 10 miles & encamped for the night"[12]

"...the direct rout would be covered with swamps"[3]
— White Crow, Winnebago Indian Guide

WEDNESDAY, JULY 11, 1832

clear, north wind

Thermometer: 7 A.M. - 75°
2 P.M. - 79°
9 P.M. - 66°

"Before my arrival at Fort Winnabago I [Henry Dodge] had ascertained if I returned to Rock River by by the same rout[e] I marchd to that place I would Loose [lose] the greater part of my men"[1]

"...we [Dodge's troops] reached Fort Winnebago on the evening of the second day...."[2] "we arrive here on the 11th. Late in the evening I [Henry Dodge] found the distance at least sixty miles the white crow our pilot stated the direct rout[e] would be covered with swamps"[3]

"Genl Dodge arrived with 230 Militia of Ioway [County, Michigan Territory] Capt. [Gideon] Low [commander of Company D, 5th Infantry Regiment, U.S. Army] arrived."[4]

Meanwhile, the troops of Brigadier General James D. Henry and Brigadier General Milton K. Alexander were moving on more slowly. "go to fort winnebago for provisions about 12 miles from the river Praierie set in land good and roling and hilly timbre reasonably plenty of a scruby groth springs of the best water to be found in abundance"[5]

"March thirty miles & encamped for the night."[6]

In Captain Jesse Claywell's Company of Colonel James Collins's Fourth Regiment of Henry's Third Brigade, John H. Wilcoxen[7] [or Wilcoxson[8]] was "Elected 1st Lieut 11 July"[9] to replace Sawyel Cox who "Resigned July 10th 1932"[10] In the same Company, Rezin H. Constant was "Elected 2nd Lieut 11 July"[11]

"On arriving at the fort, Gen. Dodge at once set to work to find out the position of the enemy from a number of Winnebago Indians who were at that time at the fort. This he effected through Pierre Poquette, a half-breed and their interpreter, over whom he had great influence. Through him he learned that the enemy were encamped on Rock River, at a place now known as Hustis' Rapids."[25]

—Lt. Charles Bracken, Adjutant,
Michigan Territory Militia

THURSDAY, JULY 12, 1832

clear, north wind
Thermometer: 7 A.M. - 75°
2 P.M. - 78°
9 P.M. - 70°

"We [the Second Brigade of Brigadier General Milton K. Alexander and the Third Brigade of Brigadier General James D. Henry] continued our march for three days having the best water to drink and good grass into which we could spansel our horses a while but was (th[r]ough fear of loosing) obliged to take up the poor weary creatures and tie them by the neck and cut a little grass with our knives for them to eat thro the night."[1]

"I [Major William Lee D. Ewing of Henry's Spy Batallion] was dismounted before I reached this place [Fort Winnebago] by reason of my horse becoming lame."[2]

In Captain Bennet Nowlen's Company of Colonel James Collins's Fourth Regiment of Henry's Third Brigade, John Yowell was "elected 1st Lieut. 12th July 1832"[3] to replace 1st Lieutenant Jesse Scott who "Resigned 10 July 1832".[4]

"...while on the march from fort Kaskanong on Rock-

River, to Fort Winnebago Wisconsin Territory* on the 11th or 12th day of July 1832, said [Corporal] N. [Nathaniel] Highsmith being then in the service of the United States**, and in the line of duty as a soldier was taken sick, with what was then thought to be an ordinary Diarrhea, but said complaint continued till it resulted in a confirmed case of the piles, which rendered him almost wholly unfit for duty the ballance of the Campaign***...."[6]

The troops of Alexander and Henry "Marched twenty three miles Come to Fort Winnebago a beautiful fort, or garrison"[9]

Juliette Kinzie, wife of the Sub Agent for Winnebago Indian Affairs, had followed this route the year before (in 1831) when she returned to Fort Winnebago from Fort Dearborn (Chicago). She described this section of the journey as follows: "Our next morning's ride was of a more tranquil character than any that had preceded it; for at an early hour we entered upon what was known as the 'Twenty-mile Prairie,' --and I may be permitted to observe that the miles are wonderfully long on the prairies. Our passage over this was, except the absence of the sand, like crossing the desert. Mile after mile of unbroken expanse--not a tree--not a living object except ourselves."[7]

---

* Michigan Territory in 1832. Wisconsin Territory was established in 1836 with Henry Dodge serving as its first and then its last Governor.

** He was in the Company of his brother, Captain William Highsmith, in Colonel Samuel Adams's Second Regiment of Alexander's Second Brigade of Illinois Mounted Volunteers.[5]

*** "--and since the campaign up to the present time [January 6, 1851] said N. Highsmith has not been able owing to said complaint still afflicting him--to support his family by farming which is his usual calling."[6] He died in 1853. In 1857 his widow, Elizabeth, after many petitions and affidavits was granted a U. S. pension of $8 a month.

Juliette Kinzie, Author
of *Wau-Bun: The "Early Days" in the North-West*

According to her editor, Louise Phelps Kellogg, "This prairie was what is now Northern Dane County and southern Columbia County. Starting from somewhere near the present village of Sun Prairie, the travelers crossed it in a north-west direction through Bristol and Windsor townships in Dane County, and Leeds township in Columbia County."[8]

Before she left Fort Winnebago on July 4, 1832, for the greater safety of Fort Howard at Green Bay, Juliette Kinzie saw the situation as follows:

"The bold promontory on which Fort Winnebago was built looked down upon the extended prairie and the Fox River on one side, and on the other stretched away into the thickly-wooded ridge that led off to Belle Fontaine and Lake Puckaway.

"In front lay an extent of meadow, across which was the Portage road, of about two miles in length, leading between the Fox and the Wisconsin Rivers. Teams of oxen and a driver were kept at the [Winnebago Indian] Agency by the Government, to transport the canoes of the Indians across this place, which at many seasons was wet, miry, and almost impassable."*[10]

---

* Moses Pauquette described the portage as follows: "...my father, who was employed by the American Fur Company, had a trading house and barracks for the five or six men whom he then engaged in the business of portaging boats across the almost two miles of marsh which here separate the Fox and Wisconsin rivers. Boats coming up the Fox would be beached at a point near the mouth of the present canal. The beach on the Wisconsin river was very near where, at a later period, the Carpenter house was built. The intervening marsh was in those days often a mere quagmire, the transportation of heavily-laden Mackinaw boats across it being a task involving much expenditure of time and patience. It took four or five yoke of oxen to haul one of these craft, which would be slung upon a huge reach cut out of a tree and mounted on broad wheels."[11]

Fort Winnebago, Portage, Wisconsin,
Painting by Juliette Kinzie

"Fort Winnebago was not picketed in; there were no defences to the barracks or officers' quarters, except slight panelled doors and Venetian blinds--nothing that would long resist the blows of clubs or hatchets. There was no artillery, and the Commissary's store was without the bounds of the Fort, under the hill.

"Mr. [John] Kinzie [Sub Agent for Winnebago Indian Affairs] had, from the first, called the attention of the officers to the insecurity of their position in case of danger, but he generally received a scoffing answer."[12]

"In a few days our friends waked up to the conviction that something must be done at once. The first step was to forbid any Winnebago coming within the garrison, lest they should find out what they had known as well as ourselves for three months past--namely, the feebleness of the means of resistance. The next was to send fatigue-parties into the woods, under the protection of a guard, to cut pickets for inclosing the garrison.

"There was every reason to believe that the enemy were not very far distant, and that their object in coming north was to break a way into the Chippewa country, where they would find a place of security among their friends and allies. The story that our Indian runners brought in most frequently was, that the Sauks were determined to fall upon the whites at the Portage and Fort and massacre all, except the families of the Agent [Kinzie] and Interpreter [Paquette]".[13]

"At night we were all regularly armed and our posts assigned us. After every means had been taken to make the house secure, the orders were given. Sister Margaret and I, in case of attack, were to mount with the children to the room above, while my husband and his men were to make good their defence as long as possible against the enemy. Since I had shown my sportsmanship by bringing down accidentally a blackbird on the wing, I felt as if I could do some execution with my little pistols, which were regularly placed beside my pillow at night; and I was fully resolved to use them, if necessity required. I do not remember to have felt

Fort Winnebago in 1834,
Oil Painting by Ira A. Ridgeway (1896)

The view is from the southwest. The building to the right of the gate is the guardhouse; to the left, the armory. On the opposite side of the square, to the left, were the officers' quarters. The peaked-roof building at the left corner was a blockhouse. A similar structure was in the corner diagonally opposite. The magazine appears in the corner adjacent to the guardhouse, and at the side of it to the right were the soldiers' quarters. The log building near the end of the bridge over the Fox river, to the right, was Henry Merrill's sutler's store. The low structure a little to the east of it, was the ice cellar. A little further along was the surgeon's headquarters (a portion of which is still standing), and a little to the right of it was the hospital. In the distance, looking between the hospital and the surgeon's quarters, may be seen the old stone bakery. At the left of the bridge is a commissary building. Just in the rear of it was Jones's sutler's store. To the far left, out of the picture, was the Indian Agency building.

the slightest compunction at the idea of taking the lives of two Sauks, as I had no doubt I should do; and this explains to me what I had before often wondered at, the indifference, namely, of the soldier on the field of battle to the destruction of human life. Had I been called upon, however, to use my weapons effectually, I should no doubt have looked back upon it with horror."[14]

"About fifty lodges had come at the commencement of the disturbances and encamped around our dwelling, saying that if the Sauks attacked us it must be after killing them; and, knowing them well, we had perfect confidence in their assurances.

"But their vicinity, while it gave us a feeling of protection, likewise furnished us with a channel of the most exciting and agitating daily communications. As the theatre of operations approached nearer and nearer, intelligence was brought in by their runners--now that 'Captain Harney's head had been recognized in the Sauk camp, where it had been brought the day previous,' next, that 'the Sauks were carrying Lieutenant Beall's head on a pole in front of them as they marched to meet the whites.' Sometimes it was a story which we afterwards found to be unhappily true, as that of the [May 24th] murder of their Agent, M. [Felix] St. Vrain at Kellogg's Grove*, by the Sauks themselves, who ought to have protected him."[15]

"The fort [Winnebago] was beginning to look very respectable; and there was a nice frame-house** for the subagent on the same side as the post of the American Fur Company. There was another house, where William Gourdain, the blacksmith, was living; and still another, occupied by Louis Managre.*** At the other end of the

* Near today's Kent, Illinois.

** The historic Agency House in Portage, Wisconsin, built in the Summer of 1832, was not yet under construction when the Black Hawk war troops were there.

*** When there was enough distance between them, he was sometimes called "mon nĕgre" by a fellow worker.

Portage, a little north of the landing, Pierre Grignon resided, half-brother to Captain Grignon."[16]

"we [the troops of Alexander and Henry] at lenghth arrived at the fort on the third day after we left the new fort (Koskanong*) our quarter master soon had plenty of flour and pork and we soon satisfied our craving appetites turned our horses into the grass struck up camp"[17]

"Here, when we got to Fort Winnebago, we were still surrounded by the Winnebagoes."[18]

Their situation was described by Spoon Decorah, a Winnebago Indian, who said, "During the Black Hawk War, I lived at the Portage. When we heard of the trouble, I wanted very much to go and join the Americans. I knew the officers at Fort Winnebago, and was friendly to them.

"But my friends got around me and said that the Sacs were friends of the Winnebagoes. So I was persuaded not to go.

"In July, ten families of us started out on our summer's hunt, on the Roche-a-Cri River. We had got as far as [today's] Friendship [Wisconsin], when Ochpiyoka (The Spaniard), one of our friends, came into camp much excited and told us what had happened down in the Illinois country, saying that the Sacs were headed our way. We had gone out on our hunt in strong numbers. Knowing that the war was going on, we feared that the Sacs might come into our territory. For there was some fear of the Sacs, all the while, although we had been told of their friendliness. They knew that some of our people were with the Americans. We felt that if the Sacs were

---

* Construction of the stockade called Fort Cos-co-nong at today's Fort Atkinson, Wisconsin, was started by the U. S. Army Infantry troops under the command of Colonel Zachary Taylor on July 11, the day after the Illinois militia left to get food. It was finished by the time Brigadier General Alexander got back with his Second Brigade on July 17. For details, see the Eye-Witness Series volume ahead of this one, *Hunting A Shadow: The Search for Black Hawk.*

driven into our hunting-grounds they might be revengeful, and then it would go hard with our hunting parties unless we were prepared for attack. So when The Spaniard came and told us that the Sacs were really headed our way, we were much afraid. He told us that the center of attack would be Portage. We had left many of our old people and women here. So we at once returned to Portage. The other hunting parties, to which runners had also been sent out, did so too. This was a few days before the battle on the Sauk bluffs [the battle of Wisconsin Heights].

"Our party camped on the rise of ground just back of what is now [1887] the city end of the Wisconsin River bridge, in Portage. Nearly the whole tribe was camped about Portage. There were three large camps, on both sides of the river, about where the bridge now is.

"The principal chiefs in these camps were: Black Wolf, his son Dandy, Tahneekseeickseega (Fond of Tobacco), White Eagle, White Crow, and Ahsheeshka (Broken Arm). Black Wolf was the uncle of Gray Eagle's Eye, my [Spoon Decorah's] present squaw; Dandy was her cousin; White Crow was a one-eyed chief, who had a village at the Four Lakes,--he died a few years after the Black Hawk war; Broken Arm fought under Tecumseh, and also died a few years after the Black Hawk War.

"The white Captains [Dodge, Henry and Alexander] were in Portage when we [the Winnebago hunting parties] got there; they had brought news from White Beaver's [Brigadier General Henry Atkinson's] camp, that caused our return."[19]

General Henry reported, "I arrived here [at Fort Winnebago] on the evening of the 12th after passing over some Verry bad road and traveling sixty miles or more"[20]

"Generals Alexander & Henry arrived with 1920 Illinois Militia Lt. [Alexander S.] Hooe arrived Lt. Johnson [1st Lieutenant Alexander Johnston, commanding Company F, 5th Infantry Regiment] arrived 1st 5th & 6th Regt Detach[ment] of [U. S. Army Infantry] Regulars...arrived 12th July"[22] "on the day after our arrival we [Dodge's squadron] engaged the Bakers* to prepare our Bread in the evening Generals Hen[r]y and Alexander arrive their men complained much of Hunger we gave them the Bread prepared for ourselves"[24]

"On arriving at the fort, Gen. Dodge at once set to work to find out the position of the enemy from a number of Winnebago Indians who were at that time at the fort. This he effected through Pierre Poquette, a half-breed and their interpreter, over whom he had great influence."[25]

"Pierre Paquette was the trader at the Portage, in those days. He was a large, powerful man. His squaw was a daughter of Joseph Crelie. Our tribe [the Winnebagoes] had great respect for him. His mother was a Winnebago woman, and he was a good man in every way,--very friendly to our people. I [Spoon Decorah] was his friend, and he once gave me a pony."[26]

Satterlee Clark, a resident at Fort Winnebago, described Pauquette in detail: "I now come to that part of my recollections in which the people of Portage and the Fort Winnebago region, feel the greatest interest, and have the most curiosity. I allude to my acquaintance with Peter Pauquette. His strength was so immeasurable, and his exploits so astonishing, that while relating what I have seen I shall tell only the exact truth, I will promise not to be offended if some of my readers should be a little skeptical.

"Peter Pauquette was born in the year 1800 of a French father and a Winnebago mother; the latter was buried nearly in front of the old agency house opposite the fort. He was

* When the U.S. Rangers visited Fort Winnebago the following summer, "The settlement there consisted of those in the Fort, and one man without, who kept a bakery for the accommodation of the garrison. The local currency used was common playing cards, cut in strips, issued by the baker with his name written on the back--every spot good for one shilling or a loaf of bread. If it was not quite a specie paying bank, bread--the staff of life--was always paid on demand."[23]

Satterlee Clark

thirty years old when I first knew him, and was the very best specimen of a man I ever saw. He was six feet two inches in height, and weighed two hundred and forty pounds--hardly ever varying a single pound. He was a very handsome man, hospitable, generous and kind, and I think I never saw a better natured man.

"I had heard much of his strength before I left Green Bay, and of course, was anxious to see him perform some of the wonderful feats of strength of which I had heard. From my first acquaintance with him to the day of his death, I was his most intimate friend, and consequently had a better opportunity to know him than any other person. I will now endeavor to give an idea of his strength and activity, which to me seemed also super-human. He often told me that all persons seemed alike to him. When I was nineteen or twenty years old, my business kept me constantly in training, and though I weighed less than one hundred and fifty pounds, my muscles were like iron; notwithstanding he often said it was no more trouble to take me across his lap than a child one year old, and so it seemed to me. I was told that on one occasion when he was making the portage [between the Fox and Wisconsin rivers] with a heavy boat, one of his oxen gave out, and he took the yoke off, and carried the end against an ox all the way over. I did not see this, but I asked him if it was so, and he replied it was.

"I once saw him take hold of the staple to a pile driver weighing 2,650 lbs., and lift it apparently without any exertion, and swing it back and forth a minute of time. I have several times seen him get under a common sized horse, put his arms round the hind legs, his back under the horse's stomach and lift the horse clean off the ground. A great many other things I have seen him do which would tire the reader's patience were I to relate them. It can readily be imagined, however, that scarcely anything could be impossible to such a man."[27]

Henry Merrell, the sutler at Fort Winnebago, gives a similar description of his friend Paquette:

"Pierre Paquette lived opposite Fort Winnebago on what was called the Agency Hill. I considered him the best specimen of Nature's noblemen I ever met.

"He was born, I think, in Missouri, and engaged in the Indian trade at an early day. When I knew him he was six feet two inches in height, large, and fleshy, but his flesh was hard, and felt more like my knee-pan than common flesh. I once took my handkerchief and measured around his thigh, and it just reached around my waist. He was the strongest man I ever knew; he would pick up a barrel of pork and throw it into a wagon as easily as a man would a ten gallon keg. I had a cask of dry white lead at my door, with eight hundred pounds of lead in it, and I was told by my clerk that he took it by the chimes, and lifted it off the ground.

"At one time, I was informed, he was hauling a boat across the Portage with ox-teams, and one of the oxen gave out and would not pull. He took off the bow, pushed the ox one side, and taking hold of the yoke, he pulled beside the other ox across the Portage. Many other feats of his strength are related. He was of a mild disposition, could neither read nor write; but had as fine a sense of honor as any gentleman I ever knew; and all who knew him would take his word as soon as any man's bond.

He and a companion (as he told me) were trading among some Indians in the Northwest until some others, the Flat Heads, I think, took them prisoners, and determined to burn them; they tied them each to a tree with their arms around it, then piled brush and wood around them, and set fire to the pile around his companion. He thought his time had come; but witnessing the excruciating sufferings of his fellow, he gave one superhuman pull at his thongs, and felt them give way. As he did so, an old squaw, the only one near him, caught him by the arm and gave a scream. He tried to shake her off, but could not; so he caught her hatchet and imbedded it in her head, which loosened her hold, and he jumped and ran, the Indians at his heels after him; but he could outrun almost any man, and outstripped them. Night coming on, he secreted himself, and finally got to a trading-post, after three days.

"He finally settled at Portage in the Indian trade; and at the time I knew him, he had such influence over the chiefs of the Winnebagoes, that he was considered at the head of the nation. He could talk the Winnebago, French and English languages fluently, and was the only good Winnebago interpreter in the country. He was with Colonel Dodge in the Sauk war...."[28]

"I [Henry Merrell] was told that in the Sauk war, there was a company of rangers, I believe from Illinois, who encamped on the bank of the Wisconsin River, and Pauquette was walking around, looking at them when a large man kicked a little dog following Pauquette, who said to him, 'Don't kick that dog, as he is mine.'

"The man replied, 'I'll kick you if you say much. Who are you?'

" 'My name is Pauquette.'

" 'Ah!' said the man, 'you are the very fellow I want to see. I have heard of you, and came up here on purpose to lick you.'

"Thereupon he pitched at Pauquette, who struck the man but once, pealing the skin from his cheek, knocking him down, when Pauquette caught him by the throat, raising him to his feet, and shaking him like an aspen leaf, asking him if he called himself a man.

" 'I was where I came from, but I see I ain't here,' was his reply.

"Thus it ended. He concluded he would not whip Pauquette."[29]

"A half breed Indian by the name of Poquet, told us he thought we might find Black Hawk by going around the head of Fox river, a stream of considerable size which empties into Green Bay; and offered to go with some of the Winnebagoes as a pilot."[30]

"Through him he learned that the enemy were encamped on Rock River, at a place now known as Hustis' Rapids*."[31]

"Pauquette with a few of the Winnebagoes say they can

* At today's Hustisford, Wisconsin.

pilot me [Henry Dodge] from this place to that point on Rock River in Less than two days...."[32]

"Paquette was engaged by the white captains to take them across the country to Black Hawk's camp, on the headwaters of the Rock River.

"Paquette wanted a party of Winnebagoes to go with him as guides. He sent Nahheesanchonka (Man Who Thinks Himself of Importance) into the camp to get volunteers. Nahheesanchonka told us [Winnebago Indians] that if we would go into the war we would make a name for ourselves, and get presents; also win the good opinion of White Beaver [Atkinson], and the Big Father at Washington [President Andrew Jackson].

"But there was still among us a strong feeling of friendliness toward the Sacs. This feeling was of friendly pity, not a desire to help them fight. So only six young men, none of them chiefs, went with Paquette as guides. Of these were Pawnee (Pania Blanc), Nahheesanchonka, Notsookega (Bear that Breaks up the Brush), Ahmegunka, and Tahnichseeka (The Smoker). As I think again, perhaps White Crow went with Paquette on this expedition, but of this I am not sure.* Anyway, White Crow fought on the American side, at the Sauk bluffs.**"[33]

John A. Kinzie, Sub Agent of Winnebago Indian Affairs at the portage, anticipated difficulties from Brigadier General Henry Atkinson's requisition for food supplies. Kinzie sought relief for his Indians through the Governor of Michigan Territory, George B. Porter:

---

* White Crow did not go with Paquette. He guided Alexander's Second Brigade and the sick and dismounted of Henry's Third Brigade back to Fort Cosconong.

** White Crow's son, White Pawnee (Pania Blanc), fought uncovered like a white man at the battle of Wisconsin Heights on July 21. White Crow himself was then back with Atkinson returning from near today's Palmyra, Wisconsin, where they had been trying for the second time to get around Bark river.

John Kinzie, Sub Agent
of Winnebago Indian Affairs
at Fort Winnebago

"Fort Winnebago, July 12, 1832

His Excelly: Gov: Porter, Detroit.

"Sir, The present state of affairs in this country, between our Government and the disaffected Sac & Fox Indians has placed a very large proportion of the Winnebagoes in a state of demi-starvation. I have done all in my power to relieve their immediate wants, by drawing for provisions on the military at this post. This relief cannot now be afforded any longer, as Genl. Atkinson has sent to this place for a large supply of provisions. Upwards of Two thousand mounted men, with a number of pack horses are now here for rations of pork & flour; and will leave this [place] to-day and to-morrow, for Genl. A's encampment on Rock River, about 10 miles above *Kosh-ko-nong*. The Sacs have retreated towards Lake Michigan, in the direction of Milliwalkie.* The country they now occupy, abounds in Lakes thickets and marshes. They are said to be about 600 to 700 strong-- have 8 or 900 horses & subsist upon roots and horse flesh. Genl. A. is determined to follow & overtake them. Genls. Dodge, Henry and Alexander are here in command of the mounted men.

"In consequence of this trouble with the Sacs, the Winnebagoes of Rock river, and others near

---

* The Wednesday, July 18, 1832, issue of *The Galenian* newspaper at Galena, Illinois, reported: "July 17--From information received this morning, by Mr. [John] Marsh, it appears that the trail of the Indians has taken an eastern direction from Rock river, and in the direction of Winnebago lake, or Mil-wa-ke, agreeably to Gen. Atkinson's expectation. It is thought, that by a forced march, the Indians might be able to reach Mil-wa-ke in a day or so, and it is possible, when there, they can obtain canoes (in exchange for horses) from the Menomonees, Ottawas & Pottawattomies, and cross the lake (Michigan) in whatever direction they may choose."

here, have been required to leave their villages, and to come in this neighbourhood, out of the way of the Sacs & our people. They are not well acquainted with the country to subsist by hunting, and game is scarce. I would therefore, suggest to your Excellency, the propriety of Governments supplying them with corn sufficient to enable them to subsist through the ensuing winter, as their corn fields have been destroyed and abandoned. I think the subject properly represented to the Secty: of War, will ensure these poor creatures timely relief. From two to three thousand bushels of corn, delivered here or near this place, in October or sooner, and properly distributed, would suffice.

"Very respectfully, Sir, Yo. obt. Sevt. Jno. H. Kinzie Sub-agt. Ind. affs."[34]

With night approaching, the troops "turned our horses into the grass struck camp and went to sleep but...."[35]

"horses run this night"[36]

"the horses start running in the night"[37]

"After encamping the Horses took fright and great numbers run...."[38]

"During the night succeeding our arrival at this place, the horses of the two Brigades took flight."[39]

"At this place we met with a misfortune which we had been very much troubled with during our march, which I [John Wakefield] omitted mentioning before. Our horses were given to fright and running in a most fearful manner; the army was constantly in danger of suffering great damage by their taking those frights. There is no one can tell what a horrid sight it is, to see two thousand horses coming at full speed toward an encampment in the dead hour of night. This night they got more scared than common. There were about three hundred head on this night, that run about thirty miles before they stopped; and that, too, through the worst kind of swamps."[40]

Lieutenant James J. Justice wrote, "...we were soon Roused from our slumbers by the Runing of the horses which had taken fright and were Runing through our encampment with a nois equal to thinder [thunder] and appearantly without Regard to what should be before them and we were evidintly in great danger of being Run over and killed but fortuneately the horses passed through the encampment without hurting any person and some of them Run aRound the encampment a great many times and then stopped others took the trail back a few was finally lost or cripeled others went Back to fort coskanong"[41]

"Satterlee Clark reported, "The second night the horses took fright (probably at some Winnebago Indians), and there was a regular stampede. Probably some of my readers may not thoroughly comprehend a stampede; and it may be proper to describe it, if possible, though only an eye witness can properly appreciate how terrible it is. Some horse, or may be a few horses get frightened and start to run; the entire drove may see nothing to alarm them, but presuming there is danger, they fall into line, and once fairly under way nothing can stop them.

"Those in front cannot stop without being run over, and those in the rear run to keep up. On this occasion several hundred horses started with a noise like thunder, running so close together that when one is so unfortunate as to face a tree he was either killed or so badly injured as to be unable to proceed, and was run over by the whole drove; so if a horse was unable to keep up he was knocked down and killed; between the bank of the Wisconsin and the point of land between there and the fort, thirty-seven horses were found dead. They took the trail they came on, and ran to the prairie, a distance of about sixteen miles, over sixty horses were killed, and it was late next day before those recovered were brought back.[42]

Governor John Reynolds* wrote, "The first night the army camped at Fort Winnebago they experienced a

---

* Governor Reynolds, en route to Fort Hamilton (at today's Wiota, Wisconsin) was not present, but he undoubtedly got first-hand reports from those who were at the Fort Winnebago stampede for inclusion in his history of Illinois, *My Own Times*.

John Reynolds, Governor of Illinois

calamity worse than an ordinary battle with the Indians. About a thousand horses were grazing near the encampment; and it is supposed that some thieving Indians were trying to steal some of the horses, which caused a general, most furious, and dangerous *stampede* among the quadrupeds. The soldiers being tired, were fast asleep in their tents, which were pitched near one another, mostly not more than three feet apart. It is understood by the reader that in these stampedes the horses are scared until they are *crazy,* and run, at the top of their speed, over any opposing obstacle they are able to surmount. One thousand horses running at once, with race horse speed, make not only appalling noise, worse than a tornado, but there is absolute danger in being trampled to death in the furious race. The horses behind force those before onward, so that if the foremost horses wished to stop, or to divert their course, they cannot do it.

"The first flight of the horses ran with the violence and fury of a tempest, *pellmell* over the camp of the troops, knocking down tents into the faces of the sleeping men, and battering into the ground the arms, tent poles, men, and all articles in the camp. The picket guard, sentinels, and officers of the day, all entered the camp with the horses, and all supposed it was an attack of the Indians. Many of the men were bruised and crippled, and almost unable to stir. The bugles and drums sounded to arms, and those who were able were in the utmost confusion in the dark to obtain their arms, which had been so scattered, and many broken by the horses. This was a second edition to the confusion at the Tower of Babel; only this at Fort Winnebago caused more bruised bodies.

"The stampede took a northern direction, and the Wisconsin river stopped their race in that course, but not their fury. The horses then changed their direction back, and ran the second time directly over the camp. The soldiers by this time were awakened, and attempted to stop the crazy animals; but only a few were arrested from this dangerous stampede.

"It is supposed that most of the horses must have run thirty miles in this race, which did the service much injury at this crisis. It required great trouble to find the horses, and many were never found. The trail the army made to the fort was followed back fifty miles in search of the lost horses. Many of the horses were crippled, and all injured and fatigued by the stampede."[43]

In Captain John Arnold's Company of Colonel Samuel Adams's Second Regiment of Alexander's Second Brigade, Private Joseph O. Buchannan "Lost a grey mare at fort Winebago 12 July 1832".[44]

In Captain John F. Richardson's Company of Major William McHenry's Spy Battalion of Alexander's Second Brigade, Private Samuel White "lost his gun & Blanket (private property)"[45] "The loss, valued at $14, occurred on July 12, 1832".[46]

In Captain Samuel Houston's Company of Major William Lee D. Ewing's Spy Battalion of Henry's Third Brigade, Private John Beasley "Lost horse on the 12th of July"[47] and Private Mordica Flemming "Lost hi[s ho]rse on the 12th of July".[48]

The event even earned mention in the notes of the "Diary of the Weather" at Fort Winnebago: "Some hundred horses lost on the night of the 12th which reduced the force."[49]

"This of course occasioned another delay, and it was not till the fifth day, that they left the fort in pursuit of the Indians."[50]

"Having ascertained the position of the enemy, his [Dodge's] next object was to prevail on Generals Henry and Alexander to disobey their orders from Gen Atkinson, by varying the line of march in returning to his camp, so that, by striking Rock River above the enemy, they would place them between Atkinson and themselves and it was known that the Indians were encumbered with their women and children, they could be forced into a battle."[9]

— Lt. Charles Bracken, Adjutant,
Michigan Territory Militia

FRIDAY, JULY 13, 1832

clear, north west wind
Thermometer: 7 A.M. - 72°
2 P.M. - 82°
9 P.M. - 67°

Because of the stampede last night, the militia "Remained there"[1] [at Fort Winnebago]

"This circumstance caused us to stay here two days, trying to recover our horses, but all could not be found."[2]

We "drew 12 days provision, men look for their horses [Private] John Wilson's mare runs off and broke her leg. Col. [of the First Regiment of Milton K. Alexander's Second Brigade, James M.] Blackburn's mare trimed a beautiful creek here."[3]

In Captain Andrew Bankson's Company of Colonel Gabriel Jones's Third Regiment of Henry's Third Brigade, 1st Sergeant Henry L. Roper had "horse lost 13 July & another bought".[4] Privates Joshua T. Bradley and John Omelvany also "lost horse 13" July & bought another".[5]

Major William Lee D. Ewing of James D. Henry's Third Brigade wrote, "Thirteen of those [horses] belonging to my [Spy] Battalion are (I apprehend) irrecoverably lost. Those that were recovered from the flight are more unfit for service than such as refused to join it, although it is well understood that the best horses generally are the first to take fright & run. I was dismounted before I reached this place by reason of my horse becoming lame. It however ran with the rest and is lost after the most vigilant search.... The horses which refused, or did not join in the flight were generally unable from disability."[6]

"General Alexander has drawn his provisions...."[7].

"Arriving at Fort Winnebago [on July 11], Col [Henry] Dodge ascertained, through the Winnebagoes, that the Sauks and Foxes had moved up Rock River, and were then at the Rapids*."[8]

"having ascertained the position of the enemy, his [Henry Dodge's] next object was to prevail on Generals Henry and Alexander to disobey their orders from Gen. [Henry] Atkinson, by varying the line of march in returning to his camp, so that, by striking Rock River above the enemy, they would place them between Atkinson and themselves and it was known that the Indians were encumbered with their women and children, they could be forced into a battle.

"The negotiation on this subject was opened first with Gen. Henry by Maj. James W. Stephenson, of the Galena company, serving under Gen. Dodge. Between Henry and Stephenson the closest intimacy existed; they had been arraigned together at Edwardsville, Ill. for a high crime, of which, however, they had been honorably acquitted. Maj. Stephenson possessed great influence over Gen. Henry, and on this occasion he used that influence to induce him to embrace warmly the plans of Gen. Dodge."[9]

"From this point Gen. Dodge was certainly the mainspring, the life and energy of the army, suggesting and planning all its movements; and none could be mistaken in this particular who were present, and unprejudiced. This was but natural, and can be said without any just prejudice to the reputation of Gen. Henry. Gen. Dodge had acquired a high reputation as a military man, and as an Indian fighter.

* At today's Hustisford, Wisconsin.

Major James W. Stephenson,
Illinois Mounted Militia,
Serving under Henry Dodge

Colonel Henry Dodge,
Commander of the Iowa County
(Michigan Territory) Militia

He was well acquainted with the country, with the Winnebagoes (who were our guides), with Mr. Poquette (who was our interpreter); and Gen. Henry was not so vain-glorious, as to be unwilling to be governed by the suggestions of Gen. Dodge."[10]

"Generals Henry and Dodge had by this time, come to the conclusion to go back around the head of Fox river, to see if they could not fall in with Black Hawk, and stop his passage to the north; as they supposed he was intending to make his way to the Chippeway nation."[11]

"The co-operation of Henry being secured the subject was then submitted to a council composed of the superior officers of the two brigades."[12]

"...having received their supplies, a consultation was had by the officers, on the route of return. Colonel Dodge suggested the idea* of crossing Rock River higher up, so as to throw the Indians, if they were in the vicinity, between themselves and the rest of the army under General Atkinson."[14] Dodge's thinking was this, "if the enemy continues to retreat in the direction of Lake Michigan might we not fall on him and if Hard pushed get a supply of provisions at Chicago or green Bay."[15]

---

* Peter Parkinson, Jr., wrote in later years," "...it is not true, as stated in Gov. Ford's History, that Gen. Dodge endeavored to avoid going from Fort Winnebago to the rapids of Rock River (where the enemy was then supposed to be) in consequence of the worn down condition of his horses; neither did he refuse to go without written orders from Gen. Henry.

"The facts are, that Gen. Dodge was the first to suggest and urge this course to Gens. Henry and Alexander--Gen. Henry assenting, and Gen. Alexander dissenting. This was the universal understanding at the time by all parties. I have since been informed by Col. Daniel M. Parkinson [his father], of Lafayette county, who commanded a company under Gen. Dodge at the time, and who was an intimate friend of both Gen. Dodge and Gen. Henry, that such was the fact, that he was present and heard the conversation."[13]

Brigadier General Milton K. Alexander,
Commander of the Second Brigade,
Illinois Mounted Militia

"He [Dodge] immediately called a council of his own officers, and those of the other two commands at which he communicated the intelligence he had derived from the Winnebagoes, and proposed to return to Gen. Atkinson's camp by way of the Rapids.[16]

"Alexander and the officers of his brigade altogether refused to join the expedition...."[17]

"Gen [Milton K.] Alexander objected, stating that it would be a violation of Gen. Atkinson's orders, which were to return immediately...."[18] Both Order No. 51 (written on July 9 to Brigadier Generals Alexander and Henry) and Order No. 55 (written on July 10 to Dodge) contain identical orders, "...return to these Head qrs. without delay."[19]

"...and Col. Dodge rejoined, that as there was no route specified in the orders, he thought they might return by any route they should deem proper.

"Gen. Henry coincided with this opinion, and he and Col. Dodge agreed to return with the[i]r commands, by way of Rock River Rapids, leaving Gen. Alexander to take the back trail."[20]

"General Alexander concluded that it was best to obey General Atkinson's order."[21]

Meanwhile, Dodge learned that President Andrew Jackson had nominated him to command the new army cavalry unit, the U. S. Rangers, recently established by Congress, that the United States Senate had confirmed his nomination, and that his fellow-officer James D. Henry had been authorized to raise one of the six companies.

The Galenian newspaper of July 18 approved his appointment to head up the new cavalry unit:

"It will be seen by the following official annunciation, that the nomination of Gen. Dodge to take the command of the battalion of mounted Riflemen, has been confirmed by the Senate. The nomination of Gen. Dodge must, and will, afford universal satisfaction, as there can be no one found more efficient in the discharge of duty:--

"The nomination of HENRY DODGE, to command the battalion of mounted rifelemen for the protection of our frontier has been confirmed, and it is understood that the following gentlemen have been authorized to raise companies: B. V. Beekes and S. Ford, of Indiana; J. B. Brown and Mr. Jas. D. Henry, of Illinois; N. Boone*, of Missouri, and Capt. Been, of Arkansas.--*Globe*"[23]

Dodge's immediate reaction was that "it will take at least two months before the Mounted Battallion can take the field"[24]

Captain Nathan Boone,
United States Army Rangers

* Nathan Boone was the youngest son of Daniel Boone. Daniel Boone died at this son's home in Missouri in 1820.[22]

Act of Congress

Chap. CXXXI.—An Act to authorize the President to raise mounted volunteers for the defence of the frontier. June 15, 1832.

Be it enacted by the Senate and House of Representatives of the United States of America, in Congress assembled, That the President of the United States be, and he is hereby, authorized to raise, either by the acceptance of volunteers, or enlistment for one year, unless sooner discharged, six hundred mounted rangers, to be armed, equipt, mounted, and organized in such manner, and to be under such regulations and restrictions as the nature of the service may, in his opinion, make necessary.

Sec. 2 And be it further enacted, That each of the said companies of rangers shall consist of one captain, one first, one second, and one third lieutenant; five sergeants, five corporals, and one hundred privates; the whole to form a battalion, and be commanded by a major.

Sec. 3. And be it further enacted, That the said non-commissioned officers and privates shall arm and equip themselves, unless otherwise ordered by the President, and provide their own horses, and shall be allowed each one dollar per day as a full compensation for their services and the use of their arms and horses. The commissioned officers shall receive the same pay and emoluments as officers of the same grade in the army of the United States, and the officers shall be allowed forage for their horses, and be entitled to the same rations as those of the same grade in the army of the United States, respectively.

Sec. 4. And be it further enacted, That the officers, non-commissioned officers, and privates raised pusuant to this act, shall be entitled to the like compensation, in case of disability by wounds or otherwise, incurred in the service, as has heretofore been allowed to officers, non-commissioned officers, and privates in the military establishment of the United States; and shall be subject to the rules and articles of war, and such regulations as have been or shall be established according to law for the government of the army of the United States, as far as the same may be applicable to the said rangers within the intent and meaning of this act, for the protection and defence of the north-western frontier of the United States.

Sec. 5. And be it further enacted, That the President of the United States, by and with the advice and consent of the Senate, is hereby authorized to appoint all the officers proper to be appointed under this act; which appointments may be made during the recess of the Senate, but shall be submitted to the Senate at their next session, for their advice and consent; and that the sum of fifty thousand dollars be, and the same is hereby, appropriated for the purpose of carrying this act into effect.

Approved, June 15, 1832.

"Many of the officers, also, of the brigade of Gen. Henry were not inclined to march with their General; and all the officers of the regiment of Col. Fry, except the gallant Col. himself, signed a remonstrance to Gen. Henry against the violation of orders, and marching with him. This paper was presented to the General by the Lieutenant Colonel of the regiment. This was the crisis--the governing pivot of the whole campaign--and General Henry was equal to the emergency."

—Illinois Governor John Reynolds

SATURDAY, JULY 14, 1832

clear south wind

Thermometer: 7 A.M. - 77°
2 P.M. - 86°
9 P.M. - 70°

Early in the morning, Henry Dodge reported his situation to Brigadier General Henry Atkinson:

"Fort Winnebago July 14th. 1832 7 Oclock A M.

"Dear General we arrive here on the 11th. Late in the evening I found the distance at least sixty miles the white Crow our pilot stated the direct rout would be covered with swamps on the day after our arrival we engaged the Bakers to prepare our Bread in the evening Generals Hen[r]y and Alexander arrive their men complaineed much of Hunger we gave them the Bread prepared for ourselves

"Finding the men of my squadron unwilling to return by the rout we came and that I was in danger of Lossing [losing] them I determined to return by the rapids of Rock River* Pauquette with a few of the Winnabgoes say they can pilot

---

* At today's Hustisford, Wisconsin.

me from this place to that point on Rock River in Less then two days and I have sent this express to you Hoping he would be able to return and meet us at the rapids with your Orders. Knowing the difficulties you would Have to encounter in procuring provissions and the necessity of acting as Efficiently as possible while our provisions Lasted I proposed to Gen[e]rals Alexander & Henry to take the rout to the rapids of Rock River at which point we could march Either way as you might Direct

"General [Milton K.] Alexander has drawn his provisions yesterday and General [James D.] Henry is Drawing his rations this day if the enemy continues to retreat in the direction of Lake Michigan might we not fall on him and if Hard pushed get a supply of provisions at Chicago or green Bay. these are suggestions of mine submitted to your better Judgement.

"it will take at least two months Before the Mounted Battallion [of U. S. Rangers*] can take the field for the present I will accept the command selected for me by the President [Andrew Jackson] it becomes my Duty to report myself to Genl [Winfield] Scott or yourself commanding the army of the Frontier for duty**

* Created by Act of Congress on June 15, 1832.

** Major General Winfield Scott was commander of the Eastern Department of the U. S. Army, just as Brigadier General Henry Atkinson was commander of the Western Department of the U. S. Army. On June 14, 1832, General Scott was ordered to "assume command of the regular troops & militia in the service of the United States, operating upon the frontiers of Illinois, Indiana & Michigan, against the hostile Indians."[1] Because Henry Dodge knew that the plague of Asiatic Cholera was preventing Scott from taking over command from Atkinson, Dodge here reports for duty as head of the new cavalry to either of them as commanding the Army of the Frontier.

"I am with great regard your friend & Obedient Servant H. Dodge

"Genl Henry Atkinson Commander in Chief of the army of the Frontier"[2]

Brigadier General James D. Henry of the Third Brigade also wrote a note to Atkinson indicating that he was sending back to Fort Cosconong* those of his troops who were without horses:

"Fort Winebago July 14th 1832

"Brig Genl Atkinson

"Sir I arrived here on the evening of the 12th after passing over some Verry bad road and traveling sixty miles or more

"After encamping the Horses took fright and great numbers run away but we have succeeded in getting all but ninety One and Hunters are still out

"I have drawn 14 days Rations and intend starting in the morning in company With General Dodge for the Rapids of Rock River, which movement I hope will meet your entire approbation, as information Respecting said rout has been Recd [received] from Responsible source and will be communicated to you by Gnl Dodge

"My men that are afoot will return with my baggage train in company with Brig Gnl Alexander on the Rout we came under an Officer who will Report himself to you on his arrival at your camp**

---

* At today's Fort Atkinson, Wisconsin.

** First Lieutenant William Scott of Captain Allen F. Lindsey's Company of Major William Lee D. Ewing's Spy Battalion of Henry's Third Brigade.

Major William Lee D. Ewing,
Commander of Spy Battalion, Third Brigade,
Illinois Mounted Militia

"Any Orders from you I will expect to Receive at the Rapids of Rock River which is said to be Twenty miles* from where we Left you encamped

"I have the Honor to be Sir your Most Obt Servt

"James D. Henry Brig Gnl comdg 3r Brig M V." [Brigadier General commanding the Third Brigade of Mounted Volunteers][3]

Major William Lee D. Ewing of Henry's Spy Battalion also wrote to Atkinson:

"To Brigadier Gen. H. Atkinson Commander in Chief of the Army of the Frontier now at the Mouth of White Water of Rock river

"Sir. It is a duty which I regret most sincerely to apprise you that my ballation [battalion] is rendered utterly unfit for service by reason of sickness, lost and disabled horses.* During the night succeeding our arrival at this place, the horses of the two Brigades took flight. Thirteen of those belonging to my Battalion are (I apprehend) irrecoverably lost. Those that were recovered from the flight are more unfit for service than such as refused to join it, although it is well understood that the best horses generally are the first to take fright & run. I was dismounted before I reached this place by reason**

---

* Actually 35 miles.

** Neither of these letters was sent to Atkinson immediately, even though the entire Second Brigade under Alexander and other units were returning directly to his camp.

*** For instance, in Captain Samuel Houston's Company of Major William Lee D. Ewing's Spy Battalion of Henry's Third Brigade, Private Henry Smith "Lost his horse on the 14th of July".[4]

of my horse becoming lame. It however run with the rest and is lost after the most vigilant search of a day & a half. The horses which refused, or did not join in the flight were generally unable from disability. In a word, I regard the Corps as useless to the service. The highest gratification that my ambition aspires to, is the assurance of the approbation of my Commander in Chief, and other superior officers. Whatever of service that myself & corps have performed I believe, is approved by them.

"These and other considerations induce me to solicit their and my discharge. Since I have been writing this note my horse and two others belonging to the Corps have been brought in, but unfit for service.

"We have received our provisions and are compelled to pack them or the most of them on our horses--the consequence is that the greater part of the Corps are compelled to walk--at least Two thirds.

"I am anxious to engage in the ranging service [just created by Congress] and should I succeed in obtaining a situation in the contemplated corps, the pressing nature of my private concerns at home absolutely requires my presence there before the first day of August.*

"I would not make the request I do unless it were for reasons of an uncontrollable character. If I know myself, I believe I would disobey no order nor avoid any service which a Commander in whose ability I have so much confidence, would prescribe or direct.

"I am aware of the great & unforeseen difficulties which have been encountered and of

* Ewing was a successful candidate for state senator in the August 6 election.

the unceasing efforts made by you to overtake and whip the enemy, and properly appreciate them.

"As it regards myself, altho I remain at great personal sacrifice, I do not wish or ask for a discharge or furlough without the whole corps is, or such as wish to be.

"Entertaining for you the highest respect & consideration I have the honor to be your obt. Servt.

"Wm. Lee D. Ewing Maj. Spy Bat. 3rd Brig. Ill. M.V. [Mounted Volunteers]

"N.B. Mr. Scott Lieut. in Capt. Lindsey's company of my command will report the invalids and foot to you by order of Gen. Henry W L D Ewing Maj. &c."[5]

Colonel William Hamilton, en route to Green Bay to enlist the services of the Menominee Indians against Black Hawk, arrived at Fort Winnebago with Captain William Gordon and his company. They were operating under Atkinson's orders of July 12.

"Col. Hamilton on his arrival stated you [Atkinson] would probably march up the Rock River with the army..."[6]

John H. Kinzie, Sub Agent for Winnebago Indian Affairs, wrote a hasty note to George B. Porter, Governor of Michigan Territory:

"Fort Winnebago, July 14, 1832

"His Excelly: George B. Porter Detroit Col: Hamilton has just arrived from Genl. Atkinson's camp, on his way to Green Bay, for the Menomonie Indians. The Sac & Fox Indians, I understand are making for Milliwalkie and that vicinity, and it is conjectured intend making good their retreat in canoes (which they can procure along the Lake), to Drummond Island &c. Col: H will cross from Green Bay to Lake Michigan to intercept them, if possible, and I think Genl

Colonel William S. Hamilton,
Commander of a Company of Michigan Territory Militia
and Indians

Dodge will leave here today for that direction. I have written a few lines to Col: Boyd, and suggested the propriety of sending a notification to Mackinac of the Probable approach of the Sacs in that quarter.

"I am, Sir, in great haste, Yo. obt Sevt Jno H. Kinzie Sub agt. I. aff [Sub agent, Indian affairs]"[7]

Dr. Addison Philleo, Surgeon of the 27th Regiment of Illinois Militia Volunteers of Galena, wrote a letter back to *The Galenian* newspaper, of which he was the editor:

"Fort Winnebago, 13th July.*

"Dear Sir:--Col. Wm. S. Hamilton arrived here about an hour ago, from Gen. Atkinson's head quarters, on his way to Green Bay, to collect all the Menomonees, and proceed immediately down the lake, to intercept the retreat of the Sacs. He states that the hostile Indians had moved in the direction of Mil-wa-ke, on Lake Michigan, to occupy, (it is supposed,) an extremely small swamp. Today at 2 o'clock, the brigades commanded by Generals Henry and Alexander, together with the command of Gen. Dodge, will start into the woods--move down Rock river, where it is thought the Indians are,--and thence to the camp of Gen. Atkinson.

"We take with us 12 days provisions; and we hope before that is gone, the fatal blow will have been struck.

"We have had some hardships to endure in marching after the enemy--among them might be mentioned, our total want of provisions of any kind, (except fresh beef without salt,) for *four* days.

---

* John Kinzie's letter dated July 14, says, "Colonel Hamilton has just arrived..." Addison Philleo's letter dated July 13 says, "Col. Wm. S. Hamilton arrived here about an hour ago..." Which is correct?

"I will endeavor to keep you regularly advised of the movements of the army."[8]

Meanwhile, a touch of mutiny:

"Some soldiers, and some of the officers in the [Third] brigade of Gen. Henry became disaffected by their intercourse with the brigade of Gen. Alexander, and did not want to march with the General against the Indians. The brigade of Henry was now reduced to about five or six hundred strong--and one-third of them were without horses.

"Many of the officers, also of the brigade of Gen. Henry were not inclined to march with their General; and all the officers of the [Second] regiment of Col. [Jacob] Fry, except the gallant Col. himself, signed a remonstrance to Gen. Henry against the violation of orders,* and marching with him. This paper was presented to the General by the Lieutenant Colonel [Jeremiah Smith] of the regiment. This was the crisis--the governing pivot of the whole campaign--and General Henry was equal to the emergency. This crisis showed Gen. Henry to be an extraordinary man. One brigade had mutinied, and decided to return to Atkinson: the privates in his own brigade at the brink of open mutiny, and

---

* Governor John Reynolds, who was not present, later wrote, "About this time, Capt. [James] Craig, from Galena and the vicinity, reached Fort Winnebago with a fine company of mounted men, and joined the battalion of Gen. Dodge, which made his force number one hundred and twenty men. This addition put to rest all murmuring in his corps as to their marching with Gen. Henry in search of the enemy."[9]

But Charles Bracken, Dodge's Adjutant and Aide de Camp, pointed out his error: "He was not reinforced here by Craig's company from Galena; but that company, however, subsequently joined him and did good service after we had crossed the Wisconsin River in pursuit of the enemy to Bad Ax."[10] A July 26 item in *The Galenian* reported, "Capt. James Craig, with about 50 mounted men, left town [Galena] today to join Gen's Henry & Dodge."[11]

the officers of one regiment, all but the Colonel [Jacob Fry] himself, had signed a document dissenting from his order. Thus was left this gallant officer almost alone to oppose the symptoms of open mutiny of two brigades. His situation, and determined firmness, forcibly reminds us of the condition of General Jackson in his military campaigns against the Southern Indians. The determined courage and firmness of the two Generals are similar and striking. Jackson posting himself on a bridge, and with a pistol in hand defying the troops to pass the bridge while he was alive; and Henry forcing the brigade to pursue the Indians.*

"In this crisis, as well as in all others, Henry was cool and reflecting; possessing not the least bluster or parade. He reflected thoroughly on what was right: and when he was right, he possessed the firmness and iron will to maintain

---

* Peter Parkinson, Jr., age 20 at the time, wrote years later, "Neither is it true, that Gen Henry's men and officers attempted to mutinize at this place. I deem it quite unfair as well as ungenerous in the extreme, to detract from the merits of Gen. Henry's men and officers, and every body else, for the purpose of making a Gen. Jackson of Gen. Henry--a thing which Gen. Henry would never have done; he was a brave and generous man, and no man esteemed him higher than I did. I had know him from my boyhood, and he had been one of my father's warmest and most intimate friends for more than ten years. But at the same time, many of his friends and officers were my friends and intimate acquaintainces, and are yet living, and it is but justice to them that I should repel this slander."[12]

Lyman C. Draper, Editor of the *Wisconsin Historical Collections,* felt constrained to add the following footnote to the above:

"It would appear that there was , after all, something that squinted towards mutiny among a portion of Gen. Henry's troops. We have Gov. Ford's statement corroborated by Gov. Reynolds in his *Life and Times.* In General Bracken's strictures allusion will also be found to it."[13]

his position, against all earthly power, so far as his strength was able. This campaign showed Henry to be an extraordinary man, such as in ages may not again appear on the public stage. He hesitated not a moment, but ordered all of the officers signing this remonstrance to be put under arrest and to be marched off to General Atkinson under the guard of Colonel [James] Collins and his [Fourth] regiment [of Henry's Third Brigade]. This efficient and decided order from a man whom they knew had the moral and physical courage to execute it, made the officers reflect, doubt, and finally to repent. The Colonel presenting the shameful paper denied knowing the contents of it. All the officers, by the prompt and decisive course of Gen. Henry, came to a sense of their duty, and performed it nobly during the balance of the campaign.

"The character of Gen. Henry was such that the officers and soldiers loved as well as obeyed him. He was exceedingly kind, and attentive to the comforts of his brigade, and nourished the sick and supplied the wants of all with everything that was in his power."[14]

"Preparations were immediately made for proceeding. All the worn down horses that were regarded as unfit for the expedition, were sent home to the Mining county, and Maj. [James W.] Stephenson's company, with himself at their head, nearly all leaving, thus reducing Col. Dodge's effective force to about one hundred and fifty; and Gen. Henry's force was also greatly reduced so that both commands did not, at this time, exceed six hundred men.--"[15]

"Alexander and the officers of his brigade altogether refused to join the expedition, and the officers of one regiment of Henry's brigade also refused to march in that direction, but were finally prevailed on to do so."[16]

"Atkinson commanded at Whitewater, Alexander and Posey obeyed him; Dodge and Henry disobeyed."[17]

"General Alexander concluded that it was best to obey General Atkinson's order. He accordingly returned [on July 15] the same way we came, to join General Atkinson; taking with him twelve days' provision. We drew the same number of days' rations."[18]

"Dodge and Henry having agreed on their line of action, preparations were immediately made for a march. All the men of their respective commands who were riding horses that were unfit for the expedition were discharged. In Dodge's command these amounted to about twenty-five men."[19]

However, Dodge himself wrote, "about fifty of my men left me at Fort Winnabago"[20]

"Having secured the services of Poquette and a number of Winnebago Indians as guides, the expedition, numbering about seven hundred men, marched on the 15th of July, in the direction of the enemy on Rock River."[41]

—Lt. Charles Bracken, Adjutant & Aide de Camp,
Michigan Territory Mounted Volunteers

SUNDAY, JULY 15, 1832

clear south wind

Thermometer: 7 A.M. - 82°
2 P.M. - 89°
9 P.M. - 74°

"We have received our provisions and are compelled to pack them or most on them on our horses--the consequence is that the greater part of the Corps [returning to Brigadier General Henry Atkinson's camp] are compelled to walk--at least Two thirds."[1]

Many personnel changes took place as the troops got reorganized before moving out.

In Captain John F. Richardson's Company of Major William McHenry's Spy Battalion of Alexander's Second Brigade, 2nd Sergeant John Wilson "lost his horse Saddle & Bridle".[2] "The loss, valued at $78, occurred on July 15".[3]

4th Sergeant Robert Davidson of the same Company also "lost his horse".[4] The "Horse gave out, & was left at Fort Winnabago Valued at $75.00 July 15, 1832".[5]

In Captain Soloman Hunter's Company of Colonel Hosea Pierce's Third Regiment of Alexander's Second Brigade, Private Francis B. Thompson was "Furloughed July 15th 1832".[6]

In addition, many troops of Brigadier General James D. Henry's Third Brigade of Illinois volunteers were discharged from the service at this time.

Records show that two men were discharged from Colonel Jacob Fry's Second Regiment:

Fry received the "Resignation of Capt Alexander Smith July 15th 1832",[7] and in Captain Aaron Barrow's Company, 4th Sergeant James Doddy was "Discharged for Disability 15th. July".[8] "James Doddy discharged in consequence of inability--15th of July"[9]

Seven men were discharged from Colonel Gabriel Jones's Third Regiment:

On the staff of Colonel Jones, Benjamin Bond Pay Master resigned 15 July.[10] Private Martin W. Doris [Doriss] was promoted "Pay Master on the 15 of July".[11]

From Captain David Baldridge's Company, Private Alexander Anderson was "Discharged July 15th. at Winnebago on Surgeon Cer[tificate]".[12]

From Josiah S. Brigg's Company, 3rd Corporal Richard Bradley had "horse lost Discharged at Winnebago 15 July".[13]

From Captain James Burns's Company, 3rd Corporal William Minson was discharged "On the 15th of July on Sergt [Surgeon's?] Certificate"[14]

From Captain Jacob Feaman's Company, Privates Lewis V. Bogy, John Ohara, and Birral Phillips were discharged "on the 15 of July". [15]

Three men were discharged from Colonel James Collins's Fourth Regiment of Henry's Third Brigade:

From Captain Ozias Hale's Company, 4th Corporal John Cross, and Privates David Cole and James O. Pryor were discharged "Juley the 15".[16]

One man was discharged from the Spy Battalion:

In Captain Samuel Houston's Company of Major William Lee D. Ewing's Spy Battalion of Henry's Third Brigade, Private Benjamin D. Moore was "Furlowed on the 15th of July".[17]

"...the sick and dismounted [were] ordered from Fort Winnebago to Fort Cos-co-nong--280 in number about the 15th. June [actually July]".[18]

Brigadier General James D. Henry wrote Atkinson, "My men that are afoot will return with my baggage train in company with Brig Gnl Alexander on the Rout we came under command of an officer who will Report himself to you on his arrival at your camp"[19]

In command of the approximately 150[20] sick and dismounted troops from Henry's Third Brigade was 1st Lieutenant William Scott. "Mr. Scott Lieut. in Capt. Lindsey's company of my command will report the invalids and foot to you by order of Gen. Henry", Major William Lee D. Ewing wrote.[21]

Among the 150 sick and dismounted were the following from Colonel Jacob Fry's Second Regiment:

From Captain Aaron Barrow's Company were Privates Alfred Rule, James Hart, and John F. Hart.[22]

Among the 150 sick and dismounted were also the following from Colonel Gabriel Jones's Third Regiment:

From Captain William Adair's Company 2d Lieutenant John Hansford, 2d Sergeant Bartley Anderson, 1st Corporal Abraham Cokenhour, and Privates Payton Brown, Hiram Casey, James Huggins, Bowen Keath, Rezin Keath, Thomas J. McDowel, Abner Pyle, Peter Srance, George Terry, and Nicholas Woodrum.[23]

From Captain Josiah S. Briggs's Company were 2d Lieutenant John Thompson[24] and Privates Eneas Christie and Bryant B. Jernigan[25]

From Captain James Thompson's Company was Private William Parks.[26]

Among the 150 sick and dismounted from the Third Brigade Spy Battalion were the following:

From Captain Samuel Houston's Company of Major William Lee D. Ewing's Spy Battalion were Privates Henry Smith and John Beasley."[44]

From Captain Allen F. Lindsey's Company of Major William Lee D. Ewing's Spy Battalion were 1st Lieutenant

William Scott, 4th Sergeant David Thornsberry, and Privates Jesse B. Garrett, William Matthews, and James Taylor.[27]

1st 5th & 6th Reg[iment] Detach[men]t of [U. S. Army Infantry] Regulars who arrived 12th Inst, left, with provisions also, Genl [Milton K.] Alexanders [Second] brigade, for the Seat of War. Lt Johnson [Alexander Johnston?, commanding Company F, 5th Regiment] left here with the Regulars above.- Genl [James D.] Henry's [Third] Brigade, also Capt [Gideon] Low, and Genl [Henry] Dodge's detach[men]t departd for the seat of war with 12 days provisions. The whole force about 900. Force of Alexan[der] about 900. Some hundred horses lost on the night of the 12th which reduced the force.- 4 militia left here Sick*, also 1 Regular of the 1st Regt [Regiment] Co[mpany] A.-"[30]

"on Sunday the 15th day of July Allexander with his Brigade and all those of Henrys which had lost thier horses and others with horses to carry their provisions set off for General Atkinson...."[31]

"Our road back the way we had come, was hunted for upwards of fifty miles [for horses still missing after the July 12 stampede]; and still a great number of them were missing."**[32]

On July 15, the troops with General Alexander "Marched 17 miles & encamped for the night. Camped at our old encampment, soil good in places."[34]

---

*Including 1st Lieutenant Samuel Barber of Captain James Thompson's Company of Colonel Gabriel Jones's Third Regiment of Henry's Third Brigade. He was "Sick, left at fort Winnebago July 25".[28] Private James Barbour of Captain Josiah S. Briggs's Company was "left to attend Saml. Barbour Sick at Winnebago".[29]

** Horses were still showing up at the end of the month. Indian Sub Agent Henry Gratiot's diary reports for July 31: "White Crow, Little Priest, Bull head, and 20 and others came to get provisions [at Gratiot's Grove, 1 mile south of Shullsburg, Wisconsin] for their families. They brought as far as Hamiltons Fort several Stray Horses which belonged to the Militia."[33]

"On the 15th of July, the brigade was reviewed, and all inefficiency of men or material was discharged, and the troops marched with honor and duty to guide them to victory. Poquette, the half-breed, and a Winnebago chief, 'the White Pawnee,' were selected for guides to the camp of Black Hawk and band."[35]

"A few reliable Winnebagoes under Peter Pauquette and myself [Satterlee Clark] were secured for scouts."[36]

"Taking Mr. Poquette with us as interpreter, and some Winnebagoes as guides, we set out..."[37]

"White Pawnee (Pania Blanc), a son of the one-eyed chief White Crow, accompanied my father [Pierre Pauquette] as a guide during the Black Hawk war."[38]

"In the summer, about the tenth or twelfth of July, I [John T. De La Ronde] went with Pierre Pauquette, Kaukishkaka, or White Crow, commander of the Indians, Rascal Dekaury, Paneewahsaka, or Pania Blanc, and a dozen other Winnebagoes, to the Fox and Sauk war. We joined Colonel Dodge, accompanied by a detachment of soldiers from the Portage, under Lieutenant [Alexander Seymour] Hooe,* perhaps the whole of his company. We went to Rock River..."[39]

"July 15th. We took up the line of march on this day, with General Henry at our head, with the intention to try and see if we could not hunt out Black Hawk. But on account of our horses taking fright on the night of the 12th, our brigade was very much weakened.[40]

"Having secured the services of Poquette and a number of Winnebago Indians as guides, the expedition, numbering about seven hundred men, marched on the 15th of July, in the direction of the enemy on Rock River."[41]

"...General Henry with his Brigd. and Dodges squadron took up their march for the Rapids of Rock River**and marched about twelve miles and took up camp."[42]

---

* This is highly unlikely. Lieutenant Hooe, returning from leave, probably went to Fort Cosconong with his Captain (Gideon Lowe).

** At today's Hustisford, Wisconsin.

"The feeling of contempt which the army officers entertained for the militia, extended itself to their subordinates and dependents. After the visit of the Ranger officers to Fort Winnebago, before the battle of the Wisconsin, the officer of the mess where they had been entertained called upon his servant one day to inquire into the sutler's accounts. He was the same little 'Yellow David' who had formerly appertained to Captain Harney.

" 'David,' said the young gentleman, 'I see three bottles of cologne-water charged in the month's account of the mess at the sutler's. What does that mean?'

" 'If you please, lieutenant,' said David, respectfully, 'it was to sweeten up the dining-room and quarters after them milish' officers were here visiting.' "[43]

"...finding that the army had commenced moving, and fearing that they might come upon and surround our encampment, I concluded to remove my women and children across the Mississippi, that they might return to the Sac nation again."[7]

—Black Sparrow Hawk

MONDAY, JULY 16, 1832

clear, south west wind
Thermometer: 7 A.M. - 80°
2 P.M. - 90°
9 P.M. - 74°

The troops of Milton K. Alexander's Second Brigade "Marched 28 miles [toward the camp of Brigadier General Henry Atkinson*] & encamped for the night. Camped on mud creek [Crawfish river?]. Captain [Isaac] Sandford [of Colonel James M. Blackburn's First Regiment of Alexander's Brigade] & others hear of Indians camped at the Lakes [of Madison, Wisconsin] go to them find them Winnebagoes, find 22 of our horses & bring them in."[1]

On the staff of Colonel Gabriel Jones of Henry's Third Brigade, "Benjamin Bond [was] Appointed Pay Master on the 21st. June & Resigned on the 16th July".[2] He was replaced by "Martin Doriss Pay Master 16 July".[3]

In Colonel Jacob Fry's Second Regiment of Henry's Third Brigade, "Gershom Patterson [was] promoted to Capt[ain] 16th. July 1832"[4] after the "Resignation of Capt[ain] Alexander Smith July 15th 1832."[5]

---

* At today's Fort Atkinson.

In Captain Samuel Houston's Company of Major William Lee D. Ewing's Spy Battaltion of Henry's Third Brigade, Private Charles Enos "Lost his [horse] on the 16th of July".[6]

"The next morning after we [the troops of James D. Henry's Third Brigade and Henry Dodge's squadron of Michigan Territory militia] started [for the Rock river rapids*], the morning report was made out: General Henry had six hundred effective men; and Colonel Dodge's corps was reduced to one hundred and fifty, or nearly so, but their weakness did not discourage these true men, nor any of their officers.

"We had now the brave General Henry at our head, and our intention was to find the enemy, if they were to be found in this region of the country. We now went with more speed than we had done before; the men appeared to have imbibed new spirit. They had a prospect of falling in with the enemy, and they well knew, that, if we went back to Gen. Atkinson by the way we came to fort Winnebago, there would be but a very slight chance of ever seeing an Indian; for they now had been watching him for some time; and being intimately acquainted with the situation of the country, they could dodge from swamp to swamp, and bid him defiance. We now thought that while they were watching Gen. Atkinson, we could steal upon old Black Hawk and take him by surprise.**

"We had Poquet, the half-breed, whom I have mentioned before, and twelve Winnebago Indians with us as pilots, and

---

* At today's Hustisford, Wisconsin.

** Not a chance. Black Hawk's scouts were watching *all* of the troops. In his autobiography, he wrote, "...finding that the army had commenced moving, and fearing that they might come upon and surround our encampment, I concluded to remove my women and children across the Mississippi, that they might return to the Sac nation again. Accordingly, on the next day, we commenced moving, with five Winnebagoes acting as our guides, intending to descend the Ouisconsin."[7]

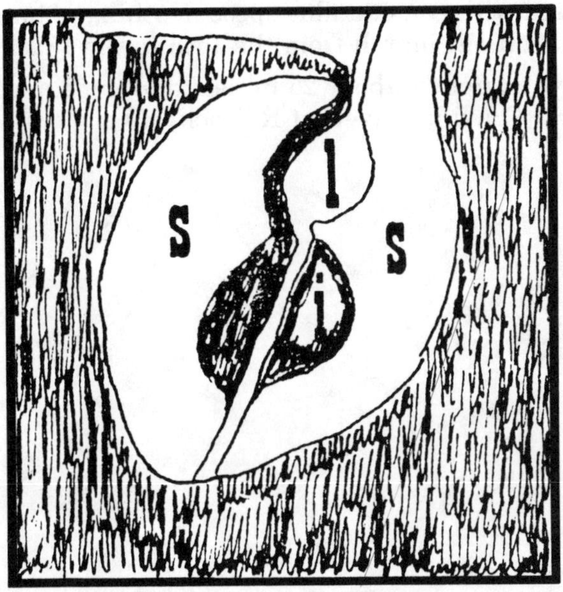

"The above is a bungling attempt to give our readers an idea of the stronghold of Black Hawk and his gang. It is copied from a diagram presented to us, and which is said to be nearly correct. I — The open space in the center is intended to represent an island and a peninsula, between which Rock River passes and which spreads into a lake immediately above. The isthmus which is indicated by an open space connecting the peninsula with the main land, is only about twenty feet wide and a mile long. S — The swamps are from a mile and a half wide, and are represented to be impassable for a man or beast.

"It thus appears that Black Hawk can be approached at only one point in his stronghold. Should our troops attempt to force their way over the narrow pass they would do it at an imminent hazard."

—*The Sangamo Journal*

When Black Hawk was about to leave this hide-away, "Once they [the Winnebago Indians] urged the Sacs to go with them and attack the fort at Cosh-ke-nong—the Sacs said they could not stop and starve, they must go on."[11]

progressed with considerable speed. Nothing of importance occurred* on our march from the 15th to the 18th."[9]

"...we marched about 25 m[iles] and encamped on the mud fork [Crawfish river] of R [Rock] River"[10]

*Illinois Governor John Reynolds, who was not present but who was given many first-hand reports for his book, wrote in *My Own Times,* "On the second days' march, the spies seized two unarmed Indians, who said they were Winnebagoes; but the white spies considered them Sac Indians, and also spies of Black Hawk. With this impression, the Indians were confined with the army."[8]

"...they left Gen Dodge on Tuesday, about 30 miles east of Fort Winnebago, pursuing in the direction of the enemy..."[7]

—*The Galenian* newspaper

TUESDAY, JULY 17, 1832

clear, south west wind
Thermometer: 7 A.M. - 72°
2 P.M. - 86°
9 P.M. - 76°

Brigadier General Milton K. Alexander's Second Brigade and the dismounted troops of Brigadier General James D. Henry's Third Brigade "Marched to Cos Cosconong a fort built* by Atkinson troops [of U. S. Army Infantry regulars under the command of Colonel Zachary Taylor] whilst we were gone 12 miles-- encamped for the night"[1] "Marched to Coskonong, find [Private] James Shaw [of Captain Royal A. Nott's Company of the First Regiment of Alexander's Brigade] & others there, & S [1st Sergeant Stephen] *Archer's mare*"[2]

"on tuesday we [the troops with James D. Henry's Third Brigade and Henry Dodge's squadron of Michigan Territory militia] marched about 30 miles mostly through high Rolling Prairie which was Rockey and scarce of water and at night encamped in a very Barrony place"[3]

---

* At today's Fort Atkinson, Wisconsin.

"I [Henry Dodge] sent 35 of them [my men] Home owing to their Horses being unfit for service"[4] "...they left Gen. Dodge on Tuesday, about 30 miles east of Fort Winnebago..."[5]

The Galenian newspaper of July 25, 1832, reported their arrival in town as follows:

"July 22--Lieut. Col. James W. Stephenson, and several gentlemen* belonging to Capt [Enoch] Duncan's company, who have been under the command of Gen. Dodge, returned home this evening from the army. They state that they left Gen. Dodge on Tuesday, about 30 miles east of Fort Winnebago, pursuing in the direction of the enemy: Gen. D. [Dodge] could not have been far from the swamps where the Winnebagoes had discovered the encampment of Black Hawk, when they [Stephenson's troops] left."[7]

From the staff of Colonel James Collins's Fourth Regiment of Henry's Third Brigade, Quartermaster Sergeant Servilious Blanchard (apparently left behind) "Deserted 17th. July from Fort Winebago".[8]

* Probably including Privates Benjamin Burbridge, Thomas Chichester, and James Hays, all of whom were "19 July Discharged".[6]

"they came upon a large fresh trail, which they soon learnt, by its appearance, and the signs and gestures of Little Thunder, their pilot, was that of Black Hawk and his whole army making their escape."[18]

—Surgeon's Mate John A. Wakefield,
Spy Battalion, Third Brigade,
Illinois Mounted Volunteers

WEDNESDAY, JULY 18, 1832

clear, southwest wind, high wind
Thermometer: 7 A.M. - 80°
2 P.M. - 90°
9 P.M. - 82°

"We this day came to a small Winnebago village,* on Rock river; having reached that river once more, though some distance above Gen. [Henry] Atkinson."[1]

"Arriving at an old Indian village on the river on the third day, no indications of the enemy were found other than some trails that appeared to be several days old."[2]

"...and on the third day arrived at the Rapids (now Heustisford); but, to our great surprise, found no Indians there, except some emaciated Winnebagoes, who told us that the Sauks and Foxes had moved further up the river, to the Cranberry Lakes [Horicon Marsh]."[3]

"on wednesday we Reached the Rapids of Rock River where the friendly Indians told us that we would find Black hawk but on our arrival we found a party of Indians who said they were Winebagoes but who I [James Justice] believe

---

* At today's Hustisford, Wisconsin.

to have been sacks & winebagoes who were married together This Idea I took from their having the dress of some white woman which had a bullet hole in it near the waist seam and some of the men had on shirts which I thought had been the shirts of white men whom they had murdered"[4]

"Generals [James D.] Henry and [Henry] Dodge here called a halt, and had a talk with this nation of the forest--for forest it really was. It might have been supposed, from the appearance of the place they were in, that they had tried to hide from all the world, as their bark wigwams were in the midst of a very large growth of timber, in a bend of the river, and the earth was covered with an almost impenetrable undergrowth."[5]

"we were told different stories by them concerning Black Hawk which few of the soldiers believed."[6]

"Gen. Dodge who was well acquainted with the Winnebagoes, attended strictly to the examination. They were asked where Black Hawk and his band were?--

They replied that they were above, on Rock river, at a place called Cranberry Lake, about a half a day's travel from where we then were."[7]

"it may not be considered a digression to state, here, the reasons we had for believing that the Winnebagoes were telling us the truth; for we had been a long time very suspicious that they were secret allies of Black Hawk, as we caught them in many lies.

"There was one fellow, who, on examination, stated that he had come from Black Hawk only two days before.

"He was then asked what he had been up there after?

"He replied that he had two sisters married to Sac men, and that each of his sisters had six daughters, who were also married to Sac men, and that he had been up to see them.

"This was a very reasonable story, and we thought that it might be true. But, at the same time, it went to show that they were to some extent, allies of the Sacs, as they were intermarried so much with each other."

Hustisford, Wisconsin, Monument
Marking July 18 Army Encampment.

"Generals Henry and Dodge consulted with the officers generally, in relation to the course most proper to pursue. They came to the conclusion to send an express to Gen. Atkinson, informing him that they had learned where Black Hawk was, and that they would march against him the next day. We were then, from the best information we could obtain from the Indians, about thirty-five miles above Gen. Atkinson where he was still engaged in building a fort, at Lake Kushkanong"*[8]

Dodge wrote a letter explaining the situation to General Atkinson:

> **"Rapids of Rock River. July 18th 1832**
>
> **"Dear General Before my arrival at Fort Winnabago I had ascertained if I returned to Rock River by by the same rout I marchd to that place I would Loose [lose] the greater part of my men Col. Hamilton on his arrival [at Fort Winnebago] stated you would probably march up the Rock River with the army and from the information through him Genl Henry & myself concluded we would proceed to this place and await your orders the Winnabagoes here state the socks are at cranberry Lake not to exceed 20 miles above this place and that my Express could reach you in half a days Ride Knowing the difficulty you would have in providing for so Large a Mounted Force that it would be proper to pursue the Enemy as far as pessible with the stock of provisions we have on hand Pauquette and seven or Eight of the Winnabagoes are with us they are raising Corn near theis place they must know where the socks are about fifty of my men left me at Fort Winnabago I sent 35 of them Home owing to their Horses being unfit for service my command is about 150 men**

* Actually on Rock river, just below the mouth of Bark river, at today's Fort Atkinson, Wisconsin.

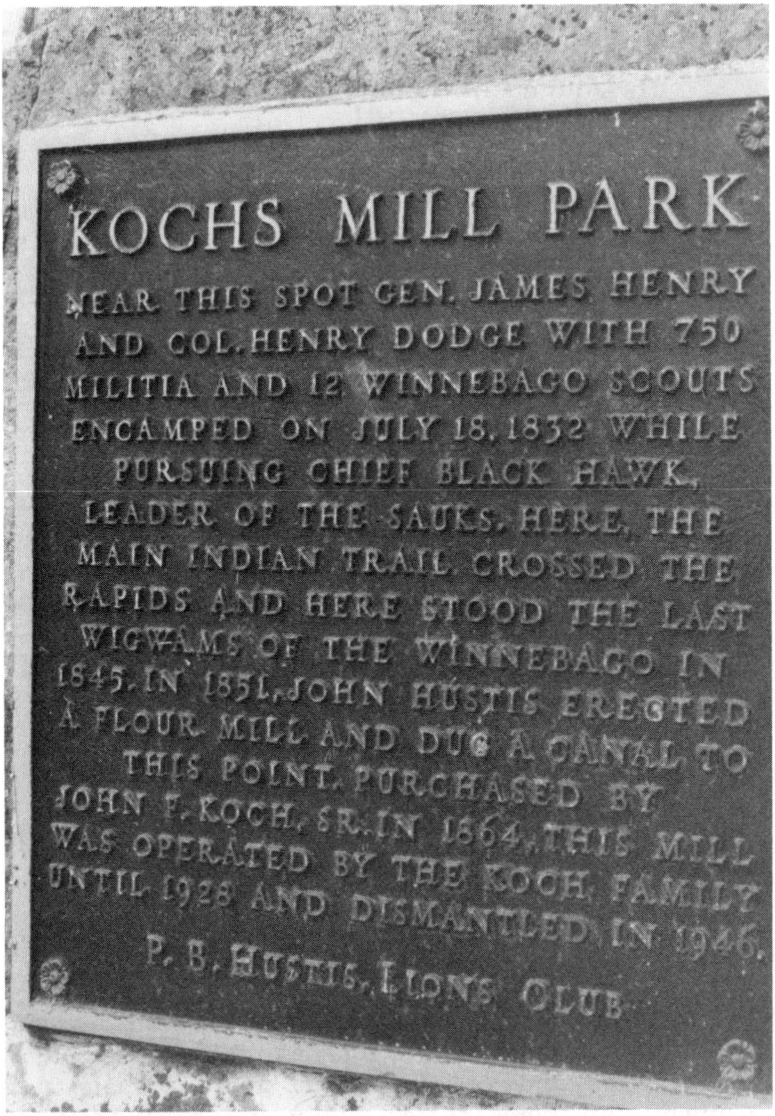

Hustisford Historical Marker
Composed and Developed
by Herbert Neuenschwander

"With sentiment of Esteem & Regard I am your Obedient servant

"H. Dodge Col. Commanding Iowa [County, Michigan Territory] Militia

"Genl Henry Atkinson"[9]

General Henry wrote a note on the back of his July 14 letter to General Atkinson for which he had been unable to find an express:

"Rock River July 18, 1832

"Brig Genl Atkinson You will perceive that this Letter is dated 15 July* at ft Winebago the particulars of our march will be communicated by Dodge. We have had Verry good road

"J D Henry B Gnl Comg 3d Brig [Brigadier General commanding the 3d Brigade of Illinois Volunteers]"[10]

"Generals Henry and Dodge now made application for a pilot to go with two of our men to Gen. Atkinson, to inform him where the Indians were, and that we were going in pursuit of them the next day.

"After some Indian chat among themselves, they reluctantly consented that Little Thunder should go.

"The next thing was, to get two of our men, possessed of sufficient courage and perseverance to go. Dr. E. [Elias] H. Merryman, Adjutant of Col. [James] Collins's [Fourth] regiment [of Brigadier General James D. Henry's Third Brigade], and Mr. W. [William] W. Woodbridge, Adjutant of Gen. Dodge's squadron, were the men who volunteered to perform this important and hazardous service."[11]

"We thereupon encamped for the night, posting both a double guard, and a double picket guard; dispatching, meanwhile, an express to Gen. Atkinson, born by Adjutant Woodbridge of Dodge's battalion, and Dr. Merriman, one of

* The letter was sealed, and Henry apparently forgot that it had been dated July 14.

Gen. Henry's adjutants, with a Winnebago chief for a guide."[12]

"They started about 2 o'clock P.M., in company with Little Thunder as their pilot, intending to reach Gen. Atkinson's camp that night; but they had not proceeded more than eight miles* before they came upon a large fresh trail, which they soon learnt, by its appearance, and the signs and gestures of Little Thunder, their pilot, was that of Black Hawk and his whole army making their escape.--They pursued their course a little further, intending to go on with the message; but this Indian petitioned them to go back, intimating by signs that they would soon be killed if they went on. The expresses could not speak his language, nor could he speak theirs; but they made signs for him to proceed with them, but they did not succeed in getting him more than

---

* Although John Wakefield says "eight miles", twelve miles may be more accurate.

Dodge wrote to Atkinson, "...after traveling about 12 miles fell in with Two Large Trails..."[13] *BHW* II:525.

James J. Justice wrote in his journal, "we took up camp and started an express to Gen. Atkinson to inform him that we were at the Rapids The express was Born by adjutants Woodbridge [and] Merriman piloted by an Indian They proceeded through the woods about twelve miles and discovered a trail and at first concluded that some of atkinson scouts Had been there but on pursuing it some further they discovered where the Indians had been takeing the Bark off of the trees"[14]

Captain Daniel M. Parkinson wrote, "When they had proceeded about eight or nine miles, they came across one of the main trails of the enemy, plainly pointing out their route as making towards the west."[15]

Charles Bracken wrote, "...this express, after proceeding a few miles down the river, fell in with a fresh trail of the enemy, evidently bearing towards the Wisconsin River, and immediately returned and reported their discovery."[16]

two miles further, when he suddenly wheeled his horse to the right-about, and giving him timber, left them. It was now nearly night, and the country they were in impassable to a stranger; the ground being covered with prickly ash and white thorn; and in the midst of these thickets were the worst kind of swamps. They were therefore compelled to return to their camp. It was some time before they overtook their pilot; and after dark when they got back. On entering the encampment the sentinels fired at one of them, and came very near killing him*. They now told the joyful news, that they had discovered the trail of Black Hawk and his band making out of the swamps, which seemed to give new life to every heart; as now there appeared to be a prospect of bringing our toils and troubles to a speedy issue.

"Orders were accordingly given for all hands to be ready for an early march next morning in pursuit of the enemy."[18]

"In the confusion of the army, the two Indians, the prisoners and spies [captured two days before], made their escape, but were recaptured.

"Major [Murray] McConnel [Brigade Inspector on the staff of Brigadier General James D. Henry's Third Brigade] had been out about dark reconnoitering some distance from the main army with another person, and found the Indian trail of Black Hawk. The individual returned alone to the army and reported the fact. Just at dark--McConnel was still reconnoitering--two Indians came through some brush wood, within ten yards of him, and one of them gave an Indian whooh, evidently showing great alarm. McConnel supposed the Indians were the enemy, and was about shooting when one of them cried out in tolerable English, 'Good Indian, me! good Winnebago!' McConnel immediately discovered that they were the two prisoners [captured on July 16] who had been marching with the army. He captured them, and tied their hands behind their backs and marched them to the camp. In this enterprise with the Indians, and

* "They at once returned, and as they approached the camp, they were fired upon by one of the picket sentinels, and Adjutant Woodbridge was barely missed."[17]

Major Murray McConnel,
Brigade Inspector, Third Brigade,
Illinois Mounted Militia

throughout the whole campaign, Major McConnel displayed efficiency and courage as a soldier and an officer, which won for him the approbation of the whole army.

"The Indian prisoners confessed their guilt; that they were spies from Black Hawk. They expected to be shot; but the General did not proclaim their guilt, and they were spared. The General acted with humanity, as the army was then nearly on the Indian trail, and the spies could do no injury to the whites, and to destroy two deluded, unarmed human beings, after their having been prisoners for some time, seemed to be a cruel act. The General was compelled to exercise much care over the Indians, or some volunteers might have shot them if the fact had been know."*[19]

* Charles Bracken, Dodge's Adjutant and Aide de Camp, believed no part of this story reported by Illinois Governors Ford and Reynolds (neither of whom were present) in their separate Illinois histories. Bracken ridiculed the tale as follows: "Poquette and the Winnebago Indians, from the time we left the fort, at all our halts and encampments, invariably made their camp-fires close to that of Gen. Dodge. No man who knew him, ever suspected the honesty or patriotism of Poquette. He possessed unbounded influence over the Indians; treachery could not have existed among them in our camp without his knowing it; and none in that encampment ever heard before it was printed in Ford's History, that Major Murray McConnell had discovered those Indians were treacherous; that he had single handed

and alone, stopped more than a dozen of warriors in their flight from our camp, carried them to the quarters of General Henry, where they confessed their treason--and all this too without the assistance of Poquette, their Interpreter, the only man in the camp who could render into English a single word they said!"[20]

Lyman C. Draper, the respected, long-time editor of *Wisconsin Historical Collections* footnoted Bracken's remarks with the following comments: "Whether Gov. Ford has made some mistake in this matter, we know not, but Gov. Reynolds, in his recent [1855] *Life and Times,* seems to corroborate it [in the passages quoted above]. * * * Maj. McConnell still lives [1856] and is a well known citizen of Illinois."[21]

"Thickets and swamps of the worst kind we had to go through; but the men had something now to stimulate them. They saw the Sac trail fresh before them, and a prospect of bringing our campaign to an end."[13]

—Surgeon's Mate John Wakefield,
Spy Battalion, Third Brigade,
Illinois Mounted Volunteers

THURSDAY, JULY 19, 1832

cloudy, west wind, heavy rain, violent storm at night, tremendous storm of rain, wind, thunder and lightening
Thermometer: 7 A.M. - 83°
2 P.M. - 82°
9 P.M. - 75°

"At the dawn of day the bugle sounded. All now were up, making ready with great eagerness for a march."[1]

Brigadier General James D. Henry "Issued a General Order this morning after consultation with the Cols & Maj Spy B.* to the commandents of Corps to be ready to march at an early Hour in pursuit of the enemy and Leave all the waggons Harnuss and Heavy and cumbersome articles which was implicitly Obeyed."[3]

"...the General...gave orders to the field offi[c]ers to have their men Immediately on the march in pursuit of the enemy

---

* Colonels Jacob Fry, First Right of the Second Regiment; Gabriel Jones, Second Left of the Third Regiment; James Collins, Second Right of the Fourth Regiment. Not present was the First Regiment under Colonel Samuel T. Matthews, which remained stationed at Dixon, Illinois. Also consulted was Major William Lee D. Ewing of the Spy Battalion.[2]

there was a great change made on the men when they heard this Report from men on whom they could Rely The evening before there was nothing appeared to the soldiers that animated them in any degree they had hitherto been led on by the Indians* who professed to be friendly to the wh[i]tes but from the way that they led us it was appearant that they designed to lead us in a different diRection from that in which we should have went in order to find Black Hawk The soldiers had began to dispair of ever seeing an Indian without a white knapkin on his head and the word good Winebago or Potawatamie in his mouth but on the Inteligence of the express finding the trail and that we were to follow on in pursuit the soldiers were seen gathering their horses and sadling them with as much cheerfulness as if at home and gearing them to go to plowing after a fine season of Rain they then felt as if they would shortly overtake the savage foe and give him a scurging and then Return home"[5]

Both Generals reported the situation to Atkinson. Henry Dodge wrote,

"July 19th 1832

"Dear General I yesterday addressed you from the rapids of Rock River my adjt [adjutant William W. Woodbridge] directed by an Indian Guide after travelling about 12 miles fell in with Two Large Trails no doubt the greater part of the Socks from the appearance of the Trails it must be the Main Body of the Enemy the direction is about South West Course they have peeled the Bark of the Oaks and have Dug in different places in search of Wild Potatoes Genl. Henry who is acquainted with the trail of the socks having followed it from the mouth of Rock River believes it to be the Main Body of the Enemy also**

"Your friend in great Hast H. Dodge

"Genl. Atkinson

---

* "The Winebagoes were until that time our pi[lots]."[4]

** Toward today's Watertown, Wisconsin.

Brigadier General Henry Atkinson,
Commander, Right Wing of the Western Department,
United States Army Infantry

"P.S Genl Henry and myself will pursue the trail as fast as our Horses will carry us ys, H D."[6]

General Henry also wrote to Atkinson:

"July 19t 1832

"Brig Genl Atkinson

"Sir You will find enclosed a Letter [written by General Henry on July 14] which was designed to be forwarded to you by Express but a carrier Could not be found (--from fort Winebago)

"Haveing pursued our march to the Rapids of Rock River which place we arrived Yestereday and started an express to you which after travelling 10 or 12 miles discovered Large trails makeing S.W. supposed to have beem made yesterday

"I accordingly Issued a General Order this morning after consultation with the Cols & Maj Spy B. to the commandents of Corps to be ready to march at an early Hour in pursuit of the enemy and Leave all the waggons Harnuss and Heavy and cumbersome articles which was implicitly Obeyed

"This movement I hope will meet your entire approbation and the destruction of the enemy

"We will continue the pursuit untill prudence dictates Otherwise

"We are now on the trail

"James D Henry Brig Genrl con 3rd Brig M V [Brigadier General commanding 3rd Brigade of Mounted Volunteers]

"Dr. [Elias H.] Merriman will hand you the Letter"[7]

"Having by the discovery of the express got hold of something tangible with regard to the whereabouts of the enemy, the pursuit commenced early next morning. It was rapid and persevering...."[8]

"This new information entirely changed our plan of operations, for instead of marching up the river as we intended, we marched down it early the next morning, and at a rapid pace. The express was continued to Gen. Atkinson, by the same men selected the previous day for that service. We advanced rapidly upon the trails, which consisted of three--one main center and two flanking trails."[9]

"Here we had to leave every thing that was calculated to retard our march. Five baggage waggons, sutlers' stores and a number of other valuable articles were left, in order that we should have nothing to impede us on our march."[10]

"accordingly we left our bagage waggons and took up our march early in the morning and marched about 12 miles and thro a desperate thicket and low swampy land and came on the trail of the Indians which appeared to be about a day and a half or two days old and afforded us a much better guide than the Winebagoes were   it was some place places tollerably wide   at others the Indians had (where the woods were open) marched in seven lines and consequently made seven trails which were narrower than where they had marched in one or two lines   there was very little of the sign made by the Indians that escaped our notice   we were all anxious to make what discoveries we could with Regard to the strength of the Enemy and the length of time they had been gone"[11]

"The army marched through a marshy and swampy country, which very much impeded their progress. At every swamp horses were lost in the mud, and left to die."[12]

"July 19th. This day we had, for about twelve miles, the worst kind of road. To look at it, it appeared impossible to march an army through it. Thickets and swamps of the worst kind we had to go through; but the men had something now to stimulate them. They saw the Sac trail fresh before them, and a prospect of bringing our campaign to an end. There was no murmuring, no excuses made; none getting on the sick report. If we came to a swamp that our horses were not able to carry us through, we dismounted, turned our horses before us, and stepped in ourselves, sometimes up to our arm-pits in mud and water. In this way we marched with great celerity."[13]

"We crossed the Mud lake fork of Rock [Crawfish] river at about 2 Oclk P M on the 19th. where the Sacks had encamped in a body."[19]

"Thus we marched on till the afternoon when there come on a very heavy Rain which continued an hour or two the clouds then Broke away and the Rain ceased for a short time and we halted for a short time and dryed our guns as well as we could (as for my own part I [James Justice] had just before we stoped droped my gun into a Creek* and could not dry it in so short a time as was allowed us to rest) after Resting a short time we set off again and was soon in another shower of Rain which was very heavy and continued till after night"[14]

"In the evening of this day, it commenced thundering, lightening, and raining tremendously. We stopped not, but pushed on. The trail appeared to be still getting fresher, and the ground better; which still encouraged us to overcome every difficulty found in the way. It continued raining until dark, and indeed until after dark."[15]

"we continued our march through the Rain and passed by one of the Indian encampments near a Lake which I supposed to be about fifteen miles in circumference and at dark we struck camp some made fires others lay down without"[16]

"The first night we camped on the trail, we were literally drenched with rain; and it was with the greatest difficulty that we were enabled to make any fire by which to cook our supper."[17]

"Mr. [Abel] Rasdell was one of the fourteen men who were sent forward as a scout, when Gen. Dodge was pursuing Black Hawk from Rock River westward, before the battle at Wisconsin Heights. His party encamped about ten miles east of the Catfish [Yahara river]."[18]

---

* Probably Crawfish river near today's Aztalan, Wisconsin.

** Rock Lake at today's Lake Mills, Wisconsin.

Lake Mills, Wisconsin, Historical Marker

"...our scouts discovered a large force of Indians, who made a feint to attack us, when we at once formed into order of battle. Seeing this movement of ours, they made a precipitous flight into the woods surrounding the lake."[12]

—Captain Daniel M. Parkinson,
Michigan Territory Volunteers

FRIDAY, JULY 20, 1832

cloudy, south wind

Thermometer: 7 A.M. - 74°
2 P.M. - 89°
9 P.M. - 77°

"...The next morning* we arose the most of us leaving a puddle of water where we had lay"[1]

Henry "Dodge fared no better than his men. He never had a tent. Our object was to save the country; men women and children."[2]

"We now saw the want of our tents in the morning; a great number of us having left this necessary article behind, in order to favor our horses. The rain ceased before day, and it turned cold and chilly. In the morning we arose early, at the well known sound of the bugle, and prepared in a very short time our rude breakfast, dried our clothes a little, and by seven o'clock were on the march at a quick pace."[3]

"after discharging our guns and puting dry loads in them and geting some thing to eat we again set off on a force march and passed several encampments [of Black Hawk]"[4]

---

* Near Rock Lake at today's Lake Mills, Wisconsin.

"On this day some of our scouts took an Indian as a prisoner. On examination he was found to be a Winnebago. He stated that Black Hawk was but a little distance ahead of us, and that he had seen some of his party not more than two miles ahead. But it was a bad piece of conduct on our part, that this Indian was not kept as a prisoner of war, but was set at liberty, and let go: no doubt, he that night informed the Sacs of our pursuit.

"We halted, and the order of battle was formed, as we expected we would overtake them this evening. The order was as follows: General [Henry] Dodge and Major [William Lee D.] Ewing were to bring on the battle. Major Ewing was placed in the center, with his spy battalion; Captain [James H.] Gentry and Captain [Benjamin W.] Clark's companies on our right; and Captain [Hosea T.] Camp [with the remaining troops of Captain Stephenson's Galena company] and Captain [Daniel] Parkinson on our left. Our own battalion (Major Ewing's) was reduced to two companies, (as Captain [Henry L.] Webb and his company had been left at Fort Dixon*;) Captain [Allen F.] Lindsey, of our [Spy] battalion, was placed on the right, and Captain [Samuel] Houston's company on the left; Colonel [Jacob] Fry and his [Second] regiment on the right; and Colonel [Gabriel] Jones with his [Third] regiment on the left; and Colonel [James] Collins in the centre [with his Fourth Regiment]. In this order we marched in quick time, with all possible speed, in hope that we would overtake the enemy on that evening. We were close to the Four Lakes [of Madison, Wisconsin], and we wished to come up with them before they could reach that place, as it was known to be a strong hold for the Indians; but the day was not long enough to accomplish this desirable object. We reached the first of the Four Lakes about sun down. General Henry here called a halt, and consulted with Poquet, [Pierre Paquette] our pilot, as to the country we were approaching. Poquet, who was well acquainted with this country, told him he could not get through it after night; that we had to march close to the

* At today's Dixon, Illinois.

margin of the lake for some distance, as the underwood stood so thick, one man could not see another ten steps.[5]

"...we reached the Third Lake [Lake Monona], early in the afternoon of the second day [from Rock river rapids]. Here Gen. Henry refused to advance, until a neck of land, formed by the junction of a creek* with the lake, over which the trail of the Indians led, and which was covered with a heavy growth of underbrush, had been examined by our spies, under Capt. Jo. Dickson."[6]

"General Dodge sent Captain Dixon [Joseph Dickson] on ahead with a few men, to see if they could make any discovery of the enemy, who returned in a very short time, and stated that they had seen the enemy's rear guard about a mile and a half distant."[7]

"After this was effected, it was deemed too late for a further advance that evening, and we encamped for the night on the bank of the lake."[8]

"General Henry concluded to encamp here until the break of day."[9]

"Our encampment, on the night of July 20th, was in the woods, about a quarter of a mile north of the northeast end of Monona (or Third) Lake, and about one mile northeast of the present crossing of the Catfish (or Yahara)."[10]

"The second night we encamped on the east end of the Third Lake [Lake Monona]; and, previously to our arriving there, our scouts discovered a large force of Indians, who made a feint to attack us, when we at once formed into order of battle. Seeing this movement of ours, they made a precipitous flight into the woods surrounding the lake. We then advanced a short distance, and took up our encampment."[11] "...and encamped at the four lakes while the

* Catfish river, today called Yahara river, which flows through all four lakes of Madison, Wisconsin.

Indians were (some of them) on the opposite side of the lake"*[12]

"General Henry gave strict orders for every man to tie up his horse, so as to be ready to start as soon as it was daylight. The order was strictly obeyed**, and after we took our frugal supper, all retired to rest, except those who had to mount guard; for we had marched a great way that day, and many were still wet by the rain that fell the preceding night; but being very much fatigued we were all soon lost in sleep, except those on guard."[13]

"That night our scouts discovered many Indians..."[14]

"we were under armes the greater part of the night"[15]

* At today's Pheasant Branch in Middleton, Wisconsin.

** Not really. See July 21.

"A warrior will duly appreciate the embarassments I labored under—and whatever may be the sentiments of the white people, *in relation to this battle, my nation, though fallen, will award to me the reputation of a great brave, in conducting it."*[313]

—Black Sparrow Hawk

SATURDAY, JULY 21, 1832

cloudy, east wind, cold and beating rain, rained all day

Thermometer: 7 A.M. - 71°
2 P.M. - 68°
9 P.M. - 64°

"Early the next morning the pursuit was renewed."[1]

"July 21st. At the break of day the bugle was sounded, and all were soon up, and in a few minutes had breakfast ready; and after taking a little food, we mounted our horses, and again commenced in pursuit."[2]

"The next morning--the memorable 21st of July--we were upon their [Black Hawk's] trail by sunrise,* with every

---

* Lieutenant Richard H. Magoon of Captain Benjamin W. Clark's Company from White Oak Springs recalled a considerable delay:

"The camp was early astir, breakfast was gulped hurriedly, and accouterments donned so as to be prepared at a moment's notice. The morning wore away without any command being issued, and the impatience of the men manifested itself in murmuring at the protracted delay. At 9 o'clock, orders were issued to mount. The order of march was Ewing's battalion in the lead, the mounted miners, and then Gen. Henry's regiment."[3]

expectation of overtaking them soon. The march or pursuit was consequently rapid."[4]

"...the next morning which was the 21st of July we took up our horses which we had allowed to Run at large thro the night* (not withstanding we were not far distant from the Indians) and commenced our march passing through the narrows of the four lakes...."[6]

"Part of the 3d Brigade, together with the squadron under the command of Gen. [Henry] Dodge, moved from its encampment at the Four Lakes [of Madison, Wisconsin], on the 21st inst. at quick time."[7]

"The advance, from the time we left Rock River, preceded by Capt. Jo. [Joseph] Dickson's spies, was led by Col. W. L. D. Ewing's [Spy] battalion of [Brigadier General James D.] Henry's [Third] brigade, the order of march being in two columns."[8]

"...and the next morning crossed over the ground between the Third [Monona] and Fourth [Mendota] Lakes....[9]

"The pursuit was renewed on the day after reaching the Lakes, where one or more of the Indians was killed."[10]

"We entered what is now Madison the next morning, between the Third and Fourth Lakes, crossing the Catfish [Yahara river] at or near where the bridge now [1859] spans that stream, nearly south of the former residence of Wm. Welch, Esq. After crossing the Catfish, the Indian trail led along the slight ridgeway between Monona or Third Lake and the marshy land on the west."[11]

"The last spot where Black Hawk's force halted was on the site of Madison, and they are said to have thrown up a brush or log breast-work on University Hill."[12]

"...it appeared from information received the next morning from a Winnebago, that about one half of the main

---

* In spite of General Henry's order the night before "for every man to tie up his horse, so as to be ready to start as soon as it was daylight."[5]

body of the Sauks and Foxes took post near the crossing of the Catfish [Yahara], on the eastern confines of the city of Madison, with the intention of there attacking us, should we attempt a night pursuit; but as we did not, they left about midnight."[13]

"At this point the Indians had selected an excellent position for a battle, as was discovered when we came to it, by the marks of their bodies where they had laid on the ground. There were two banks, one above the other, and each forming a natural breastwork, with a ravine through which passed a small creek these formed great natural defences, and in all probability, if the army had not encamped the night before, but had proceeded on the trail, a decisive battle would have been fought at this place, which it was evident had been selected by the Indians."*[15]

"We soon found that the pilot [Pierre Pauquette] had told us no lie, for we found the country that the enemy was leading us into, to be worse if possible, than what he told us. We could turn neither to the right nor left, but were compelled to follow the trail the Indians had made; and that too, for a great distance at the edge of the water of the lake."[16]

"They crossed the creek, and were marching over the present site of Madison, when a gunshot was heard on the banks of the lake, to the left."[17]

"About ten o'clock A.M., a party of scouts from the squadron, discovered and killed the first Sac warrior."[18]

"Reaching the point where the 'Lake House' hotel formerly stood, just above S. L. Sheldon's agricultural depot, a lone Indian was killed."**[20]

"An Indian who was sick and unable to travel, was shot the moment the eye of Capt. Fred Dickson [Dixon], of Capt. Jo Dickson's company of spies, fell on him, he not being

* Peter Parkinson, Jr., wrote, "I can recall nothing about the Indian ambuscade formed near the crossing of the Catfish; but Indian signs were fresh and plenty."[14]

** "...the killing of an Indian on the bank of Third Lake, near where the Lake House now [1856] stands, a circumstance known to all of the first settlers of Madison."[19]

aware that the Indian was sick. This Indian was killed on the bank of the Third Lake, within less than one half mile of where the Capitol now stands."[21]

"Pushing on they discovered a solitary savage seated near the shore of Third Lake, a little east of the foot of King street. Suspecting him to be connected with some ambush, they shot him at once. This precipitation they afterwards regretted, and the more since they observed that he was lying on an Indian grave."[22]

"They left their encampment early in the morning, and preceded the main body about two miles, crossing the Catfish just below where the bridge leading out of Williamson street, Madison, now stands. When they arrived at the point, near where Parker's planing-mill stands, an Indian was seen coming up from the waters' edge, near the present watering-place, below the Lake House, who seated himself upon the bank apparently indifferent to his fate. In a moment after, his body was pierced by several balls, one of which passed in at the temple, and out at the back part of his head. From Mr. [Abel] Rasdell's description of the position of the wound, I [Professor C. B. Chapman, M. D.] have little doubt that the skull of this Indian is now [1859] in my possession. He said the Indian proved to have been seated upon a grave, where he probably seated himself with the heroic intention of ending his days upon the grave of some dear friend or kindred. This he thought, occurred about 8 o'clock in the morning, possibly earlier. The Indian was seated with his back partly towards the party, and was turning, apparently to look at them, when he received the shot. If the party had more fully appreciated the character of their victim, his life would, most likely, have been saved; but so frequent had been the deceptions practiced upon the whites, that it was not deemed safe to trust him, and they were, at the time, impressed with the idea, that he was one of a party laying near in ambush."[23]

"On the bank of the Third Lake [Monona], near where the Lake House in Madison now [1856] stands, our advance guard killed an Indian, who, the Winnebago Indian before alluded to, informed us, was sitting upon the grave of his wife, who had perhaps died of fatigue, hunger and exhaustion, and her disconsolate companion had resolved to await the advancing foe, and die there also; and he boldly bared his naked breast, and presented a full front, as a willing target for the balls of the scouts. He but too soon met the death he coveted. This may be thought to have been cruel on the part of the scouts; but it will be recollected that our motto, was, *'no quarter;'* and besides, in such an exciting pursuit, there was little time to deliberate as to their course of action in such a case, even had they then been aware of the attending circumstances."[24]

"In a few minutes the shot was explained by the appearance of the regimental surgeon [Dr. Addison Philleo] bearing in his hand a trophy in the shape of a fresh Indian scalp, reeking with blood. He had surprised the Indian trying to draw a bead on some ducks, and had popped him on the spot. Seeing the Indian fall, he rushed from cover, and, gaining possession of his tomahawk and scalping-knife, began to rend the scalp from the head. The pain partially revived the victim, who muttered some words in his native gutteral, which elicited from the surgeon the following: 'If you don't like being scalped with a dull knife, why didn't you keep a better one?' He then dispatched the Indian and returned to camp."[25]

"We had not marched more than five miles, before Doctor Phileo came back, meeting us, with the scalp of an Indian. He had been on ahead with the front scouts, and came on this Indian, who had been left as a rear guard to watch our movements. There were several shots fired at him about the same time, and I suppose all hit him, from the number of bullet holes that were in him; but Doctor Philleo scalped him; so he was called Philleo's Indian; which reminds me of the hunters: He who draws the first blood is entitled to the skin, and the remainder of the carcase, if there are several in the chase; which was the case at this time."[26]

"But I am not done with Dr. Philleo yet. I will show you that he is a good soldier, and something of an Indian fighter."[27]

"Here it may not be uninteresting to the reader, to give a small outline of those lakes. From a description of the country, a person would very naturally suppose that those lakes were as little pleasing to the eye of the traveller, as the country is. But not so. I [John Wakefield, Surgeon's Mate of Henry's Spy Battalion] think they are the most beautiful bodies of water I ever saw.

"The first one we came to [Lake Monona], was about ten miles in circumference, and the water as clear as crystal. The earth sloped back in a gradual rise; the bottom of the lake appeared to be entirely covered with white pebbles, and no appearance of its being the least swampy.

"The second one that we came to [Lake Mendota] appeared to be much larger. It must have been twenty miles in circumference. The ground rose very high all around;--and the heaviest kind of timber grew close to the water's edge.

"If those lakes were anywhere else, except in the country they are, they would be considered among the wonders of the world. But the country they are situated in is not fit for any civilized nation of people to inhabit. It appears that the Almight intended it for the children of the forest.

"the other two lakes we did not get close enough for me to give a complete description of them; but those who saw them, stated that they were very much like the other.

"I am disgressing and leaving my subject too long; so I will go back and pursue our march."[28]

"we followed on in pursuit passing on by the lakes which would have afforded a delightful vew to the traveler who was exploreing the country but we had only time to take a passing vew of the Romantic beauties of the wilderness and pass on from the beautiful sandy shores of the lakes into the Broken and Barrony woods...."[29]

"Mr. Rasdell was one of fourteen men who were sent forward as a scout, when Gen. Dodge was pursuing Black Hawk from Rock River westward, before the battle at Wisconsin Heights."[30]

"This party, which was commanded by Capt. [James H.]

Madison, Wisconsin

Surgeon's Mate John Wakefield wrote of the lakes of Madison, "If those lakes were anywhere else, except in the country they are, they would be considered among the wonders of the world. But the country they are situated in is not fit for any civilized nation of people to inhabit. It appears that the Almighty intended it for the children of the forest."[28]

Gentry, was sent forward in order to reconnoiter and prevent a surprise by the main body, for they were well assured that the main body of Indians was but a short distance in advance, as was after-wards proved, for this was the morning of the memorable 21st of July, near the evening of which, was fought the battle of Wisconsin Heights."[31]

"They hastened forward, passing a little north of the Capitol Park, in Madison, and along the lake near the University."[32]

"Then turning nearly due west, we pursued almost precisely over the ground where the Capitol now stands-thence nearly due west, leaving the summit of University Hill slightly to the north."[33]

"Having passed this defile, the brigade entered an open country thinly covered with over cup oak, on the right bank of one of the four lakes."[34] "...and followed the trail round the southern end of the Fourth Lake to where Slaughter's farm is now [1854] situate."[35]

The army continued the march on the trail which followed around the south side of the upper lake [Mendota]. They [Black Hawk's band] had camped on the southwest side of the lake, and their cold camp-fires showed they had several hours' move of the soldiers."[36]

"In our pursuit, we passed an encampment on what is now called Pheasant Branch, at the head of the Fourth Lake [Mendota], where was a freshly made Indian grave, where a squaw was buried, supposed to have died the night before."[37]

"The signs now began to get very fresh, and we mended our pace very much."[38] "Hitherto the march had been conducted at a walking pace, and now it was altered to a quick trot."[39]

"...we...commenced our march passing through the narrows of the four lakes where the spis come on two Indians and killed them one only of which I [James J. Justice] saw which was the first man I ever saw that had been killed"[40]

"From that time the pursuit became greatly animated; a struggling Indian or two was seen, and killed...."[41]

"They killed 3 indians on the last day, one Kickapoo on

Bascom Hill Black Hawk Trail Marker

In spite of the inscription, no U. S. Army regular troops were involved in this chase to Wisconsin Heights.

the 1st 4 Lake & two Sacs just in the rear of the enemy...."[42]

"Proceeding on the trail of the enemy a few miles further in advance at the head of our line, three other hostile Sacs were discovered, two of which were killed: the other made his escape.--"[43]

"We had not proceeded more than ten or fifteen miles further, before our fighting Doctor [Addison Philleo] run afoul of two more Indians; he showed his bravery in assisting to kill them. I suppose he killed one, and Mr. Sample Journey [of Benjamin W. Clark's Company] the other; so there was a scalp for each."[44]

"Another sick or disable Indian who begged for quarter was shot by Dr. Philleo during the pursuit."[45]

The Galenian reported, "We have heard from a number of gentlemen who were in the late battle with the Indians, that the *Editor* of this paper* was fortunate enough to kill and *scalp* TWO Indians before the engagement commenced in the evening. It appears that he went in advance of the army some distance, for about half a day, in close pursuit of *three* Indians, until he got them in a good position for attack.--He then asked for *five* men to assist him in killing them--his request was doubly granted by Gen. Dodge, who sent to his aid ten men."[46]

"Col Dodge ordered ten men from Capt. [Benjamin W.] Clark's detachment to advance and kill him. With cocked rifles, the detail advanced."[47]

"They continued to pursue them,—the Editor in advance—who came up within 20 paces of the hindmost Indian, and shot him through the body, the ball entering immediately under the heart."[48]

---

* Dr. Addison Philleo, Staff Surgeon of the 27th (Galena) Regiment of the Illinois Militia, was on leave from his duties as publisher of *The Galenian,* weekly newspaper of Galena, Illinois. His substitute back at the paper, John B. Patterson, later published Black Hawk's autobiography.

"Learning of their presence and his prospective fate, the Indian stoically retreated to a tree, where he steadied his rife, and, after taking deliberate aim, fired."[49]

The Galenian continued, "Our informants state that, after the first Indian had received the contents of the Editor's *short gun,* (a ball and three buck shot,) he staggered back a few paces, leaned against a tree, levelled his piece, fired and wounded one of our men before he fell, although the lead had passed entirely through his body!--It is said he played the part of a *Tactician* in a considerable degree."[50]

"In falling, the Indian discharged his gun, and wounded a young man of Clark's company, of Dodge's command."[51]

"...one of those miserable wretches sold his life dear as possible. He, in the act of falling after he was shot, fired, and shot three balls into a gentleman who was himself in the act of shooting at him. The balls were all small, one went through his thigh, one through his leg, and the other through his foot. I [John Wakefield] am sorry that I have forgotten the gentleman's name; he belonged to General Dodge's squadron."*[52]

"The Indian's rifle had been charged with six rifle-balls,

---

* Peter Parkinson, Jr., recalled, "During the chase of the 21st, occurred the incident mentioned by Wakefield, in his work on the Black Hawk war, of one of Dodge's men having received three wounds from one shot of a wounded Indian. It took place about fifteen miles west of Madison, and not far from the route of the present road to Sauk Prairie. The Indian was on foot, and a straggler, and when discovered by our advanced men, he attempted to deceive them by crying out, Winnebago! Winnebago! It was regarded as a weak device--and if really a Winnebago, he was found in bad company, in the wake of the flying foe, and was immediately shot; and while in the act of falling, he raised his gun, and shot a young man of Capt. Clark's company, of White Oak Springs, whose name I have forgotten. I was near by, and witnessed the incident--the soldier received but one ball, and that in the thigh."[53]

the entire number lodging in the thigh of a soldier named Isam Hardin."[54]

"Troops came across 2 Indians. One shot a man from behind tree. Spies killed him. There were 20 spies. Another Indian shot a man in hip, Isham Harding. We killed the Indians."[55]

"About five miles from [Pheasant Branch], our scouts killed an Indian, who said he was a Winnebago; and when in the act of falling, he fired his rifle, wounding one of the volunteers of Capt. [Benjamin W.] Clark's company."[56]

"When near Pheasant Branch; they saw an Indian in advance of them, who continued for the same distance for a short time, with no apparent definite purpose; when he suddenly placed himself behind a tree, from which he fired at them. As he had plainly exhibited his intentions, their course was very plain, and he was soon slain by a shot from one of the party. By spreading out to right and left, his refuge from them was of little avail, and in an effort to escape he was shot down."[57]

"Clark's men replied [to the wounding Isam S. Hardin][58] with a volley, which they followed up with a bayonet charge."[59]

"The first Indian killed was walking along ahead of the troops, with a pack of meat on his back. A soldier fired but missed him, he turned and threw down his gun, but was bayonetted after his surrender, by Sam Journey."[60]

"The Indian seized the nearest bayonet in his naked hands and attempted to wrest it from the soldier, who, by a powerful effort threw the Indian, face down, on the ground. With great agility he recovered his position, and again seizing the bayonet,* he was forced to release his grasp, and the weapon descended with such force as to penetrate through the body and pin it to the ground. The hapless Indian strugged to release himself, but the brutal volunteer

* The published source incorrectly puts a period after the word "bayonet" and begins a new sentence.

sprang on the body, and, with merciless ferocity, extracted the bayonet and inflicted seven additional thrusts through the body.

"A parcel enveloped in the folds of an antiquated blanket composed a portion of the Indian's equipment, but no man had the temerity to investigate the contents, fearing contagion or vermin. In the next fall, a hunter named Rowan visited the scene, and prompted by curiosity, opened the package, which displayed to his astonished gaze the gold watch owned by Lieut. [George] Force at the time of his death at Blue Mounds."[61]

"So hot was their chase, that no time was appropriated to the examination of his body; but some weeks afterwards, and after the prairie had been burned over, on examination of his body, the watch which was taken from the body of Mr. [George] Force [on June 20 at the Blue Mounds] was found among his effects.

"The watch was the more readily recognized, as it had been used at the fort at Blue Mounds to regulate the service of sentinels. Mr. [Abel] Rasdell, with his party, hastened onward, after their adventure with the Indian near Pheasant Branch, and was engaged with the army under Generals Dodge and Henry, at the Wisconsin."[62]

"One old man left to die at foot of an old Oak tree so was shot and scalped by a surgeon, that kept his scalp as a trophy of his valor."[63]

The Galenian reported, "By one of our informants, who was close at hand when the Editor shot and scalped his Indians, we received the scalps, sent us." "It is not common for *Editors* to fight with weapons more potent than the *goose quill!*—and, when they do, it is the duty of the press, taking precedents for example, to note them.—Ed. pro tem."*[65]

---

* The *Cincinnati Chronicle* commented, "We trust that the Galenian is the only paper in the Union that could boast of such a feat, and that its editor is the only one of the fraternity capable of perpetrating so disgusting and cruel an act."[64]

"These circumstances raised the hopes of the Brigade to the belief that the wily Hawk and his desperate followers, could and would be overtaken: its movements consequently were greatly accelerated."[66]

"From this point [where Dr. Philleo killed the second Indian], our scouts were continually chasing the Indians, and being in turn chased by them. Consequently the march became almost a flight in pursuit of the enemy."[67]

"A man who was passing two months afterward to that [Wisconsin] river from Fourth Lake, says the trails of the Indians were still distinct, sometimes they would all converge into a broad and plain path, and then radiate in different directions dwindling [to] a mere trace. This method of travel was adopted in order to deceive pursuers in regard to their true route, and also to help them escape in case of attack."[68]

"In the mean while a chilling rain began to fall and continued until night, which rendered the time exceedingly unfavorable for the anticipated fight."[69]

"The after part of the day was Rainy and the utmost care was necessary to keepe the armes dry and notwithstanding in spite of all that could be done there were a number of guns which was incapable of use"[70]

"The pursuit continued; the advance was commanded by Colonel Wm. L. D. Ewing [commander of the Spy Battalion of Brigadier General James D. Henry's Third Brigade of Illinois Militia], but Colonel [Henry] Dodge's command becoming dissatisfied with what they considered a tardy march, broke off to the right and left, and took the front.*[72]

"Dodge's command becoming dissatisfied with the slow gait at which Ewing's battalion led the pursuit, reasoned

* Captain Daniel M. Parkinson denied this: "...the facts are, that Col. Dodge's command marched in front *all that day,* as well as on all the previous days of the pursuit...."[71]

among themselves that it was safer to dash ahead, overtake the enemy, and fight them on *terra firma,* than to suffer them to reach the islands of the Wisconsin [river], where if we advanced on them, we would be without cover and liable to be shot in the water. They therefore insisted on Gen. Dodge's taking the lead and engaging the enemy with his command. For this purpose the heads of our columns, striking off at a brisk trot, were inclined to the right and left of Ewing's battalion. On seeing this movement, that officer urged his men forward with blows and curses, and succeeded in keeping up with us, and held a position in our centre."[73]

"We now doubled our speed, all were anxious to press forward, and as our horses were nearly worn out, we carried nothing, only what was actually necessary for us to eat; camp kettles, and many such articles were thrown away."[74]

"The trail was now literally, in many places, strewed with Indian trinkets, such as mats, kettles, &c.,; which plainly told us that they knew we were in pursuit. We too, saw from the face of the country that we were drawing close to the Wisconsin river, and our object was to overtake them before they could reach it; so we now went as fast as our horses were able to carry us;—but this was too severe for our poor horses; they began to give out; but even this did not stop a man. Whenever a horse gave out, the rider would dismount, throw off his saddle and bridle, and pursue on foot, in a run, without murmur. I think the number of horses left this day, was about forty."[75]

For example, in Captain Earl Peirce's Company of Colonel Jacob Fry's Second Regiment of Henry's Third Brigade, 2d Lieutenant Loring Ames had "Horse & Equipments Lost 21st. July"[76] and Private Albert Felt had "Horse Lost equipments Lost July 21st. on forced march."[77]

In Captain Andrew Bankson's Company of Colonel Gabriel Jones's Third Regiment of Henry's Third Brigade, 2d Corporal John Carter was "Dis [Discharged] on Surgn Certf. [Surgeon's Certificate] 21. July horse lost".[78] In addition, 3d Corporal Meredith T. Nichols, 4th Corporal John T. Donaldson, and Private William Baker had "horses & Equipages all lost for[c]e march".*[79]

"...meantime we were pushing on hard after them and some of our men who had broke down their horses kept the march on foot while those that were mounted went on in a full trot"[80]

"...we had only time to pass on into the Broken and Barrony woods where from the top of one stupendous hill we could vew nothing but the savage wilds of high hills and narrow Vales untill the afternoon when our spies could discover when they were on one of those high stony hills the Indians on another"[81]

"...occasionally small parties of Indians were seen on the surrounding eminences; the route was through oak openings from the time of leaving the Fourth Lake."[82]

"the enemy began to show itself from the heights on the right and left. The enemy threw back a party of mounted warriors to occupy a position on the left; this movement occasioned a temporary halt, and formation of the line of Battle."[83]

"Two hours subsequently [to the Indian's shooting Isam Hardin] a view was had of thirty mounted Indians, about eighty rods to the left. One of Henry's regiments was detached to follow them, while the main body continued on the trail. This troop of mounted Indians were making in a southerly direction, while the others were continuing due west."[84]

"...they showed themselves freequently on the surrounding hills to divert our attention."[85]

"...we advanced rapidly, halting and forming once or twice to meet the enemy, who appeared in some numbers in our front, until we arrived near the Wisconsin bottom...."[86]

---

* Ames, Felt, Nichols, Donaldson, and Baker must have acquired other horses and continued on. They were all "Furloughed" on August 12, well after the war was over.

"Upon one occasion, we were thrown into order of battle, but the enemy immediately receded, and a running fire was then kept up almost constantly by our scouts and the rear guard of the Indians, until the main battle was fought."[87]

"the rear guard of the enemy began by this time (about three o'clock P.M.) to make feint stands; and as the timber stood thick, we did not know but that the whole army of Black Hawk was forming for action; in consequence of which, we got down and formed as often as twice, before we found out that their object was to keep us back until they could gain some strong position to fight from."[88]

"It was however, soon discovered to be a characteristic stratagem of the Sac leader, and the Brigade moved forward."[89]

"Our front scouts now were determined not to be deceived any more; but the next they came to, they stopped not for their feigned manoeuvre, but pursued them to the main body of the enemy."[90]

"Fearing a decoy, Henry's regiment was re-called, and the whole army descended into a valley opening toward the Wisconsin River. The march was continued cautiously, the scouts maintaining a lead of thirty yards."[91]

"The Indians were overtaken, and followed down, and along a long hollow, or ravine, being the first one east of Black Earth Valley...."[92]

"As the army defiled down the valley, the width increased and the bank on the right dwindled in proportions until equalized with the surrounding surface."[93]

"We had no difficulty in following the trail, and gained upon them rapidly, overtaking them on the bank of the Wisconsin about twenty-five miles below [Fort Winnebago], where the battle of Wisconsin was fought."[94]

"...in the evening we approached the hights of the ou[i]consin where the Indians having chosen their ground were Ready for Battle"[95]

"...at this point the Ouisconsin was in sight on the right, a succession of lofty peaks on the left, and less elevated

Wisconsin Heights Battle Grounds
This landscape by Milwaukee artist Samuel M. Brookes is owned by the State Historical Society of Wisconsin.

heights on the right; the Brigade occupying an uneven plain; in front lay the second step of the river, thinly covered with low over-cup oak; on the left and between the position of the Brigade and the above mentioned Sacs, runs a deep ravine from left to right, diagonally across the front and bounding the aforesaid step; before this lies a marsh covered with the most luxuriant growth of grass, which continues to the margin of the river, being interrupted only by one slight elevation of sandy ground.

"Thus was the situation of the country when it was discovered that the whole force of the enemy was advancing."[96]

"He [Dodge] came upon the main body about half an hour after five oclock in the evening of the 21st. inst: near the Soc Prairie on the Wisconsin...."[97]

"Here we overtook them, and found them as willing to fight as ourselves."[98]

"...the Engagement took place just about sundown & on the Ouisconsin swamp about a mile from the Bank....[99]

"Our men [in Captain Daniel M. Parkinson's Company of Dodge's squadron] led the chase, next after the scouts, who were continually firing at the Indians. The Indians continued to retreat, until they reached the Wisconsin River, where some made a stand and showed a fight, while the others crossed the river."[100]

"It was immediately discovered that the close pursuit and daring courage of the scouts from the squadron had brought the enemy at bay—"[101]

"...our spies met with three [Indians] & pursued them within a mile of their camp, our men were pursued in turn by the enemy on horseback."[102]

"Here the scouts were retreating down the valley, vigorously applying whip and spurs, to escape a score of Indians in pursuit."[103]

The main battle "was brought about by the chasing of our scouts, who were commanded by Capt. Joseph Dickson, now [1856] of Grant county, by a large body of the enemy

Captain Joseph Dickson,
Commander of Spy Company,
Michigan Territory Mounted Militia

who had been secreted in the low bottom of the Wisconsin River."[104]

"Captain Joseph Dickson, (of Platteville,) who was in command of the spy company, had preceded them, and had encountered a large body of Indians, who drove them in."[105]

"I [Captain Joseph Dickson] with my spy company, commenced the attack on a band of Indians who were kept in the rear of the retreating Indian army, and chased them to the main body of the Indians, when we were fired at several times, but without injury, and I returned to the advancing army without loss or injury to my command."[106]

"They [Dickson's Spy Company] returned to us in great haste, and informed General Henry that the Indians were forming for action."[107]

"At this natural outlet, the alarm was communicated from the scouts, who shouted, 'Here they come, thick as bees'."[108]

"The enemy occassionally shewing itself in front and flank until the advance columns composed of General Dodge's squadron and Maj. Ewing's Battalion of spies halted. This step was taken in consequence of a scattering and skirmishing fire heard on the left."[109]

"Dodge saw them & being with his Battalion & the advance guard of spies under Majr Ewing dismounted & found the horses being held in the rear by a few men"[110]

"On arriving at the edge of the heights, or bluffs of the Wisconsin, the troops were dismounted."[111]

"We then came on prairie. Indians were on horses behind thicket. Our men, Maj. Ewing ahead, got off horses."[112]

"...believing the main body of the enemy near us, I [Colonel Henry Dodge] dismounted my squadron of horse, which formed the right & left columns of the advanced guard, the centre was composed of the spies commanded by Colo. [William Lee D.] Ewing."[113]

"The right and left columns of the advance under the command of Gen. Dodge, and the centre column under Maj. Ewing, were immediately formed in line of Battle, by their respective commanders*...."[115]

"I [Dodge] ordered my squadron to advance in front, and fortunately met with a good position, a natural elevation of ground which covered my men who were ordered to squat down...."[116]

"The line was immediately formed, and advanced in front of the horses, to the brow of an eminence which concealed them from the enemy, who, in the mean while, was approaching from the other side of the heights, in pursuit of Dickson, not being aware of the near presence of the army."[117]

"While they were pursuing the scouts up a long slope, the advance portion of our men were rapidly ascending from the opposite side, and, as a consequence we met near the top.[118]

"...the horse guard was told off, and the men dismounted. This had scarcely been effected, when Capt. Dickson and his spies came galloping over a ridge a little in advance of us, pursued by a number of the enemy. The columns immediately advanced, Ewing's battalion forming the centre, to the top of the ridge, and formed in line by wheeling the heads of columns to the right."[119]

---

* "The companies of volunteers under the immediate command of Colonel [Henry] Dodge at the battle of Wisconsin Heights, were Captain [James W.] Stephenson's [the remaining detail of which was now commanded by Captain Hosea T. Camp], from Galena; Captain [Benjamin W.] Clark's, from White Oak Springs; Captain [James H.] Gentry's, from Mineral Point; Captain [Daniel M.] Parkinson's from Fort Defiance; Captain [James] Jones's, from Blue River, and Captain [Joseph] Dickson's from Platteville. Lieutenant Charles Bracken was adjutant of the battalion & aid to Colonel Dodge."[114]

Wisconsin Heights Order of Battle

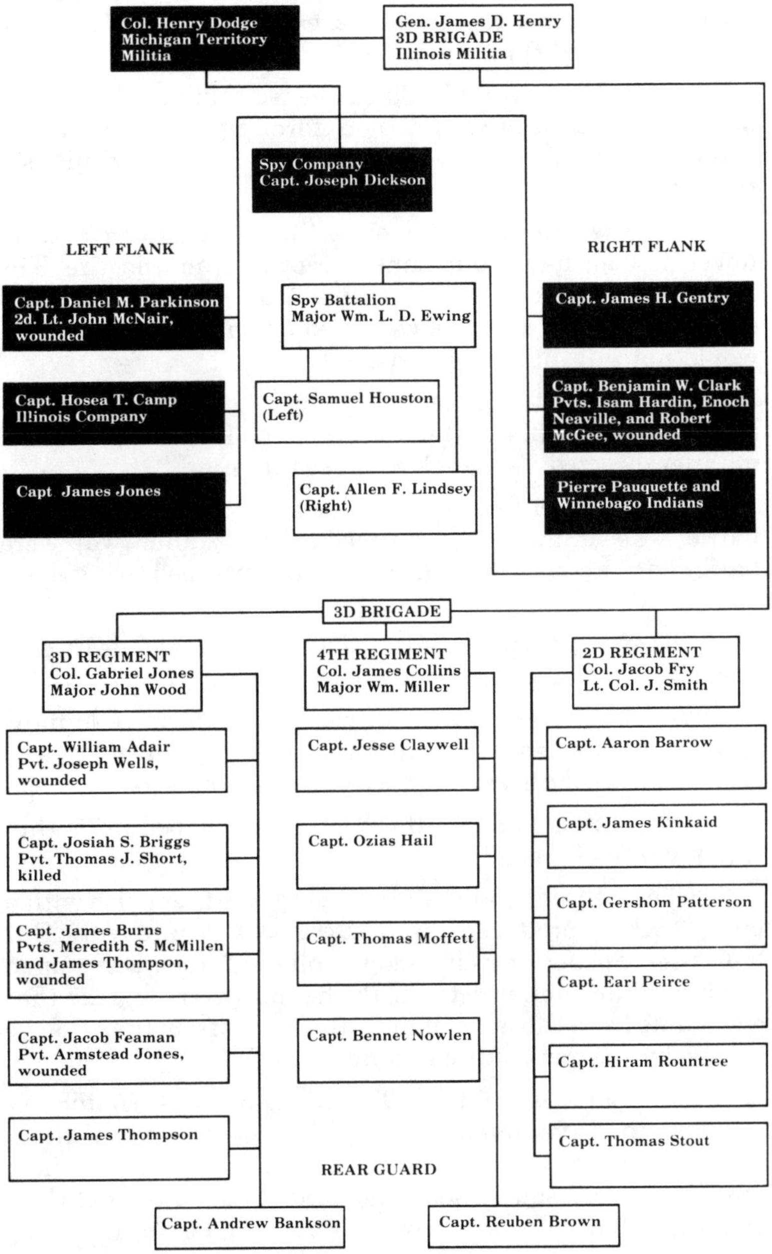

"Here we had barely time to form ourselves into battle order. Col. Dodge's command, of which my [Daniel M. Parkinson's] company formed a part, and Col. Wm. L. D. Ewing's formed the front...."[120]

"Capt. [Benjamin W.] Clark opened column to admit the passage of the scouts, and then, forming line, presented a solid front to the foe, which had approached within six rods."[121]

"Indians charged them, expecting whites to retreat. We never drilled; never had time except to load and fire. The Indians came yelling. We turned our horses loose, and emptied saddles. Indians were tied on their horses so they would not fall into our hands."[122]

"The conflict commenced, as both parties met on the bluffs..." "...at this instant the enemy in its accustomed manner directed its attack against the front."[123]

"They first endeavored to charge us in front. A line of battle was immediately formed...."[124] "...and [we] were barely face about, when the enemy commenced firing upon us."[125]

"...they were not long formed when they saw the Enemy charging on horseback over the hill raising the yell &c"[126]

"We had scarely time to form on foot, before the Indians raised the war-whoop, screaming and yelling hideously, and rushed forward, meeting us with a heavy charge."[127]

"...the Enemy raised the Yell and galloped up within thirty yards of us...."[128]

"General Dodge and Major Ewing met them also with a charge, which produced a halt on the part of the enemy. Our men then opened a tremendous volley of musquetry upon them, and accompanied it with the most terrific yells that ever came from the head of mortals, except from the savages themselves. They could not stand this."[129]

"Gen. Dodge is said [in Thomas Ford's *A History of Illinois*] to have refused to charge the enemy, without reinforcements; when the facts are that he charged them with his single squadron alone, and received almost their entire fire and killed many of their number, before any of the

Wisconsin Heights Troop Positions

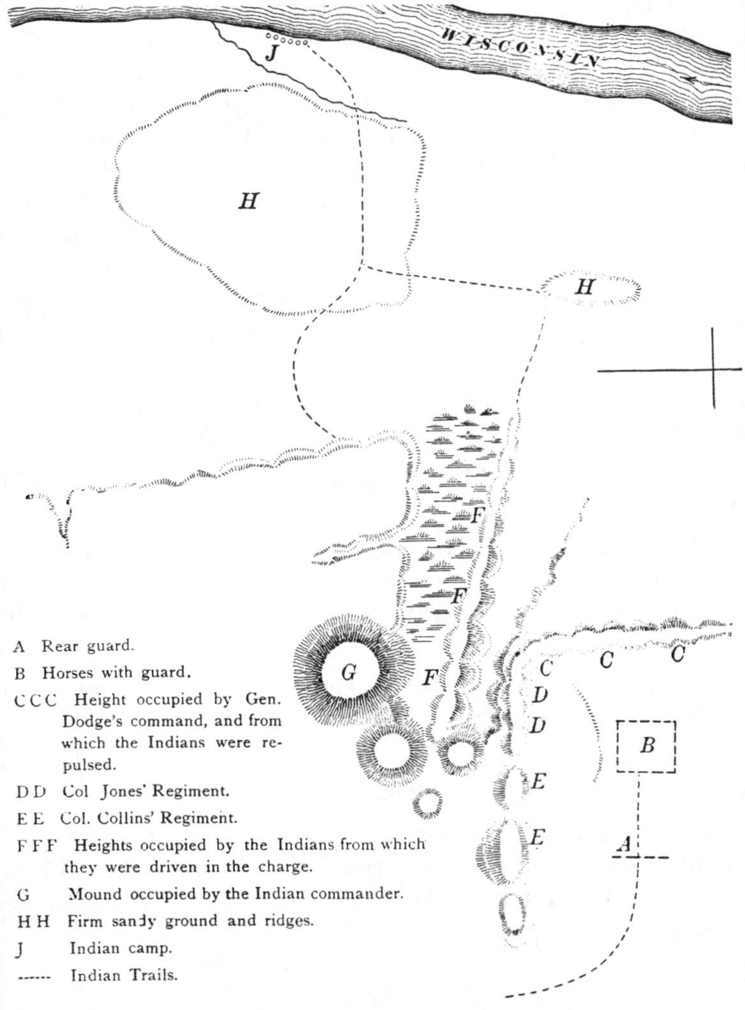

BATTLE OF WISCONSIN HEIGHTS, JULY 21, 1832.

This map appeared in *The Iowa Historical Record* for January, 1890, published by the State Historical Society at Iowa City in 1889.

Illinois forces could be brought successfully to bear upon them. This was in consequence of his position in front, where Gen. Henry had placed them for the purpose of receiving the first fire and terrific yell of the Indians; having, as Gen. Henry expressed it himself, some doubts whether his men would stand the first fire and the frightful savage yell; and well he might have some doubts of this character, as the Illinois troops had, upon two occasions, fled at the first onset of the Indians [at Stillman's Run near today's Stillman Valley, Illinois, on May 14 and with Major John Dement at Kellogg's Grove near today's Kent, Illinois, on June 25]."[130]

"Dodge & Ewings men immediately returned the scream & if any thing hollowed louder than your children* This the rascals did not look for, finding the men ready for them & hearing the white mans voice & also seeing our horses standing as well as theirs, they wheeled & ran."[131]

"These troops gallantly withstood the shock and drove back the survivors in confusion and dismay."[132]

"A volley was fired, and one Indian bit the dust. The Galena company, with a well-directed fire, demoralized the enemy, who fled in dismay to a safe position behind a ridge forty rods distant."[133]

"One fire from our line caused the Indians to retreat as rapidly as they had advanced."[134]

"...we fired on them and killed one and wounded one or two others, when they retreated."[135]

"We returned the fire with great rapidity, and with deadly aim, as it was ascertained that forty-eight of the enemy were killed in this charge."[136] "...and the enemy was repulsed."[137]

* The Indians. This paragraph is from the July 25 letter of Meriwether Lewis Clark, one of Atkinson's Aides de Camp, to his father, William Clark, Superintendant of Indian Affairs.

One soldier shouted out, "Stillman is not here!*"[138]

"The only wounded was Capt. Parkinson, Second Lieutenant [actually Captain Parkinson's Second Lieutenant], who received a bullet in the thigh."[139]

Daniel Parkinson reported, "My orderly, John McNair, was wounded in this onset, by a shot in the thigh, but was not conscious of it until the firing ceased, and the enemy had fled." "...when I directed him, after it was discovered that he was wounded, to fall into the rear, he replied, 'O, God! Captain, I must have another shot'..."[140]

"Col. Dodge ordered his men not to expose themselves or to expend a single shot without a sure target."[141]

"We occupied this position until the arrival of General [James D.] Henry with [James] Collins', [Gabriel] Jones' and [Jacob] Fry's regiments, who, owing to our rapid advance, had been left far in the rear. During this delay, the enemy were concentrating their forces on a hill that commanded our position, about two hundred yards in advance of us, and kept up a constant fire on our line for fully an hour before Henry arrived** and arrangements were made to charge them."[144]

---

* Stillman's troops fled in defeat at the battle of Stillman's Run on May 14, 1832, at today's Stillman Valley, Illinois.

** While Dodge's Aide de Camp, Lieutenant Charles Bracken, reports that Brigadier General James D. Henry was an hour late in arriving at the battle, Captain Daniel M. Parkinson says General Henry was there within ten minutes: "...Gen. Henry's entire command kept close in our rear and were there when the engagement commenced, and were in line of battle, in ten minutes at most after the first firing. But it is true, that Colonels Dodge and Ewing's commands alone received the fire of the first charge of the enemy."[142] "By this time, the remainder of Gen Henry's command, except the command of Col. Fry, a part of whom were dragoons, was brought into line of battle, and which was within ten minutes after the firing commenced."[143]

"The position of Colonel Dodge was maintained, under a constant fire from the Indians for fully an hour before the line of battle was formed by the arrival of General Henry with the rest of his brigade...."*[145]

"Dodge got ahead of Henry, going towards Wisconsin river."[146]

"Henry came up, was slow, and formed on our right and left."[147]

"In front of Dodge's command the principal part of the Indians were killed. The greater part of the Winnebago Indians who accompanied us from the fort [Winnebago], hid in sink holes or sheltered behind trees, except the White Pawnee and the son of White Crow, who together with [Pierre] Poquette fell into our ranks, and fought uncovered like white men."*[148]

"...the brigade under the command of Gen. Henry, after three days forced marching, the last of which [with our broken down horses]** we marched forty miles, and came up with the enemy at near one hour before sunset."[151]

* "The son of the White Crow.... He was in the battle of the Wisconsin Heights—his conduct on that occasion was that of a BRAVE man. General [Winfield] Scott, the great War Chief, sent him a medal, which has the likeness of his Great Father, the President [Andrew Jackson]."[149]

After the Winnebago Treaty of September 15, 1832, the Commissioners, Brigadier General Winfield Scott and Illinois Governor John Reynolds, wrote to William Clark, Superintendent of Indian Affairs, "The medals left by you, with one of the commissioners, have been disposed of as follows:—...one of the third size to the son of the *Crow*, or *Blind*, a Winnebago of the Rock-river Agency who served gallantly with General Dodge, in the late campaign..."[150]

** Brackets are in the original.

William Clark,
Superintendent of Indian Affairs

Colonel Jacob Fry,
Commander of the 2d Regiment,
Third Brigade, Illinois Militia

"General Henry arrived with his Brigade dismounted & formed in order of battle..."[152] "there was no time to spend in counsel we were ordered to form"[153]

"The Brigade advancing from the right and left and centre, by heads of Regiments, the line of battle was immediately completed, under the command of Col. Jones on the left, supported by Col. Collins, who as soon as they were dismounted, commenced and maintained a well directed fire against the enemy."[154]

"About sunset they [the Indians] returned, re-inforced, and made a most desperate effort to break our lines."[155] "They now tried their well-known practice of flanking: but here they were headed again by the brave Colonel Jones and his regiment who were on our left, where he met them in the most fearless manner, and opened a heavy fire upon them."[156]

"...the enemy rallied and commenced a fire on the left flank, his object was evidently to outflank us. the prompt movement of one of General Henrys Regiments defeated the object he had in view."[157]

"The right wing was commanded by Col. [Jacob] Fry, who advanced on the right with the first battalion and occupied a position on the high ground above the marsh, and drove back the enemy in its attempt to flank to the right of us."[158]

"Colonel Fry was placed on the extreme right. They tried his line, but were soon repulsed. Their strong position was on the left, or near the centre, where Colonels Jones, Dodge, and Ewing, kept up a constant fire upon them for something like half an hour."[159]

"...the Indians made a feint charge (in which one or two were Killed) and then Retreated into the high weedes in the hollow in which they at first formed"[160] "They then took possession of a ravine, where the grass was so high as to conceal them."[161] "The enemy here had a strong position. They had taken shelter in some very high grass, where they could lie down and load, and be entirely out of sight."[162] "The battle continued for more than one hour. The heads of the

Indians above the grass, resembled *stumps in a newly cleared forest.*"[163]

"The enemy being driven back at all points, took possession of strong positions on the sides of the heights to the left, and in the ravine at their base. Thus posted they threw a number of shot against the front and left wing, without the possibility of being reached by ours...."[164]

"They had taken a strong position, in a broken piece of ground, intending to take shelter, if compelled to retreat, under each hill in succession."[165]

"The Indians occupied a height which enabled them to kill one of Genl Henrys men & wounded one of mine [Dodge's]. [166]

"After the line of battle was now fully formed, which was upon a high eminence, and in open ground, considerable firing was kept up by the Indians, who had taken shelter in some underbrush upon the brink of the opposite declivity, by which seven of our brave volunteers were wounded, and one killed—two of the wounded belonged to Capt. [Benjamin W.] Clark's company, and the other to Colonels Jones and Collins' regiments; and the man who was killed, was named [Thomas Jefferson] Short, and belonged to Col. Jones' command."[167]

"Here we were fired on by the Indians, and one man was killed, and several wounded."[168]

"Another incident which illustrated the mode of Indian warfare was related [by Abel Rasdell], showing the necessity of meeting them with some tact. As a number of men were in close proximity to some straggling Indians in the midst of the battle, and were firing from behind boulders, logs, or anything which would afford protection, a man [Thomas Jefferson Short] who was near Mr. Rasdell would often raise his head above the log, in order to reconnoiter. While thus engaged, a ball from the gun of an Indian, who was concealed quite near them, and before unobserved, took effect just above the eye. The poor fellow thus paid a dear forfeit for his disregard of the advice given him by his more careful companions."[169]

"The commander-in-chief of the Indians, supposed to be Ne-a-pope, or Rattle-foot, was seen during the battle, mounted on a white horse, and giving orders, from the summit of a conical mound, which overlooked the battle-ground. It is supposed that five hundred or six hundred Indians were present in the fight."[170]

"During the battle, he [Abel Rasdell of Captain Gentry's Company] said an Indian of noble form stood upon a high rock, apparently engaged in cheering on his men, when a gun, considerably larger than others, was brought to bear upon him, but without effecting any injury; he soon retreated from his position. This Indian was supposed to have been the old [age 65] chief Black Hawk."[171]

"Black Hawk said, "I was mounted on a fine horse, and was pleased to see my warriors so brave. I addressed them in a loud voice, telling them to stand their ground, and never yield it to the enemy. At this time I was on the rise of a hill, where I wished to form my warriors, that we might have some advantage over the whites. But the enemy succeeded in gaining this point, which compelled us to fall back into a deep ravine, from which we continued firing at them and they at us, until it began to grow dark."[172]

At the time, the soldiers did not realize that Black Hawk himself was directing the action: "Their commander, who, it was said was Na-pope, was on a white poney on the top of a mountain in the rear of his Indians; who certainly had one of the best voices for command I [John Wakefield] ever heard. He kept up a constant yell, until his men began to retreat; when he was heard no more."[173]

"Seeing that our men were suffering more in this firing than perhaps the enemy were, though we were not idle, I [Captain Daniel Parkinson] stepped to Col. Dodge, and suggested the propriety of a charge; and he immediately suggested it to Gen. Henry...."[174]

"after consulting with Genl Henry we determined to charge the enemy..."[175]

"...the charge was at once ordered."[176]

"After fighting them in this position for at least thirty minutes, during which time Colonel Jones had his horse shot from under him, and one of his men [Thomas Jefferson Short] killed, and several wounded, Colonels Dodge, Ewing and Jones, all requested General Henry to let them charge upon them at the point of the bayonet, which General Henry readily assented to...."[177]

"We kept up a fire for about one hour on both sides, after which Gen. Henry ordered us to charge* upon the enemy, and drive them from their ambuscade."[178]

"...at this juncture, I [Brigadier General James D. Henry] ordered the left wing under Col. Jones, (whose horse was shot under him at this time) and Collins to advance at a charge and take possession of the enemy's position, and cover the heights; and Maj. [Benjamin] James, of the 2d Battalion 2d Regt., with two companies of said Battalion, was ordered to charge on the right."[179]

As soon as their position was ascertained, the order 'CHARGE' was given, and executed with such promptitude and effect, as again to compel them to *retire* from their *strong hold.*"[180]

"As soon as the whole line was thus formed, a charge was ordered and promptly made, by which the Indians were

---

* "Upon the second charge upon this occasion, it is most untrue, that Gen. Dodge and his men took no part in the charge, as the idea is clearly conveyed in the chapters [of Governor Ford's *History of Illinois*] published in your paper [*Argus & Democrat,* Madison Wisconsin]. This charge was suggested by Gen. Dodge to Gen. Henry, as I am most credibly informed, and I know upon this occasion as upon all others, where I was with the army, that Gen. Dodge's squadron was the foremost, most prompt and energetic. To say anything else of them is most ungenerous as well as most untrue. They were in their own country, defending their own immediate families and firesides, and it was expected of them that they would take the foremost rank at all times of danger, and in no instance was that expectation disappointed."[183]

Colonel Gabriel Jones,
Commander of the 3d Regiment,
Third Brigade, Illinois Militia

driven from their position into the low grounds, or Wisconsin bottoms, which were here covered with high grass..."[181]

General Henry "gave the order, 'charge!' which was obeyed by both men and officers in a most fearless manner. All were intent upon the charge."[182]

"By request of Gen. Dodge and Maj. Ewing, they were ordered to charge the enemy at the point of bayonet, lying covered in the ravine."[184]

"Col. Dodge then ordered the charge, and the force advanced with eager rapidity, without encountering any obstacles."[185]

"...my [Henry Dodge's] squadron, with the spies commanded by Colo. Ewing, & the regiment of Colo Jones charged the enemy in good order, with part* of Col Collins Regiment."[186]

"the order was promptly executed by the men under the commands of Cols. Jones and Collins, followed I believe by Gen. Dodge's troops and Col. Ewing's spy battalion. When the charge commenced, the Indians raised a most tremendous savage yell, but our troops rushed upon them with a fury that they could not withstand, and they were routed, and fled."[187]

"These movements were effected with the greatest promptitude, and in the most gallant style."[188]

"When the line of battle was formed, Dodge's command, including Ewing's battalion, formed the right wing; Fry's regiment was ordered to occupy a position on our right, to prevent the Indians from out-flanking us when we charged, consequently this regiment was not in the action. As I before remarked, owing to the delay of General Henry in coming up, the main body of the enemy had concentrated in front of Dodge's command."[189]

* Captain Reuben Brown's Company was serving as rear guard in case the Indians should successfully flank the troops.

Colonel James Collins,
Commander of the 4th Regiment,
Third Brigade, Illinois Militia

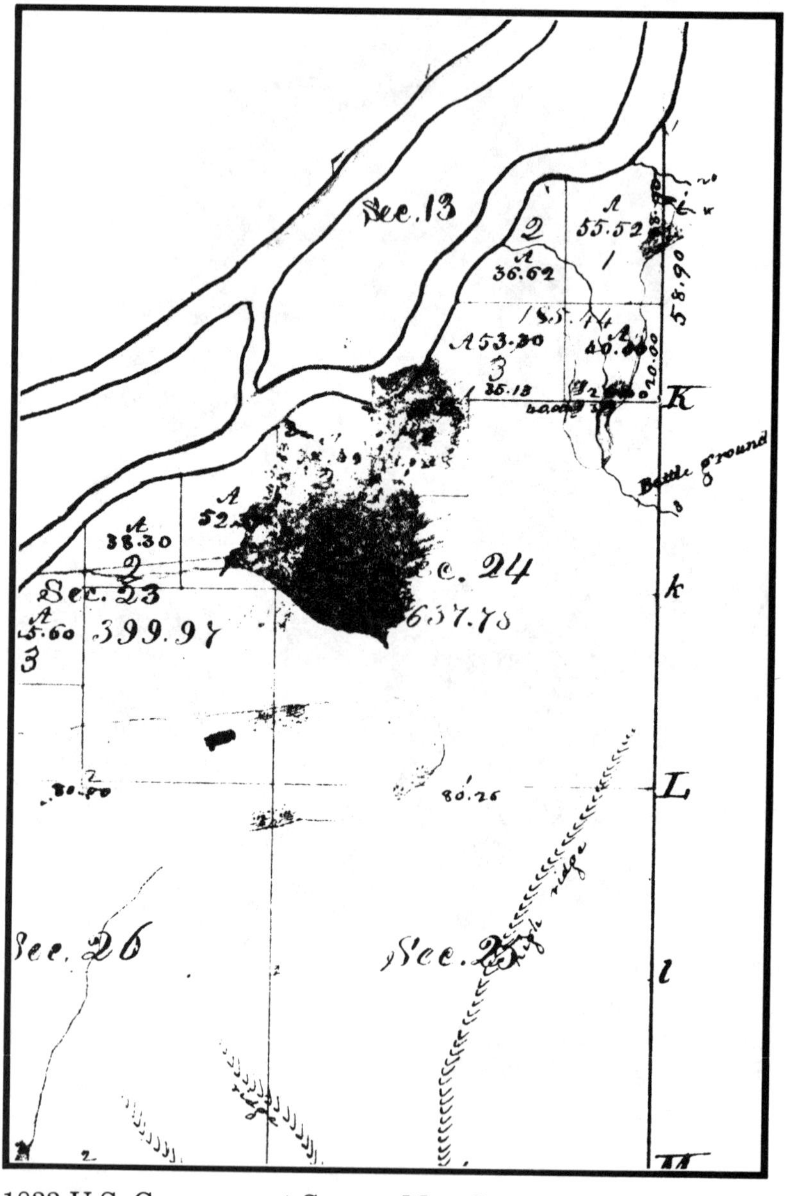

1833 U.S. Government Survey Map Section, Township 9 North, Range 6 East, 4th Meridian, Showing Battle Ground in Section 24

"When the line was ordered to advance and charge, a detachment of Henry's brigade was at the same time ordered to cover the right wing; their movement for this purpose, probably induced a belief, on the part of the Indian commander, that the intention was to cut off the women and children of the Indians, who were in their rear, on the banks of the Wisconsin River; a retreat was therefore ordered by the Indian commander, which took place as the line advanced, and to this circumstance may be attributed the small loss of life on our part."[190]

"I have no doubt but that the Indian commander, who occupied a high mound which overlooked our position, was deceived by the movement of Fry's regiment to our right. He reasonably supposed that movement was to cut him off from his women and children at the river. He was distinctly heard giving an order to his warriors in a loud voice, who immediately retreated. That the Indian commander fell into this error, is confirmed from the fact, that just previous to the charge, the hill fronting the right wing was covered with Indians, and although our advance was over open ground and in full view of the enemy, yet we had none killed and but one man wounded, in reaching the position occupied by them.[191]

"our men soon made a charge and Routed them out of their coverts and continued to charge repeatedly none of which the Indians disputed with any Kind of obstinacy"[192]

"In the meantime, another party of Indians had outflanked Capt. Clark, who, by a well-directed charge, coupled with the skillful maneuvering of his company, averted a disaster and routed his opponents."[193]

"we dislodged him from his position & drove him down the height into the high grass in the swamp. Our fire was so heavy he soon gave way, I [Henry Dodge] thought from the movement of the enemy he might aim at turning the right flank. I advanced briskly at the head of Clarks & Camps Companies to watch his movements, supported by two Companies ordered by Genl. Henry to the right flank."[194]

"After a moments examination, Genl. Dodge with a detachment of mounted men, under cover of a ravine turned the enemies flank & at a concerted signal from the flanking party, charged him with his remaining forces in Front. The enemy broke & gave way immediately & fled in great confusion, carrying off many wounded from the ground"[195]

"Col. Fry, with the first battalion of his (2d) Regiment having completely routed the enemy on our right, was withdrawn from the position he then occupied in the battle, and was ordered to guard the horses and baggage until the issue of the conflict was determined. This important duty was confided to the charge of Lt. Col. Smith, while Col. Fry was engaged on the lines."[196]

"Colonel [James] Collins was kept during this engagement, in the rear, as a reserve, and to keep the enemy from flanking, and coming in upon us in the rear, which was a very good arrangement of General Henry."[197] "two companies had been detailed as Rear guards [Reuben] Browns [of Colonel James Collins's Fourth Regiment] and [Andrew] Banksons [of Colonel Gabriel Jones's Third Regiment]."[198]

"Major [John D.] Wood, of the 3d [of Colonel Gabriel Jones] and Major [William] Miller of [Colonel James Collins's] 4th regiments, commanded and sustained the left of their respective regiments, while engaged with the enemy, on the charge, and acquitted themselves in a manner worthy of their characters as officers and men."[199]

"We made a general charge. Indians lay in grass. We lost one man killed. Don't know number of Indians killed. No women and children there. Drove them to Wisconsin river bluffs. It was getting dark."[200]

"We had to charge up a rising pieces of ground. When we got to the top, we then fired perfectly abreast. They could not stand this."[201]

"On arriving at the brow of the bluff, they [the militia] were saluted by a volley, which passed over their heads. On the return fire six Indians fell, and the remainder retreated at the top of their speed."[202]

"In a few minutes the battle became general, and the enemy was driven from the heights, fleeing down the

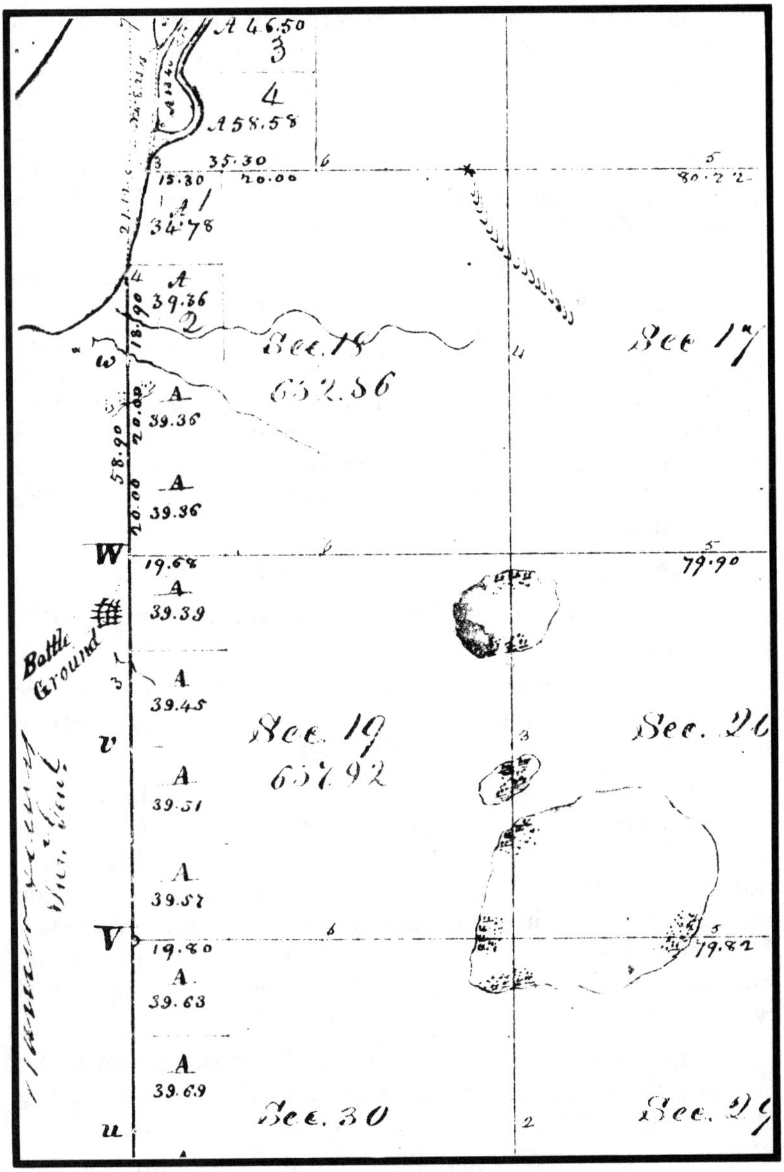

1833 U.S. Government Survey Map Section,
Township 9 North, Range 7 East,
4th Meridian, Showing Battle Ground
West of Section 19

precipitous declivities, and took refuge in the swamps, thick woods and high grass in the bottom of the Ouisconsin."[203]

"The enemy then gave way in every direction retreating to the river."[204]

"They had to quit their hiding place, and made good their retreat. When they commenced retreating, we killed a great number."[205]

Black Hawk explained his retreat as follows: "My horse having been wounded twice during this engagement, and fearing from his loss of blood, that he would soon give out—and finding that the enemy would not come near enough to receive our fire, in the dusk of the evening—and knowing that our women and children had had sufficient time to reach the island in the Ouisconsin [river], I ordered my warriors to return, in different routes, and meet me at the Ouisconsin."[206]

"The action lasted but a short time after the charge."[207]

"The enemy were seen to carry a number from the field during the action..."[208]

"We pursued them to the bottom of the Wisconsin, where we reached the tall grass, which was wet, it having rained nearly the entire afternoon of that day...."[209]

"the troops under the Several Cols [Colonels] by this time had formed & come up, charged & pursued the enemy into the swamps where the grass was so high that they could not see the enemy, & so wet that their guns would be rendered useless, they therefore retired a few steps up the hill & as the enemy rose the hill on the opposite side of the swamp, our men let loose & the way the scoundrels kicked was curious...."[210]

"...the Battle continued about an hour and a half & the Indians retreated across a swamp to the margin of the Ouisconsin...."[211]

"They fled for a swamp of tall grass cane, which afforded them suitable shelter and covered their retreat to the opposite bank, where they emerged and disappeared in the woods."[212]

The retreat led through a bottom of high grass loaded with wet, (having rained hard nearly 6 hours) which with the closing in of night rendered it prudent to draw off the pursuit."[213]

"...and as it had been, and still was raining, the men could not keep their arms dry in passing through this grass, and the pursuit ceased here."[214]

"It was now nearly sun down, and still raining as it had been all the evening; but so slow that we made shift to keep our guns dry. The enemy retreated toward the river with considerable speed. The ground they were retreating to, appeared to be low and swampy; and on the bank of the river there appeared to be a heavy body of timber, which the enemy could reach before we could bring them to another stand."[215]

"We returned their fire with effect and then charged them, killing a good many, all of whom were scalped by the wild Sucker Volunteers."[216]

"Then came the struggle for scalps. Every man could run started down the hill at his top speed, my Indian scouts and myself [Satterlee Clark] far ahead of the militia, and I was about thirty feet ahead of them all. Just as I commenced raising the hill on the other side of the valley, Pauquette passed me on horseback; and as he went by I caught his horse by the tail and held on till we reached the top of the hill, where we found four dead Indians; Pauquette took one scalp, I took one, and the Indian scouts took the other two."[217]

"The Winnebagoes scalped eleven Indians killed by the whites, and the whites took thirteen scalps..."[218]

Having no information of the probably position of the residue of the enemy, and the situation of the ground, and because of the approach of night, I [Brigadier General James D. Henry] withdrew the troops, and about eight o'clock went into the encampment on the grounds where the attack was first made by the enemy."[219]

"So General Henry concluded not to pursue them any further that night, but remain on the battle ground until next morning; and then he would not be in danger of losing so many of his men; knowing that, in the dark, he would have to lose a number; for the Indians would have the timber to fight from, while we would have to stand in the open prairie."[220]

"Owing to the late hour, it was deemed advisable to postpone the chase and recuperate for the night in camp."[221] "...and it being now nearly dark, the pursuit was continued no farther."[222]

"...night coming on & the men being fatigued & unable to pursue from the hard days march (40 miles) they encamped..."[223]

"Dodge & Henry made forced marches for three days, the last day marching 40 miles through the worst count[r]y & the [h]eaviest rain."[224]

"When the battle was over it was 7 Oclk. our men had made a forced march of forty miles many of them on foot, and exposed about six hours in the rain their arms wet and out of order. Knowing they [the Indians] had retreated to the river and that they had chosen their position and that we could not reach them before dark, after consulting with Genl. Henry it was agreed to defer a further attack on the enemy untill the next morning."[225]

"...and it being then dark the troops were called off the pursuit and encamped on the ground where we first formed and posted a strong guard expecting the Indians to give us another Battle But they kept at a proper distance"[226]

"It is believed that two hours more of day light would have enabled Genl Dodge to have completely cut up the Enemy."[227]

"The battle began, on the twenty-first of July, at five or six o'clock in the afternoon; the rain setting in about the commencement of the battle, and did not stop till after a heavy fall, about eleven at night."[228]

"The battle commenced about five o'clock in the afternoon of the 21st of July, and closed about sundown. The loss of the enemy was very severe, compared with that of the whites. The greater part of the Indians killed were found opposite Colonel Dodge's command; the only officer [of

Colonel Dodge's squadron] who was mounted during the battle was Lieutenant [Charles] Bracken [Dodge's Adjutant and Aide de Camp]; Colonel James Collins, of General Henry's brigade, was also mounted, and had a horse killed under him"*[229]

"Col. Jones horse was killed & many Indian Horses killed & 2 [Indian horses] taken prisoners—fine fat little ponies."[231]

Back at the battle site "our men bivouacked on the ground, as they had but three or four tents with them..."[232]

"We returned to camp, and just after supper, we were cheered by the arrival of Adjutant [William W.] Woodbridge and Adjutant [Elias] Merriman, who, it will be recollected, had been sent from the Rapids of Rock River, as an express to Gen. Atkinson, on Bark River."[233]

"They got to General Henry during the action, (July 21st,) but there was no time then for reading expresses, nor did those two men think of delivering expresses at that time; but immediately went to fighting. So those gentlemen performed a double duty, and deserve well of their country for the important services they rendered."[234]

"With them came Capt. James B. Estes, who claims to have been in the battle, but was, according to my [Captain Daniel M. Parkinson's] recollection, about two hours too late."[235]

Captain Estes said "he...reached the Wisconsin Bluffs, opposite the lower end of Sauk Prairie, about an hour before sundown; the battle had commenced a short time before he got to the ground; there was an extensive piece of swamp, or marshy ground, at the point where the battle was fought, about one mile south-east of the Wisconsin River."[236]

"Now for the expresses. General Atkinson directed

* "It was Col. [Gabriel] Jones who had his horse shot from under him, and not Col. Collins as stated in Gen. [William R.] Smith's History."[230]

General Henry to pursue on the trail of Black Hawk until he could overtake him and to defeat or capture him, also stating, that he would start himself, with the Infantry and General [Milton K.] Alexander's [Second] Brigade; and that Lieutenant Colonel [Powell H.] Sharp, would be left to guard the Fort; and that they would go by way of the Blue Mounds; and directed us, if we got out of provisions, to go to that place for a supply."[238]

Woodbridge and Merriman delivered this letter from Atkinson:

"Genl Atkinson. To Genl's Henry & Dodge

"Head Qrs 1st. division of the North westn Army

"Camp 12 Miles above the Mouth of White Water [Bark river] July 20, 1832.

"To Genls Henry & Dodge, I have received by express your letters of yesterday, informing me of your having discovered a Trail indicating the movement of the main body of the enemy S.W. of your purpose of pursuing with a view [of] overtaking & subduing them. I have to urge and direct that you will press on with all haste and never lose sight of the object till the enemy is overtaken, defeated & if possible captured

"I was on my march to dislodge the enemy should he have been found in the position he occupied a few days since. I shall now fall back to the mouth of White Water [Bark river] with the Regulars [under the command of Colonel Zachary Taylor] and part of Allexanders Brigade, sending however two hundred mounted men & some Indians to ascertain whether all the enemy's force have crossed Rock river.

"If I can possibly come up with you in the pursuit I shall do so with the regulars & some mounted Troops

"Signed H Atkinson Brigr Genl US Arny"[239]

The number of Indians killed in the battle of Wisconsin Heights was anybody's guess. Black Hawk said, "In this skirmish, with fifty braves, I defended and accomplished my passage over the Ouisconsin, with a loss of only SIX* men; though opposed by a host of mounted militia."[243]

"General Henry reported, "The number of the enemy killed and wounded is unknown, as the dead are scattered over a large tract of country covered with thick woods and high grass. Between thirty and forty have been found, and others are continually being discovered by our scouts. From appearances, the wounded, and many of the dead were removed during the night succeeding the battle."[244]

Henry Dodge reported, "The enemy were seen to carry a number from the field during the action, so that the numbers killed cannot fall short of forty (perhaps more) many were wounded but the number not known."[245]

---

* Only six killed makes no sense at all. At first I thought this might be a faulty translation for "sixty", but—if not—then perhaps Black Hawk is referring to Sauk Indians only. Prisoners taken later reported that the Kickapoo warriors with Black Hawk's band were all but wiped out:

"*Wee-qua-ho.* Sac woman 50 years old—related to *Pa-che-pa-ho,* the head chief of the Sacs (friendly)...[said] More than ten lodges of Kickapoos were with the Sacs, and fought with them."[240]

"*Wa-coo-se-mok* [said] There were twelve Kickapoo lodges with Black Hawk the Kickapoos fought hardest at the battle of Wisconsin"[241]

"*Puk-qua-wa—a* Sac—17 years old [said] Kickapoos were with Black Hawk all the time—many of them—nearly all he supposes were killed."[242]

"I [John Wakefield] have no doubt the Indians threw many of their dead into the river during the night after the battle; and many that were wounded and died on that night..."[246]

Colonel James Collins wrote, "The loss of the Indians was 34 slain, and certainly a great proportion wounded."[247]

Dr. Addison Philleo reported to his *Galenian* newspaper, "We killed three Indians in the pursuit, and we suppose, not less than FORTY in the battle. I am very happy to state, that we lost but one killed, and *eight* wounded."[248]

Black Hawk said, "The loss of the enemy could not be ascertained by our party; but I am of opinion, that it was much greater, in proportion, than mine."[249]

Mee-se-qua "does not know who, or how many were killed at Wisconsin—she left them just after the fight began."[250]

"Ke-Kie-e-qua. Kickapoo part Sac woman, 40 years old. [said] A great many killed at Wisconsin."[251]

"Ioway. Sac chief* —30 year old—was at battle of Wisconsin... [He said] Five Sacs were killed at Wisconsin."[252]

Wee-sheet—a Sac chief** 35 years old [said] five were killed in the first fight..."[253]

Black Hawk*** states the loss at the Ouisconsin to have been 6."[254]

Kish-kas-shoi. ½ Fox woman '½ Sac. 35 years old. [said] *Mee-ne-cau* was killed at Wisconsin. ...*Ma-cha-keet* was killed at the battle of Ouisconsin."[255]

---

* Ioway was Number 6 civil chief of the British Band of Sacs and Foxes.

** "We-shete—Sturgeons head" was Number 4 civil chief of the band.

*** Black Hawk was Number 1 warrior or war chief of the hostile party.

"Kee-po-a-qua. —Sac—the wife of Black Hawk's principal friend—and has always been near his person—25 years old. ...Has heard that ...*Me-ne-kau* and *Ma-cha-kete* [were killed] at the Ouisconsin. Did not *know* how many were killed at Wisconsin, as she was busy getting off."[256]

Wan-na-so-che a Fox—21 years old. ...Says that...*Me-ne-kau, nin-nin-ma-kee* were killed, and *ma-cha-keet* was missed after the battle."[257]

Ma-ka-se-o-ke man (The Eagle chief) a Sac 20 years old. [said] mee-nee-kau—Ma-cha-keet & Nin-na-ma-kee and many young braves were killed at Wisconsin."[258]

Puk-qua-wa said "Mee-nee-kau, one of the first braves [second in military command to Black Hawk]—Ma-cha-keet a great warrior—[and] Non-ne-na-kie—a brave were killed at Wisconsin."[259]

"Wa-coo-se-mok...has been told that men-ni-cou—Ma-chas-kete [and] a brave by the name of Thunder [were killed at Wisconsin Heights]."[260]

"A prisoner, (part menominee she says) informs that there was 68 Warriors killed in the Battle of the 21st. inst. with Genl. Dodge."[261] "She has not seen that band since the battle, says that they lost in killed 68 men."[262]

"We in this battle were very fortunate indeed. We had only one man killed and eight wounded; and we have learned since the battle, that we killed sixty-eight of the enemy, and wounded a considerable number; twenty-five of whom, they report, died soon after the battle."[263]

"night coming on our Troops were called back and the enemey saved from entire destruction, and he passed over to an Island where he had, and was in the act, of sending Women and Children."[264]

"Our interpreter, Mr. Poquette, and our Indian spies who had accompanied us from Fort Winnebago, left us immediately after the battle."[265] "All the Indians, together with Poquette, started for Fort Winnebago immediately after the action"[266] "Pierre Pauquette, the interpreter, having received orders that we, the Indian party, should return to the Portage, we started off in the night, and arrived there in the morning."[267]

One reaction of the Winnebago Indians at today's Portage, Wisconsin, to the battle of Wisconsin Heights, was given by Spoon Decorah, Winnebago: "The return of Paquette's party, a week or so later [they having left on July 15 and returned on July 22], told us of the defeat at the Sauk bluffs. We heard that those Sacs who had escaped the white bullets had crossed the Wisconsin River in a body. There was now great excitement in our camp. We feared that Black Hawk, thinking us now to be his enemies, would turn up the river and attack us at Portage. Our sympathies were strongly with the whites. Our trading interests were with them, and we were bound to them by treaties. Yet we did not like to be fighting old neighbors like the Sacs.

Some of our people wanted to move out of the way, but others wanted to stand ground against Black Hawk. And thus we argued the matter between ourselves, till the danger was passed."[268]

The reaction of the white citizens to the battle of Wisconsin Heights was given by John Kinzie, Sub-Agent for the Winnebago Indians at Portage, in a letter to his wife, Juliette (who had been sent to Fort Howard at Green Bay for safety during the war): "Generals Dodge and Henry left here a few days since, accompanied by Pauquette; they met the Sauks near the Wisconsin, on the 21st. A battle ensued, in which upwards of fifty of the enemy were killed—our loss was one killed, and eight wounded. The *citizens* are well pleased that all this has been accomplished without any aid from *Old White Beaver* [General Henry Atkinson]."[269]

"I [Charles Bracken, Dodge's Adjutant and Aide de Camp] have shown conclusively, if credit is due to any one for having overtaken Black Hawk and his forces, and defeating them at the Wisconsin, it is to General Dodge. He planned the enterprise, and owing to the generous support he received from Gen. Henry, carried it out. If he was not the actual commander, he was virtually so. He was the only officer holding the rank of Colonel (the highest rank to which he could be appointed under the Territorial law) commissioned by the Governor of Michigan [Territory] west of the lake. He was from this appointment sole commander of the militia within the territory which was the seat of war, and from the extent of his command entitled to the rank of a Brigadier General. He had been appointed in the regular service as commander of United States Rangers, in which corps General Henry had been appointed to a captaincy under him. He was by many years the senior of General Henry, and had been a Major General in the State of Missouri, and held an important command on that frontier in the War of 1812, when General Henry was in his boyhood*. That General Henry virtually yielded the command, and implicitly entrusted himself and his brigade to the direction of General Dodge, are apparent from his declining to write letters, although urged to do so, claim[i]ng the honor of the expedition and victory.**

"General Henry was truly a soldier, bravest among the brave! He was, however, young and inexperienced in warfare of any kind. Being patriotic and without vanity, and anxious to put an end to the war, he had the good sense to know, that he did not detract from his own merits by yielding to the guidance of one having the age and experience of Gen. Dodge."[271]

---

* Lyman C. Draper, Editor of the *Wisconsin Historical Collections,* provided this footnote: "And in that war, it may further be added, that Gen. Henry's father served under Gen. Dodge; and hence it is not strange, that Gen. Henry should have paid great deference and respect to the opinions of Gen. Dodge, who was so much his senior in years, and his superior in military experience."[270]

** This interpretation is upheld by William T. Hagen in "The Dodge-Henry Controversary", *Journal of the Illinois State Historical Society,* Volume L, Number 4, Winter, 1957, pp. 377-384.

Satterlee Clark said, "That battle made many heroes, and so it should."*[272]

Black Hawk said, "We were astonished to find that the enemy were not disposed to pursue us."[274]

"I [Black Hawk] was astonished to find the Ne-a-pope and his party of *spies* had not yet come in—they having been left in my rear to bring the news, if the enemy were discovered.** It appeared, however, that the whites had come in a different direction, and intercepted our trail but a short distance from the place where we first saw them—leaving our spies considerably in the rear."[276]

"The day of the fight on the Wisconsin, Napope disappeared. He did not afterwards come back, and has not been seen since or made any enquiry, after his wife or children," Kish-kas-shoi said.[277]

Napope "went to a Winnebago village of the one eyed man ('the Blind') on the waters of Rock river—this man [White Crow] wears a black silk handkerchief over his blind eye—he staid six days at this village [on Carcajou Point in Lake Koshkonong]...."[278]

But Black Hawk observed, "The balance of his party, being *brave men,* and considering our interest as their own, returned, and joined our ranks."[279]

Black Hawk said, "I would not have fought there, but to gain time for my women and children to cross to an island."[280]

---

* But Satterlee Clark's next remark makes you wonder just how accurate his observations are: "About one hundred and twenty half-starved Indians defended the pass against nearly three thousand [!] whites, while the remainder of the Indians in plain sight were crossing the Wisconsin with the women and children, and as soon as these were safe, the Indians broke and ran."[273]

** "The hunting parties went at night to the place where they expected to find the Sac camp, and came upon the American trail—they then dispersed."[275]

Ne-a-pope (Soup, Broth) Sauk Indian,
Number 1 Civil Chief
of Black Hawk's "British Band"

"The Indians crossed the Wisconsin by swimming—having to leave *all* their camp equipage."[281]

"After [actually *during*] the battle (Dodge's) the [Indian] men carried the children over from slough to slough on horses—& the last slough which was deep—they put the mats, skins, &c. together and made a raft, put the children on and pushed it over swimming."[282]

"*Puk-qua-wa*—a Sac—17 years old. He was at Wisconsin—not fighting—but assisting the women across the river."[283]

"Wa-coo-se-mok—a Fox, and a relative of Keokuk 30 years old. ...(on Wisconsin) [he] was on the Island and not in the battle...."[284]

"...as soon as the Women saw the Indians were *beaten,* they got into the Islands and made bark canoes and fled down the Rive[r]."[285]

"Mee-se-qua. Sac woman 45 years old. ...Ran off during the fight of the Ouisconsin, and knows very little of the fight."[286]

Black Hawk and his warriors "returned to the Ouisconsin, and crossed over to our people."[287]

"After the battle of Wisconsin, BH [Black Hawk] held a council and told us all—Now I will run off—if we are pursued and beaten by the Americans, I will go round between Fort Winnebago and Greenbay and get among the Ottoways or Pottowotomies," Pama-ho said.[288]

Ma-kauk said, "Black Hawk told me between the Wisconsin & Mississippi—'I am not a pure Sac—I am Ottoway & Pottowotomie, and I shall go to them in the Ottoway country."[289]

"Black Hawk after the battle, told all who had not good horses, and the women and children to go down the Wisconsin, and he would meet them at Wa-pese-per-ne-kaw crossing above Prairie du Chien, and going by Red Cedar—and ke-o-kuck would meet them there."[290]

"They were to go down the Mississippi to wa-pese-per-ne-kaw, and to go up it, and Black Hawk was to cross over above Prairie du Chien and go by Red Cedar, and meet them there—& Keo-o-kuck to meet them there* 18 miles above the head of the Rock River [?] Rapids."[292]

"One of the men says, Black H. intends to cross the Mississippi above Prairie du Chien, and that Keo Kuck is to meet him near the red cedar on the West side of the Mississippi."[293]

"Here some of my people left me, and descended the Ouisconsin, hoping to escape to the west side of the Mississippi, that they might return home. I had no objection to their leaving me, as my people were all in a desperate condition—being worn out with travelling, and starving from hunger. Our only hope to save ourselves, was to get across the Mississippi."[294]

"*Ma-ke-kon-o-wa.* a Fox—14 years old was at the battle of Wisconsin and came down the river afterwards. Black Hawk and the Prophet he heard went across to the Mississippi—he is a boy he says, and dont know much, but he heard that many young braves were killed."[295]

"Black Hawk and the Prophet crossed the Wisconsin with the Sacs—toward the Mississippi."[296]

Black Hawk said, "Myself and band having no means to descend the Ouisconsin, I started, over a rugged country, to go to the Mississippi, intending to cross it, and return to my nation. Many of our people were compelled to go on foot, for want of horses, which, in consequence of their having had nothing to eat for a long time, caused our march to be very slow."[297]

The part Menominie squaw said, "The Able Men went off up the Wiskonsin on the Horses. They have no women

---

* The trading fort on Red Cedar was at the junction of the present Cedar and Little Cedar rivers at today's Nashua, Iowa.[291]

with them.* Black Hawk was not killed or wounded. She says the Indians are whipped, and are running off for safety."[298]

"Not many men attempted to come down the Wisconsin. All that had good horses went on with Black Hawk, the Sacs, Foxes and Kickapoos—and some women who had good horses went."[299]

",,,the Foxes were coming down the Ouisconsin &...the Sacs would endeavor to cross the Mississippi above this [place, Prairie du Chien], say 20-to-60 Miles."[300]

"When the Sacs & Foxes crossed the Wiskonsin & fled N.E. the old-men Women & Children were left in the Islands of the River & are now endeavouring to escape in Elm-bark Canoes by the Wiskonsin."[301]

Wa-coo-se-mok said, "...the Winnebagoes furnished canoes for the escape of those who came down the Wisconsin after the battle."[302]

Puk-qua-wa said, "After Wisconsin battle, those who escaped down the river procured canoes from the Winnebagoes—leaving their worn down horses."[303]

"*Wan-na-so-che* a Fox—21 years old. ...Says that he was in the battle of the Ouisconsin, that he came down that river after the battle as far as the Winnebago Village and from that place he struck across the country towards the Mississippi in company with his brother ...and that he never saw Black Hawk or the Prophet after the battle but is certain that they both crossed the Ouisconsin, and that he had heard them say previous to the battle, that they intended to cross the country to the Mississippi"[304]

Wee-qua-ho "Was at the battle of the Ouisconsin, and escaped in temporary bark canoe down that river. ...has heard that after battle of Ouisconsin, B. Hawk and the Prophet with their force made for the Mississippi."[305]

"iowa...was at battle of Wisconsin, and went with the main body of the Sacs toward the Mississippi two days, and then back for the Wisconsin—came down the river in a bark

* Not true.

canoe which he made nearly to the south of the river..."[306] "...one of *Ioways* wives...told her [*Kish-kas-shoi*] that some distance down the Wisconsin, they saw some americans [U. S. Army Infantry regulars on an armed raft above the mouth of the Wisconsin river]—that *Ioway* and one of his wives and eldest daughter jumped out of the canoe and swam ashore. The rest of his family were taken then...."[307]

"...a number of Sacs, old men & wounded were taken to some of the Winnebago Villages on the Four Lakes [of Madison, Wisconsin] and to the Villages on Bar-ri-bault river, near the Wisconsin Portage, on the night after the battle of Wisconsin Heights."[308]

"Before we got to the Mppi;" Pama-ho said, "they lost many men of killed and wounded."[309]

"...a part Menominie Squaw...says that the whole of the Women and Children are coming down the Ouisconsin—that she cannot count the Canoes—That they thought they would come and give themselves up to their relations the Menominies—That there were but 7 men with her party. She does not think there were many men coming down they had gone with the main Band."[310]

"Their Canoes are all made of Elm bark and very frail and clumsy."[311]

"Many canoes turned over and sunk before they came here [to Prairie du Chien]—they were so bad, and many children were drowned."[312]

Black Hawk said, "A warrior will duly appreciate the embarrassments I labored under—and whatever may be the sentiments of the *white people,* in relation to this battle, my nation, though fallen, will award to me the reputation of a great brave, in conducting it."[313]

"we buried our slain companion, Short, and made litters for the conveyance of the wounded."[15]

—Captain Daniel M. Parkinson,
Michigan Territory Volunteers

SUNDAY, JULY 22, 1832

clear, north east wind

Thermometer: 7 A.M. - 66°
2 P.M. - 78°
9 P.M. - 68°

"Next morning, (July 22d), the troops were paraded, and put in battle order on foot, except Colonel [Jacob] Fry's regiment, and took up the line of march to the river; leaving Col. [James] Collins's regiment to guard the horses and baggage, and take care of the wounded.[1]

"The next morning we perraded and marched down to the river."[2]

"We marched down to the river, which was about one mile and a half off; but before we reached the bank, we had a very bad swamp to go through, fifty or sixty yards on this side of the timber, which stood very high on the bank of the river. We now saw that General [James D.] Henry had acted very prudently. If he had attempted to follow them the evening before, he would have lost a great many of his men."[3]

"But the Indians had got across the River"[4]

"On the morning after the battle, it was found that the enemy had all crossed the river during the night, men, women, and children, and had dispersed."[5]

"We marched from our position to the river early in the day, and found he [the enemy] had crossed the river, he had left his camp in much hurry & confusion, from the appearance of the trees, bark canoes had been prepared for the purpose of crossing the Wisconsin when they might arrive there with the main body."[6]

"...the Indians, men, women and children, had swum the river, leaving all their camp equipage."[7]

"When another day was heralded in, the enemy had disappeared having, during the night, beat a hasty retreat across the Wisconsin River, without removing their lodges. A short journey brought into sight Black Hawk's camp on the west side of the Wisconsin River, about a mile off. His camp was much larger than the camp of the military, and in the struggle of the preceeding day the whites must have been greatly outnumbered."[8]

"When we got to the bank, we found they had made their retreat across the river during the night, leaving a great many articles of their trumpery behind. We also saw a good deal of blood, where their wounded had bled."[9]

"Henry and Dodge...were unable to renew the attack in consequence of the entire absence [of] boats, canoes, or the means of constru[c]ting rafts to cross to the Island."[10]

"we went back to the [Indian] camp and after examining it was found that the Indians in the course of the night had carried off and concealed all of their dead that they could find it was supposed from what could be seen that they had lost thirty odd we however learnt afterwards that they lost sixty eight the whites lost one Killed and had nine [actually eight] wounded"[11]

"We now returned to the camp; seeing there was no chance to follow them this day across the river."[12]

From the staff of Colonel James Collins's Fourth Regiment of Henry's Third Brigade, Adjutant Elias H. Merryman and 1st Surgeon's Mate Jonathan Leighton were "Furloughed 22d July".[13]

"We continued this day on the battle ground, and prepared litters for the wounded to be carried on. We spent this day in a more cheerful manner than we had done any other day since we had been on the campaign. We felt a little satisfaction for our toils, and the thought that we had no doubt destroyed a number of the very same monsters that had so lately been imbruing their hands with the blood of our fair sex--the helpless mother and unoffending infant. We dried our clothes which then had been wet for several days. This day was spent in social chat between men and officers. There were no complaints made; all had bravely fought; each man praised his officers, and all praised our General."[14]

"we buried our slain companion, Short, and made litters for the conveyance of the wounded."[15] "We buried the brave young man who was killed, with the honors of war. It was stated that he had just shot down an Indian, when he received the mortal wound himself. His name was John Short,* and belonged to Captain [Josiah S.] Brigg's company from Randolph county. He had a brother and a brother-in-law in the same company, who witnessed his consignment to his mother earth. The wounded were all well examined, and none pronounced mortal."[17]

"...the country around was scoured--litters were prepared for the wounded--expresses were sent to General Atkinson, at Bark River, and to the Fort at Prairie du Chien."[18]

"Expresses were sent to Gen. Atkinson and to Prairie due Chien, after having marched in the morning to the Wisconsin, and ascertained that the Indians during the night had all effected a crossing."[19]

"On the morning of the 22d of July Captain [James B.] Estes was sent as an express to [Fort Crawford at] Prairie du Chien, with despatches for our officers, giving the

---

* His name was Thomas Jefferson Short. John Short, his brother, was a member of Captain James Thompson's Company of Colonel Gabriel Jones's Third Regiment.[16]

information to the garrison, that the Indians had crossed the Wisconsin."[20]

"Camp Ouisconsin July 22d. 1832.

"Capt. G. [Gustavus] Loomis.

"Sir/ We met the enemy yesterday near the Wisconsin River and opposite the old Sack village*, after a close pursuit for near 100 miles. Our Loss was one man killed and eight wounded; from the scalps taken by the Winnebagoes as well those taken by the Whites and Indians carried from the field of Battle we must have killed about 40 of them; the number of wounded is not known, we can only judge from the number killed that many were wounded; from their crippled situation I think we must overtake them unless they descend the Ouisconsin by water. If you could place a field piece immediately on the Wisconsin, that would command the river, you might prevent their escape by water. General Atkinson will arrive at the Blue Mound on the 24th with the Regulars and a Brigade of mounted men. I will cross the Ouisconsin to morrow, and should the enemy retreat by land he will probably attempt crossing some 20 miles above Prairie du Chien. In that event the mounted men would want some Boats for the transportation of their arms ammunition and provisions. If you could procure for us some Mackinaw Boats in that event as well as some provision supplies, it would greatly facilitate our views. I will refer you to Captain James B. Estes for particulars.

"Excuse great haste.

"I am Sir, with great respect your your obedient servant.

---

* At today's Sauk City, Wisconsin, where the Sauk tribe lived in the 1700's before moving to Saukenuk at today's Rock Island, Illinois.

(signed) H Dodge Comdg Michigan mounted volunteers.

"To/ Capt G. Loomis Comdg Officer Fort Crawford"[21]

General Henry wrote his report on the battle of Wisconsin Heights, which he dated July 23*:

"Camp on the Heights of the Ouisconsin, July 23, 1832.

"To Brigadier General Atkinson,

"Sir-- Part of the 3d Brigade, together with the squadron under the command of Gen. Dodge, moved from its encampment at the Four Lakes, on the 21st inst. at quick time. Having passed this defile, the brigade entered an open country thinly covered with over cup oak on the right bank of one of the four Lakes. About 10 o'clock A.M., a party of scouts from the squadron, discovered and killed the first Sac [Kickapoo?] warrior. Proceeding on the trail of the enemy a few miles further in advance at the head of our line, three other hostile Sacs were discovered, two of which were killed; the other made his escape. These circumstances raised the hopes of the Brigade to the belief that the wily Hawk and his desperate followers, could and would be overtaken: its movements consequently were greatly accelerated. In the mean while a chilling rain began to fall and continued until night, which rendered the time exceedingly unfavorable for the anticipated fight.

---

* Internal evidence shows this report was written on July 22. The July 23 date may have been applied to a copy of this report, which appeared in the *Illinois Patriot* (Jacksonville), in the *Illinois Advocate* (Edwardsville) on August 7, and in the *Sangamo Journal* (Springfield, Illinois) on August 11. The original letter received by Atkinson has not been located, according to Ellen M. Whitney in *BHW* II:860.

"Passing rapidly from this point, the enemy began to show itself from the heights on the right and left. The enemy threw back a party of mounted warriors to occupy a position on the left; this movement occasioned a temporary halt, and formation of the line of Battle. It was however, soon discovered to be a characteristic stratagem of the Sac leader, and the Brigade moved forward. The enemy occasionally shewing itself in front and flank until the advanced columns composed of General Dodge's squadron and Maj. Ewing's Battalion of spies halted. This step was taken in consequence of a scattering and skirmishing fire heard on the left. It was immediately discovered that the close pursuit and daring courage of the scouts from the squadron had brought the enemy at bay--at this point the Ouisconsin was in sight on the right, a succession of lofty peaks on the left, and less elevated heights on the right; the Brigade occupying an uneven plain; in front lay the second step of the river, thinly covered with low over-cup oak; on the left and between the position of the Brigade and the above-mentioned Sacs, runs a deep ravine from left to right, diagonally across the front and bounding the aforesaid step; before this lies a marsh covered with the most luxuriant growth of grass, which continues to the margin of the river, being interrupted only by one slight elevation of sandy ground.

"Thus was the situation of the country when it was discovered that the whole force of the enemy was advancing. The right and left columns of the advance under the command of Gen. Dodge, and the centre column under Maj. Ewing, were immediately formed in line of Battle, by their respective commanders; at this instant the enemy in its accustomed manner directed its attack against the front. These troops gallantly withstood the shock and drove back the survivers in confusion and dismay. The Brigade advancing from the right and left and centre, by heads of Regiments, the line of battle was immediately completed, under the command of Col. Jones, on the left, supported by Col. Collins, who, as soon as they were dismounted, commenced and maintained a well directed fire against the enemy.

"The right wing was commanded by Col. Fry, who advanced on the right with the first battalion and occupied a position on the high ground above the marsh, and drove back the enemy in its attempt to flank to the right of us.

"The enemy being driven back at all points, took possession of strong positions on the sides of the heights to the left, and in the ravine at their base. Thus posted they threw a number of shot against the front and left wing, without the possibility of being reached by ours; at this juncture, I ordered the left wing under Col. Jones, (whose horse was shot under him at this time) and Collins to advance at a charge and take possession of the enemy's position, and cover the heights; and Maj. James, of the 2d Battalion 2d Regt., with two companies of said Battalion, was ordered to charge on the right. By request of Gen. Dodge and Maj. Ewing, they were ordered to charge the enemy at point of bayonet, lying covered in the ravine. These movements were effected with the greatest promptitude, and in the most gallant style. In a few minutes the battle became general, and the enemy was driven from the heights, fleeing down the precipitous declivities, and took refuge in the swamps, thick woods and high grass in the bottom of the Ouisconsin.

"Col. Fry, with the first battalion of his (2d) Regiment having completely routed the enemy on our right, was withdrawn from the position he then occupied in the battle, and was ordered to guard the horses and baggage until the issue of the conflict was determined. This important duty was confided to the charge of Lt. Col. Smith, while Col. Fry was engaged on the lines. Major Wood, of the 3d and Major Miller of the 4th regiments, commanded and sustained the left of their respective regiments, while engaged with the enemy, on the charge, and acquitted themselves in a manner worthy of their characters as officers and men.

"Having no information of the probable position of the residue of the enemy, and the situation of the ground, and because of the approach of night, I withdrew the troops, and about eight o'clock went into the encampment on the grounds where the attack was first made by the enemy.

"In all these movements I received efficient aid from Col. McConnel, who in the absence of my first aid-de-camp [Alexander Pope Field, who was furloughed July 10], performed the duties of that station with coolness, promptness, and to my entire satisfaction. Assisted by Mr. Johnson [Nelson H. Johnston] and others, he communicated to the officers of the line all orders directed to be given, and accompanied Col. Fry in his charge upon the enemy upon the right.

"In short, it is with much pleasure that I have it in my power to say to you, that the officers and men under my command, without a single exception, demand and have my sincere thanks, and deserve well of their country, for the prompt obedience of orders, and unyielding bravery upon this occasion.

"At an early hour this morning the whole army was marched on foot (except the 4th Regt. left to guard camp under the command of Col.

Collins) through the swamps to the bank of the river, where we expected to find the residue of the enemy's force--but they had escaped. By means of bark canoes they were enabled to pass the river during the night, leaving behind the principal part of their effects.

"We had one man killed, and eight wounded, none mortally. The number of the enemy killed and wounded is unknown, as the dead are scattered over a large tract of country covered with thick woods and high grass. Between thirty and forty have been found, and others are continually being discovered by our scouts. From appearances, the wounded, and many of the dead were removed during the night succeeding the battle.

"The name of the person killed, is J. T. [Thomas Jefferson] Short, of Randolph County, Ill.

"Signed, &c [J. D. Henry]

"Names of the wounded in the 3d Regt. 3d Brigade.

"Meredith S. M'Millen [McMillion], from Washington co. James Thompson, do. [ditto] Joseph Wells, Perry, Armstead Jones, Randolph.

"Four more were wounded in the Squadron."[22]

Dodge also prepared his official report of the battle of Wisconsin Heights:

"Camp on the Wisconsin Thirty miles below Fort Winnebago July 22d. 1832 Brigadier General Atkinson

"Dear Sir In my last communication to you, I stated my intention to follow the hostile Sacks with General Henry. We crossed the Mud lake fork of Rock [actually the Crawfish] river at

C	2 Reg't, 2 Brig.	Ill.

James Thompson

Pvt, Capt. John Barnes Co. 2 Regt. 2 Brig.

(Black Hawk War.)

Appears on

Detachment Muster-out Roll*

of Capt. Highsmith's Det. 2 Reg't, 2 Brig., Ill. Mtd. Vols.

dated Dixons Ferry Aug 2, 1832.

Muster-out to date ...., 1832.

Enrollment:

Date of June 16, 1832.

Period 90

Pay due from enrollment

Present or absent Present

County Lawrence

Number of traveling rations drawn 12

Remarks: Wounded & left in hospital at Dixons August 2 1832

*The only roll on file for this organization.

Book mark: ....

O'Leary

(861) Copyist.

about 2 Oclk P M on the 19th. where the Sacks had encamped in a body.

"On the 20th. we made a forced march & reached the head of the 4 lakes, and on the 21st. we overtook the enemy at this place, our advanced spies killed two Sacks before we met with a body of the enemy--they showed themselves freequently on the surrounding hills to divert our attention, our spies met with three & pursued them within a mile of their camp, our men were pursued in turn by the enemy on horseback. believing the main body of the enemy near us, I dismounted my squadron of horse, which formed the right & left columns of the advanced guard, the centre column was composed of the spies commanded by Colo. Ewing, I ordered my squadron to advance in front, and fortunately met with a good position, a natural elevation of ground which covered my men who were ordered to squat down, the Enemy raised the Yell and galloped up within thirty yards of us, we fired on them and killed one and wounded one or two others, when they retreated.

"General Henry arrived with his Brigade dismounted & formed in order of battle, the enemy rallied and commenced a fire on the left flank, his object was evidently to outflank us. the prompt movement of one of General Henrys Regiments defeated the object he had in view.

"The Indians occupied a height which enabled them to kill one of Genl Henrys men & wounded one of mine.

"after consulting Genl Henry we determined to charge the enemy, my squadron, with the spies commanded by Colo. Ewing, & the regiment of Colo Jones charged the enemy in good order, with part of Col Collins Regiment.

"we dislodge him from his position & drove him down the height into the high grass in the swamp. our fire was so heavy he soon gave way, I thought from the movement of the enemy he might aim at turning the right flank. I advanced briskly at the head of Clarks & Camps Companies to watch his movements, supported by two Companies ordered by Genl. Henry to the right flank. The enemy then gave way in every direction retreating to the river.

"The Winnebagoes scalped eleven Indians killed by the whites, and the whites took thirteen scalps last night--eight were found today and three were killed in the chase. The enemy were seen to carry a number from the field during the action, so that the numbers killed cannot fall short of forty (perhaps more) many were wounded but the number not known.

"We lost one killed & seven wounded, one of our men was wounded before the battle, on our march.

"When the battle was over it was 7 Oclk. our men had made a forced march of forty miles many of them on foot, and exposed about six hours in the rain their arms wet and out of order. Knowing they had retreated to the river and that they had chosen their position and that we could not reach them before dark, after consulting with Genl. Henry it was agreed to defer a further attack on the enemy untill the next morning.

"We marched from our position to the river early in the day, and found he had crossed the river, he had left his camp in much hurry & confusion, from the appearance of the trees, bark canoes had been prepared for the purpose of crossing the Wisconsin when they might arrive there with the main body

"The conduct of the officers & men composing my Squadron was brave & cool, they advanced to the charge with a quick pace and even front, they all behaved well, and it would be difficult for me to driscriminate between them, they deserve the confidence of their country. The officers & men of Genl. Henry Brigade have met the high expectations formed of them. They have done honor to their state & themselves. I would always unite with great confidence with such brave & gallent men

"I am with sentiments of great respect Your obedient Servant

"H Dodge Col. Commanding Michigan [Territory] Mounted Volunteers"[23]

And the editor of *The Galenian* weekly newspaper, Dr. Addison Philleo, (serving as surgeon of the 27th Regiment of the militia out of Galena, Illinois) sent the following war dispatch to his editor pro tempore, J. B. Patterson*:

"Wisconsin Heights, July 22.

"The army, including Gen. Henry's Brigade of mounted Volunteers, and those from Jo Daviess, and Iowa counties, under Gen. Dodge, arrived here late last evening, after a *forced march* of several days, in close pursuit of the whole band of hostile Indians. Here we overtook them, and found them as willing to fight as ourselves. They first endeavored to charge us in front. A line of battle was immediately formed, and the Indians *repulsed.* About sunset they returned, re-inforced, and made a most desperate effort to break our lines. But our men stood

* Patterson published the substance of Dr. Philleo's letter in part of the edition for Wednesday, July 25, (Volume 1, Number 13) and issued an Extra to town subscribers. In the August 1 edition, he published the letter "as a part of our Journal of the war". He gave it a one-column headline, "A BATTLE HAS BEEN FOUGHT!"

firmly, and compelled the enemy to *retreat.* They then took possession of a ravine, where the grass was so high as to conceal them. As soon as their position was ascertained, the order 'CHARGE' was given, and executed with such promptitude and effect, as again to compel them to *retire* from their *strong hold.*

"The battle continued for more than one hour. The heads of the Indians above the grass, resembled *stumps in a newly cleared forest.* We killed *three* Indians in the pursuit, and we suppose, not less than FORTY in the battle. I am very happy to state, that we lost but one killed, and *eight* wounded.

Today we marched to the Wisconsin, about a mile and a half: the Indians, men, women and children, had swam the river, leaving all their camp equipage. We having no means of crossing, have returned to our camp, to consult upon measures next to be adopted.

"Our horses are nearly exhausted with fatigue and hunger, Many of them have given out, and been left behind, their riders following on foot. We have but one day's provision left.*

"Gen Atkinson, with his whole force, is on his way to the Mines. I do not apprehend the people of Galena to be in much danger at present.

"It is thought by some, that the Indians intend to cross the Mississippi; others believe they are pushing for the Chippeway country. A

---

* The troops drew 12 days rations at Fort Winnebago on July 13, but—when Black Hawk's trail was discovered—General Henry ordered the troops with him at today's Hustisford, Wisconsin, to "Leave all the waggons Harnuss and Heavy and cumbersome articles".[24] Some food may have been left behind at that time.

very few days will develope their plans and movements."*[25]

"We now were nearly out of provision, and to take up the line of march against them, in the condition our horses were in, told us plainly that we would suffer for something to eat before we could get it."[27]

"Late in the evening, some of our men, who had been out to see if there were any signs of the enemy still remaining near us returned, and stated that they saw smoke across the river. General Henry had been of the opinion through the day, that if the Indians did ever intend fighting any more, they would attack us that night, and this report went to confirm him in his belief more fully. That night he had a larger guard than usual. He made use of another excellent precaution. He had fires made in advance of our lines, at least forty yards, and had them kept burning all night. Orders were given for every man to sleep upon his arms: so that he could be ready for action at the shortest notice, should an alarm be given. We had scarcely got to sleep, when we were alarmed by the running of our horses; we had to parade, as usual, to keep them from Killing us. Men and

---

* This is the end of *The Galenian* report. It seems fair, yet competitive jealousies between Illinois and Michigan Territory participants surfaced after the war. The following observations by Peter Parkinson, Jr., were made later in the context of such bickering:

"As to the secret connivance of Gen. Dodge and Doctor Philleo about the publication of the battle of the Wisconsin in such a way as to rob Gen. Henry of his merit in that affair, I know nothing and moreover do not believe there is one word of truth in it. I know that the account published in that paper (the *Galenian*) of the battle, as well as all others, was substantially true, and I also know that Gen. Henry was too bold and daring a man to have passed unnoticed any such low and cowardly conduct. Neither would Gen. Dodge or Dr. Philleo (who was a brave and warm-hearted man, and an old friend and acquaintance of Gen. Henry) have been guilty of any such meanness."[26]

officers now fully expected that it was the enemy who frightened them."[28]

"we staid the 2d night on the ground and was alarmed early in the night by the horses which had taken a fright and Run up to the camp we then expected that the Indians had got their women & children to some place where they considered them in safety and was coming Back to give us Battle again"[29]

"Orders were now given, for no man to sleep that night, but for every man to stand to his arms, and be ready to receive the enemy. We all now expected to have hard fighting, and were prepared for the worst. There was not a man who shrunk from his duty. All punctually obeyed the orders of his officers, and made every preparation to receive the enemy, should he come."[30]

"there was accordingly an additional guard detailed and the Remainder of the army paraded and every man lay down on the ground he was to occupy in case the Indians should attack us and the officers were so divided that one half of them should be up at a time all night and Keep the fiers constantly burning at forty yards disdistant from the line I was up during the night and had been the Major part of the two preceeding nights"[31]

"It is claimed Black Hawk wanted to surrender. It is true. Poquette, our interpreter, had gone. Black Hawk talked loud and shrill in Winnebago. No white flag. It was at night. Later he left and crossed Wisconsin river...."[23]

—H. S. Townsend,
Michigan Territory Volunteers

MONDAY, JULY 23, 1832

clear, south wind

Thermometer: 7 A.M. - 70°

2 P.M. - 84°

9 P.M. - 70°

"Our troops, after the battle of Wisconsin, lay upon their arms with the full expectation that they were momentarily in danger of an attack. When all had become still, in the dead of night, the ear of almost every soldier caught what appeared to be an almost unearthly sound. A native had advanced within hearing distance of our army, and had placed himself upon an eminence, where he uttered loud distinct and strange ejaculations, which echoed through the camp and woods until the sound died away in the distance. The voice roused every soldier--who anticipated an immediate attack; and a bloody combat. When the Indian appeared to have satisfied himself that he was heard he then commenced distinctly, the articulation of words, and sentences. In a few moments the voice ceased.

"The effect was almost electric..."[1]

"About one hour and a half before day, on the same mountain from which the Indian Chief had given his orders on the evening of the battle, we heard an Indian voice, in loud shrill tones, as though he was talking to his men, and giving them orders."[2]

"about an hour and a half or two hours before day* there was an Indian commenced speaking on an hill at about half a mile distance from our camp and continued to speak for ten or fifteen minutes with a voice that I never heard equaled by any human voice in the course of my life"[3]

"During the night, the camp was alarmed by the voice of an Indian, who appeared to be hailing our people, with a desire to be heard. He spoke a great deal, but his language was not understood...."[4]

---

* Captain Daniel M. Parkinson, and Charles Bracken, Dodge's Adjutant and Aide de Camp, say the Indian spoke during the night of July 21-22. Lieutenant James J. Justice, Surgeon's Mate John Wakefield, and Atkinson's Aide de Camp Meriwether Lewis Clark (who go the information second hand), say the Indian spoke during the night of July 22-23. Neither Dodge nor Henry mention the incident in their reports written on July 22.

The speaker may have been Kinnekonesaut ("he that strikes the foremost"[7] or "he that strikes first".[8] Now, with the death of the number two brave, Me-ne-kau, in the battle of Wisconsin Heights, Kinnekonesaut became the number four warrior of Black Hawk's band. Later, as a prisoner after the massacre at Bad Axe, Kinnekonesaut was identified with the notation, "the man with the loud voice".[9]

But, in later years, Black Hawk said "he sought an opportunity of speaking with the Indians who were accompanying the Americans; but finding none, he went back some distance, the night after the battle of Wisconsin Heights, and ascended a tree, as near the American encampment as he thought it prudent to venture, and spoke in as loud a voice as he possibly could, desiring the American Indians to inform the white that he was not for war; that he was only endeavoring to leave the country, and hoped he would be permitted to do so in peace."[47]

"Our interpreter, Mr. [Pierre] Poquette, and our Indian spies who had accompanied us from Fort Winnebago, left us immediately after the battle. This turned out to have been an unfortunate event, for that same night, the silence of our camp was broken by the loud shrill voice of an Indian from the summit of one of the highest peaks in that vicinity, haranguing, as we supposed, his warriors preparatory to an attack on us."[5]

" 'About daybreak,' says Capt. D. S. [Daniel Smith] Harris, then a lieutenant in command of [James W.] Stepehenson's Company, 'the camp was alarmed by the clarion voice of the Prophet from a hill nearly a mile away. At first we thought it was an alarm, but soon found that the Prophet wanted peace. Although he was so far distant I could hear distinctly every word, and I understood enough to know that he did not want to fight.'

"Mr. P. [Payton] J. Pilcher, now [1878] of Elizabeth, [Illinois] who was also there [as a Private in Ewing's Spy Company of General Henry's Brigade], says that they were awakened by the shrill voice of the chief, and that he plainly understood: 'Ne—com, P-e—e-l—o-o-o;' 'Friends, we fight no more.'

"Mr. Pilcher says he told Henry what the Indian said, but Henry said 'pay no attention to any thing they say or do, but form in line of battle.' "[10]

"No attention was paid to this second* attempt to negotiate peace. It is said that the officers had no interpreter and did not know what the Prophet said until after the war closed. This excuse is exploded by the direct and emphatic testimony of Capt. Harris and Mr. Pilcher, but the starved and dying Indians must be exterminated."[11]

---

* The first of Black Hawk's three futile attempts to surrender took place on May 14, 1832, when drunk militia shot the bearer of the white surrender flag. The battle of Stillman's Run ensued, starting the Black Hawk war at today's Stillman Valley, Illinois.

"Although we were well posted, and surrounded with a double guard, yet it naturally produced some excitement, and was well calculated to test the coolness and material of our officers and men. We then thought that Black Hawk's entire force was being brought to bear upon us in a night attack--the most to be dreaded of all attacks, especially when made by an Indian enemy. Our material proved good; no man showed the white feather, and our commanders, in concert with the Indian orator, harangued their men in the most stirring manner. Gen. Henry, in particular, addressed his men in a most patriotic strain, reminding them of the discredit already brought upon the Sucker* arms by the defeat of Maj. Stillman, and other similar disasters, appealing to them in the name of their Sucker mothers, to vindicate the valor of the Suckers and the Sucker State. In fact, it was often remarked afterwards, that he made a great Sucker speech, under the impulse of which his men, no doubt, could have well vindicated, as they had the preceding day [July 21], the valor of the Sucker arms."[13]

"we very Readily conjectured that this was a signal given by him for a general attack In consequence of which our General Harangueed the soldiers on a very beautiful and spirited speech"[14]

"General Henry had his men all paraded in order of battle, in front of the tents, and the fires roused up. After all

* "...the name of 'Sucker' was given to the Illinois folks, and it was from this circumstance: Every spring, when the grass was high enough to afford pasture for their teams, large numbers would come and do all the heavy hauling during the summer, over beautiful prairies furnishing all that they could desire. But at the first frost they would all disappear not to return until the next spring. Their habits of migration being exactly timed with that of a fish, called the 'Sucker,' which abounded in all the creeks and rivers, caused the people of the upper settlements to give that name to those of the lower counties. So came the name of 'Sucker'."[12]

were paraded, General Henry addressed his men in the most beautiful manner I ever heard man speak on such an occasion. I am sorry that I cannot give the precise words, but I will attempt an outline of them. The Indian was still yelling in the most loud and terrific manner.

"General Henry commenced: 'My brave soldiers, now is the critical and trying moment; hear your enemy on the same mountain from which you drove them only on the evening before last, giving orders for a charge upon you: there is no doubt but that they have mustered all their strength at this time: now let every mother's son be at his post:

"Yes, my brave soldiers, you have stemmed the torrent of every opposition--you have stopped not for rivers, swamps, and, one might say almost impenetrable forest; suffered through the beating storm of night, amidst the sharpest peals of thunder, and when the heavens appeared a plane of lightening.

"My brave boys, hear their yells; let them not daunt you; remember the glory you won on the evening before last; be not now the tarnishers of this reputation, that you are so justly entitled to: remember that you are fighting a set of demons, who have lately been taking the lives of your helpless and unoffending neighbors.

"Stand firm my brave Suckers until you can see the whites of their eyes, before you discharge your muskets, and then meet them with a charge as you have before done, and that too with great success.'

"The Indian all this time was talking as though he was addressing his men, and appeared to approach nearer. Every officer then on the ground, was at his post, and had his particular station assigned to him, and the ground he was to occupy during the action. In this order we stood until daylight. Just before day the Indian quit talking."[15]

"we anxiously waited to Receive General Black Hawk and his suit[e] but day Broke and he did not appear"[16]

"In a few moments the voice ceased. ...and the

proceeding was an unaccountable mystery until several Indians had been taken prisoners. These Indians informed us that the native who thus addressed our troops, called for any Winnebagoes who might be in our camp, desiring them to inform the commander that they were willing to surrender themselves to the mercy of our troops."[17]

" 'The interpreter said that he said that they "had their squaws and families with them and were starving--that they did not want to fight any more, but wanted peace and would do no more harm if they could be permitted to cross the Mississippi in peace." ' "[18]

"Unfortunately no Winnebagoes were present, and the Indians made all haste to cross the Wisconsin to secure themselves from almost certain destruction which awaited them if they remained on this side of the river."[19]

"After the Indians were all collected together that we had taken prisoners*, they were examined respecting many things; and among others what it was that the Indian Chief was saying when he talked so long on the mountain at the Wisconsin. They stated, that he was telling us in the Winnebago language, that they had their squaws and children with them, and that they were starving for something to eat, and were not able to fight us; and that if we would let them pass over the Mississippi, they would do no more mischief. They stated that he spoke this in the Winnebago language, believing that the same Winnebagoes that was with us in the battle, were still there. But here he was mistaken: as soon as the battle was over, the Indians, with our pilot, Poquet, all left us; so there was no one among us, that understood the Winnebago language."[20]

"It was afterwards ascertained, however, that the Indian Chief was making propositions of peace, instead of urging or cheering on his warriors to battle, which no doubt

* During the August 2 massacre at Bad Axe river, which ended the hostilities.

would have been accepted, had the Winnebagoes been in camp. The proposals were said to have been, that the Sauks and Foxes would surrender themselves all up, at discretion, and only asked protection for the lives of their women and children. But hearing no response, and supposing the Winnebagoes were with us, they concluded that their proposals were not acceptable, and no mercy would be shown them; and consequently every effort was then made to remove as fast as possible out of the country."[21]

"it appeared afterward, that it was in the Winnebago dialect, as it was known that some of the Winnebagoes were in our camp, and they were supposed still to be there; it was thus believed that the Indian would be understood if he spoke in the language of the Winnebagoes, and that they would act as mediators for the surrender of the Sacs, which was then proposed."[22]

"It is claimed Black Hawk wanted to surrender. It is true. Poquette, our interpreter, had gone. Black Hawk talked loud and shrill in Winnebago. No white flag. It was at night. Later he left and crossed Wisconsin river...."[23]

"When it was just light enough to discover a man a short distance, the brave and fearless [Major William Lee D.] Ewing took his battalion of spies, and mounted on horseback, we were soon at the top of the mountain to see who it was that had serenaded us so long, at that late hour of the night. We found only the sign of a few horse tracks, that appeared as though they had been made that night. We marched in quick time around every part of the mountain, and found no one. We took a circuitous route back to camp, but found no one on the way."[24]

"The Winnebagoes in camp* also informed the officers

* Apparently Payton Pilcher's memory fails him here. The Winnebagoes had all returned to the Portage, leaving behind no one who could translate the request to surrender.

of the meaning of the Prophet's message, and 'early in the morning,' says Pilcher, 'they went with us to the spot where the Indian had stood, when he proclaimed peace, and there we found a *tomahawk buried*', an emphatic declaration that so far as Black Hawk and his band were concerned hostilities were ended."[25]

"our spies Reconoitered the woods arround for some distance but made no discoveries except where the Indians had taken a part of one of their horses that had been Killed in the Battle by this we knew that they were scarce of provisions and we were also growing quite scarce our selves and was obliged to quit the Indians for a while and go to some point to Replenish our stores[26]

"It was then decided to return to Blue Mounds. To facilitate the transportation of the three wounded soldiers—Isam Hardin, Robert McGee and Enoch Nevill—litters were prepared from the materials of a tent presented by Maj. W. L. D. Ewing to Capt. Clark's company. The loss was one killed and eight wounded."[27]

"It having been ascertained, that our supplies of provisions were not sufficient to enable us to pursue the enemy across the Wisconsin, and being also encumbered with a number of wounded, it was thought advisable to return to the Blue Mounds, which could be plainly seen from an eminence near the battle ground."[28]

"We were now out of provisions, and were obliged to abandon further pursuit, and go to the Blue Mounds to procure a supply. Accordingly on the 23d, we got in motion again; not in pursuit of the enemy, but for bread and meat, to satisfy our appetites--as we were now out of every thing to eat."[29]

"The Blue mounds being (as we supposed) the nearest point we set off for that Fort which we found to be about twenty five miles where we arrived some time after dark on the 23d. of July quite weary having then Marched several days without Rest and our horses were a great many of them very much broken down by the march from the Rappids on

Rock River to the ouisconsin being about one hundred and 25 miles which we traveled in three days"[30]

"The return journey to Blue Mounds was tedious, owing to general ignorance of the topography of the country."[31]

"...the whole command marched for the Blue Mounds, where we arrived at night, after one of the most fatiguing days that was experienced during the war. The difficulty of conveying our wounded men on litters for thirty miles, over almost impassable creeks, through swamps, over hills, and through thick woods, by a winding path, was attended with fatigue and difficulty of which no one can well conceive."[32]

"Our wounded this day suffered very much on account of having rough ground to pass over, and some very muddy creeks."[33]

"Here I [Captain Daniel Parkinson] must relate an amusing, and withal, at the time, an alarming incident of the day--one which I can never forget. Although John McNair's wound was a flesh one, yet it was so excruciatingly painful, that it was only with the greatest difficulty he could be conveyed in any way. Being my Orderly Sergeant, and much attached to me, he particularly requested me to stay with him, saying the boys would kill him almost, if I were not along. Desirous to gratify him, I placed my company under command of my lieutenant, Matthew G. Fitch, and remained constantly with him. After having carried him in my arms through several creeks, we at length arrived at the top of the East Blue Mound, which is almost a mountain. The litter, by this time, had become so broken, by the horses, between two of which it was swung, having to wind and twist along the narrow and devious path by which we ascended the Mound, that it would no longer answer to carry him.

"Here was a dilemma; the litter was broken up, it was dark, and McNair declaring that he could not ride on horseback; and the company was far in advance, with all the provisions and necessary materials for camping. How we could best extricate ourselves from the difficulties besetting our situation, was a question of no easy solution, and yet it must be done.

"I at length said, 'Boys, bring the horses and fragments of the litter to the foot of the Mound, and I will carry Mack down, and then we will mend up the litter so that it will carry him on to the encampment.'

"I took him up in my arms, although he weighed about one hundred pounds, and after going down the Mound, which was quite steep, I was compelled to lay him down. It seems that I either laid him on, or so near, a large yellow rattle-snake, as very much to disturb his snakeship's equilibrium, and he set up such a terrible rattling or whizzing as to frighten me much--the boys all fled precipitately, and I jumped back several paces.

"The poor fellow cried out in the most supplicating manner, 'O, Captain, for God's sake don't leave me here to be devoured by these d--d snakes! '--for, by this time, there were evidently two of them; and from the noise, in the stillness of the night, and in the midst of a dense forest, there seemed to be legions of them giving their fearful notes of warning.

"Recovering from my momentary fright, and feeling the necessity of instant action, I 'pitched in,' as politicians say, caught the poor fellow by the heels, and dragged him unceremoniously out of so dangerous a proximity to a ten times more frightful enemy than Black Hawk and all his warriors--and, remarkable to relate: the poor fellow never uttered a groan.

"After the panic was a little over, I broke the silence by asking--'Mack, don't you think you can ride on horseback *now*?'

"To which he instantly replied: 'O, God! yes--ride, or any thing,'

"And thus, in due time, we reached the camp of our company.

"Having partaken of some refreshments, I was relating McNair's conduct on the field of battle--how, when I directed him, after it was discovered that he was wounded, to fall into the rear, he replied, 'O, God! Captain, I must have another shot;' and contrasted this with his adventure with the rattle-snakes.

"He very meekly replied, 'Well, Captain, I always was d--d afraid of snakes.' "*[34]

"After the battle with the I[n]dians on the Wisconsin the Souldiers came and stayed three days close to our [Blue Mound] Fourt T[h]ey brought three men to our Fourt that had got shot in the battle and left them with us till they got well"[37]

"After the battle at the Wisconsin River they brought the wounded to our Fourt and left them there There was three men wounded John McNair Hardin Outman and one I dont recollect"[38]

"When they got to the Blue Mounds, they were very hospitably treated. There was a small fort and citizens plenty, who did not think it the least hardship to wait on those who had been shedding their blood to revenge the wrongs those people had suffered. For the Indians had killed three valuable men within one mile of this place; and one within view of the citizens who were in it,--a gentleman by the name of [Emerson] Green, of high standing in society, and who had recently emigrated from the east. I have

* "Poor Mack, he never fully recovered from the effects of his wound; as slight as it seemed to be, he was lame for life. He was an honest and worthy man, and was at the time of his death [on October 14, 1852], which was nearly four years since, and had been for many years, the Treasurer of Iowa county. The adventure with the rattlesnakes was always considered a standing joke sufficiently good, to call out a treat from Mack at any time related. This incident took place on the 23d day of July [1832], the battle having been fought on the 21st."[35]

John McNair's fear of snakes was justified. For example, Black Hawk's Number 3 civil chief, Pa-ma-sieu, died at Rock Island of a snake bite.[36]

forgotten the names of the other gentlemen*, but can say that the citizens spoke in high terms of their worth, and seemed to lament their loss."[40]

"I [Dodge] arrive[d] here at about 7 Oclock [at] night hearing Genl Posey was at Helena a point on the Wisconsin about 16 miles from this place I dispatched an express to him...with axes & augers to make rafts for the transportation of his Baggage arms &c. to take some pine Houses at that place the Logs of which will make excellent Rafts"[41]

"On our arrival there [at Blue Mounds], Dodge's command, including Stephenson's [Galena] company [now commanded by Hosea T. Camp], were ordered to their respective posts, with orders to rendezvous at Helena on the Wisconsin, as soon as General Atkinson should arrive there with the regular forces."[42]

"To gain a rest rendered necessary by a month of incessant toil, day and night, [some of] the miners removed to White Oak Springs."[43]

"I [Daniel Parkinson] may add, in this connection, that in consequence of the illness of my wife, I changed commands with Capt. [Robert C.] Hoard [of Fort Defiance, south of Mineral Point]...."[44]

* Emerson Green and Lieutenant George Force were killed on June 20, 1832, near the Blue Mound fort. Edward Beouchard buried only Green's body because George Force had refused to help him bury the body of William G. Aubrey on June 6. Beouchard said, "I had, on that occasion, asked Lieutenant Force to go with me, to get Captain Aubrey's body, but he refused to go on, and I told him if he got killed, and was only six feet off, I would not go for his body. When Force and Green were killed, on June twentieth, and I went and got Green's remains, and brought them to the fort, they asked me if I would hold spite against a dead man? I replied that I would do what I said, whether a man was dead or alive; and Lieutenant Force's body laid where it fell for four days".[39]

In Captain Samuel Houston's Company of Major William Lee D. Ewing's Spy Battalion, Private William Thompson "Lost his horse on the 23rd of July".[45]

"on the night of the 23d the capt [Andrew Bankson*] was taken with the cholrea and was thought to be out of all hopes"[46]

* Of Colonel Gabriel Jones's 3d Regiment of General Henry's 3d Brigade.

"After all their boasting, the simple fact was, that Black Hawk, although encumbered with the women, children, and baggage of his whole band, covering himself with a small party, had accomplished the most difficult of military operations,—to wit, the passage of a river, —in the presence of three regiments of American volunteers! And now they were gone—the victors *could not tell us whither."*[22]

—2d Lt. Philip St. George Cooke,
Acting Adjutant, 6th Infantry Regiment,
United States Army

TUESDAY, JULY 24, 1832

clear, northwest wind, very high wind
Thermometer: 7 A.M. - 76°
2 P.M. - 80°
9 P.M. - 67°

Early in the morning, Colonel Henry Dodge wrote a progress report to the commanding officer, Brigadier General Henry Atkinson:

"Blue Mound July 24th 1832 5 Oclock A.M.

"Dear Sir I arrive here at about 7 Oclock Last Night hearing Genl Posey was at Helena a point on the Wisconsin about 16 miles from this place I dispatched an express to him last night with axes & augers to make rafts for the transportation of his Baggage arms &c. to take some pine Houses at that place the Logs of which will make excellent Rafts we are able to furnish Genl Henry Here with five days rations and I shall be able to at my place to furnish my squadron with provision if Genl Posey has not taken it on his march to the Wisconsin

"I have sent expresses to every part of the Mining Country and will send one immediately to

praria Dechean [Prairie du Chien] I will collect as many men & Horses as possible this day and march this Evening or Early in the Morni[n]g for the Wisconsin I have advised Genl. Henry to cross the Wisconsin above about 12 Miles from this place it would Enable the Brigades to cross the Wisconsin at Two Different places at the same time

"Be assured every possible exertion will Be made to destroy the Enemy crippled as they must be with their wounded and families as well as their want of provision supplies I will follow him let them go whare [where] they will if they Leave tracks Behind them

"With sentiments of regard I am your Obedient Servant

"H Dodge Col Command Mounted Volunteers

"Brigadier Genl Atkinson Commander in Chief of the army of the Frontier"[1]

Brigadier General James D. Henry also submitted a report to his commanding officer:

"Blue Mounds July 24, 1832

"To Brig Gen'l Atkinson

"Sir In pursuance to your order I pursued the enemy at quick time and overtook them near the Ouisconsin and completely routed them from their positions in the hills and Owing to the near approach of night withdrew the troops from the charge

"My Official Report I will send you as soon as I can have it made Out

"Suffice it to say for the present that we Overtook & Routed the enemy Lost but one man had 4 in my Brig[ade] & 4 in the Squadron [of Dodge] wounded none mortally

"Between 30 & 40 of the enemy has been found on the field

"I have moved my Brigade to the Blue mound where I will draw 5 days Rations and take up the pursuit again

"I have the honour to be Sir With great Respect your most Obt

"James D. Henry Brig Gnl Comd 3rd Brig M V. [Brigadier General Commanding the Third Brigade of Mounted Volunteers]

"Genl Dodge will send you his official Roport to which I Refer you for particulars"[2]

On July 24, seven men from Henry's Third Brigade were furloughed from Blue Mound fort:

Captain Andrew Bankson of Colonel Gabriel Jones's Third regiment was "absent with leave from Gen. Atkinson from 24 July".[3]

Also furloughed from Bankson's Company were Privates James Bankson, Hiram Parker, Anderson Petty, William Talbut, and George W. White.[4] Privates Bankson, Parker, Talbut, and White each had a "horse lost".[5]

In the absence of Captain Bankson, 1st Lieutenant Godfrey Ammons was "Commanding the Company".[6]

From Captain Samuel Houston's Company of Major William Lee D. Ewing's Spy Battalion, Private Levi Davis was "Furlowed on the 24th of July".[7]

"The next morning after arriving at the Mounds, Col. Dodge's command were dismissed to their respective forts for a new supply of provisions, and Gen. Henry's troops also obtained a supply."[8]

When Henry Dodge got to his home*, he wrote a note to Major James W. Stephenson of Galena:

---

* "At Dodgeville were a cluster of eight or ten log cabins, with diggings and a [lead smelting] furnace, and one little variety store in a log cabin--these constituted the town, and this was mostly the property of Col. Dodge."[9]

"Fort Union, July 24, 1832.

"DEAR MAJOR.--I congratulate you on the bravery and gallantry of your men. They have realized the high expectation formed of them. I had the honor to lead your company, commanded by Capt. [Hosea T.] Camp, in the charge on an enemy, at a fixed position; and had the Indians done their duty, they must have killed at least twenty of our men. From a strong position, the enemy retreated in great disorder and confusion. We had but one man killed, and eight wounded. The enemy had, I think from the scalps taken, and those carried off the field, at least 40, and many wounded, the exact number I cannot say."[10]

"An express had been sent by General Atkinson to General Posey [on July 22], to march as soon as possible to a small town on the Wisconsin river, to intercept the Indians, should any of them go down the river. So, in the afternoon, General Posey, from Fort Hamilton, passed on his way to Helena;*..."[12]

"Next forenoon we [troops with General Atkinson] met expresses, who bore the news of an action on the banks of the Wisconsin, where the enemy was overtaken, and said to have been roughly handled; a gallant fight it was represented to have been."[13]

"Gen. Atkinson, who had broken up his encampment on Bark River, soon arrived with his troops...."[14]

"...and late in the evening General Atkinson and General Alexander arrived with their brigades; leaving Colonel [Powell] Sharp, with those who had lost their horses, still at Fort Kushkanong; also Captain [Gideon] Low, with one company of regulars."[15]

* Described a year later by a member of Captain Jesse B. Brown's company of U. S. Rangers (commanded by Henry Dodge): "The town of Helena, on the Wisconsin river, consisted of ten or fifteen houses; but was entirely deserted, except two men."[11]

"July 24--Arrived at the Blue Mounds"[16]

"After a forced march of four days we reached the Blue Mounds on the 24th where Henry had fallen back for supplies and was encamped. Dodge had gone to Dodgeville to recruit the strength of his Battalion."[17]

"We reached here...much fatigued after a march of 20 miles without water, which for footmen, is, as you know, very difficult."[18]

"We here found a part of General Posey's [First] brigade [Captain William N. Dobbins's Spy Company], who had been sent from Fort Hamilton, to assist in guarding this frontier place."[19]

"Some disagreeable feelings arose between the officers of the regular army and the volunteers, and it was supposed it was produced by General Henry violating his orders* and gaining the victory over the enemy without the co-operation of the regular army."[21]

"That evening we [troops with General Atkinson] formed a junction with the [Third] brigade and battalion of spies, at the Blue Mounds; whither they had *retired,* after their glorious victory, to meet us. It would be difficult to give a full idea of the proud, but modest complacency with which they all agreed--for they *must* tell the truth--in extolling the intrepidity and coolness exhibited in the battle; how they had, for example, cried out in the midst of it, 'Come forward, boys, and draw yours ponies!' by which they had playfully expressed their intention of appropriating to themselves those little animals; (which the Indians found so useful that we could not learn they had been persuaded actually to part with any of them.) 'Wisconsin Heights' fairly promised to prove a watchword, before which 'Tippecanoe,' &c., might hang its head;--'Pity it was, we had not been there;--but they could not help it,--how could they, if the Sacs *would* allow themselves to be used up?'

---

* To "return to these Head Qrs. without delay"[20] from Fort Winnebago.

"After all their boasting, the simple fact was, that Black Hawk, although encumbered with the women, children, and baggage of his whole band, covering himself by a small party, had accomplished the most difficult of military operations,--to wit, the passage of a river,--in the presence of three regiments of American volunteers! And now they were gone--the *victors* could not tell us whither."[22]

"I shall move this morning with my whole force to a point on the Ouisconsin sixteen miles below where we shall endeavour to cross the [river] by Rafts or some other means and if possible overtake the enemy and subdue him, although we are worn down with fatigue and privation. He must be much crippled, and is suffering for susistanc"[8]

—Brigadier General Henry Atkinson

WEDNESDAY, JULY 25, 1832

clear, north west wind
Thermometer: 7 A.M. - 73°
2 P.M. - 79°
9 P.M. - 65°

William B. Archer, Aide de Camp of Brigadier General Milton K. Alexander, took advantage of the brief stop at the Blue Mounds to write a letter to Jacob Harlan, the brother of Archer's wife, Elizabeth:

"Blue Mounds 57 miles from Fort Winnebago 25 July 1832.

"Genl. [Henry] Atkinson, [James D.] Henry, [Milton K.] Alexander and [Henry] Dodge are here with their respective commands--though the Brigades are reduced considerably. Atkinson and our men arrived yesterday evening and we will march to day for Wisconsin and the Mississippi in persuit of Sac Indians.

"We, our Brig[ade] has not met the indians yet. Dodge & Henry on the evening of the 21. instant came up with them on the bank of Wisconsin on their retreat over the Mississippi had a fight killed 28 indians and wounded many

others, on our side one killed and 9 wounded. the night came and the Indians got over the river with their women &c.

"Dodge and Henry retired here for provisions 18 miles leaving as they suppose the indians near the battle ground. part of our men went from our fort [Cos-co-nong on July 10 and July 21] down Rock river to Dixons. some of our men complain some of the dysentary, lost not a man as yet and none dangerous. All in good spirits when we get near the Indians.

"We have been constantly on the march and our horses are quite reduced. this projected march will leave many on foot. After 8 or 10 days I think we will be discharged. Had there been good management on the part of the Commanding Genl. the war would have been ended some time since. Our men are generally well and in good spirits but much displeased with Atkinson. It is not our fault that the Indians have not been taken are [ere] this. we have travelled this upper world over--once in three miles of them*. We may come up with them, but I fear they have now gotten too great a start. rest asured if we come up there will be fighting, our men have become desperate against them--and no troops can be more elevated in spirits than ours when we come near them. in three days we will meet I trust this band of pirates and desperadoes. I will go security that the Big Wabash troops will fight well.

"Yours &c in haste W. B. Archer**

"Jac. Harlan"[2]

* So he thought, on the night of July 2 at today's Milton, Wisconsin.

** Archer Avenue in Chicago was named in his honor.[1]

Colonel James Collins, commander of the Fourth Regiment of Henry's Third Brigade, used the down time for some public relations work. Part of the letter he wrote this morning about the July 21 battle of Wisconsin Heights appeared in the August 11 edition of the *Sangamo Journal,* Springfield, Illinois.

"Blue Mounds, Mich. Ter. [Michigan Territory] July 25, 1832.

"...the brigade under the command of Gen. Henry, after three days forced marching, the last of which [with our broken down horses]* we marched forty miles, and came up with the enemy at near one hour before sunset. They had taken a strong position, in a broken piece of ground, intending to take shelter, if compelled to retreat, under each hill in succession. We kept a fire for about one hour on both sides, after which Gen. Henry ordered us to charge upon the enemy, and drive them from their ambuscade. The order was promptly executed by the men under the command of Cols. [Gabriel] Jones and Collins, followed I believe by Gen. Dodge's troops and Col. [William Lee D.] Ewing's spy battalion. When the charge commenced, the Indians raised a most tremendous savage yell, but our troops rushed upon them with a fury that they could not withstand, and they were routed, and fled. Our loss is one killed and eight wounded--none mortally. The loss of the Indians was 34 slain, and certainly a great proportion wounded.

"We were forced to come to this place for supplies. Gen. Atkinson came up to us last evening with his regulars, and we shall take our march this day to intercept and capture, if possible, the enemy."[3]

---

* Brackets are in the source.

Meriwether Lewis Clark, one of Atkinson's Aides de Camp, dashed off a letter to his father in St. Louis, William Clark, Superintendent of Indian Affairs, explaining how he would get a scalp:

"Camp on Blue Mounds July 25 1832

"My Dear Father We reached here last night much fatigued after a march of 20 miles without water, which for footmen, is, as you know, very difficult.

"The General was on a march to drive out the Enemy from Cranberry Lake [Horicon marsh]* up the swamp when he recd [received] express from Henry Brigade telling him of the Enemey's having put off we immediately returned after dispatching a Light Battalion [under Major William McHenry on July 20] to ascertain if the enemy had fled entirely, which they had. Dodge & Henry made forced marches for three days, the last day marching 40 miles through the worst count[r]y & the [h]eaviest rain. They killed 3 indians on the last day [July 21], one kickapoo on the 1st 4 Lake & two Sacs just in the rear of the enemy, the Engagement took place just about sundown & on the Ouisconsin swamp about a mile from the Bank & 15 from here. Dodge saw them & being with his Battalion & the advance guard of spies under Majr Ewing dismounted & found the horses being held in the rear by a few men they were not long formed when they saw the Enemy charging on horseback over the hill raising the yell &c Dodge & Ewings men

* Hardly. On July 19, Brigadier General Henry Atkinson was again heading southeast from today's Fort Atkinson, Wisconsin, toward Palmyra, Wisconsin, trying to head Bark river by traversing part of the "trembling ground" (sod floating on muck or water) which sustains today's muck farms.

immediately returned the scream & if any thing hollowed louder than your children* This the rascals did not look for, finding the men ready for them & hearing the white mans voice & also seeing our horses standing as well as theirs, they wheeled & ran. The troops under the Several Cols [Colonels] by this time had formed & come up, charged & pursued the enemy into the swamp where the grass was so high that they could not see the enemy, & so wet that their guns would be rendered useless, they therefore retired a few steps up the hill & as the enemy rose the hill on the opposite side of the swamp, our men let loose & the way the scoundrels kicked was curious, night coming on & the men being fatigued & unable to pursue from the hard days march (40 miles) they encamped and remained 2 nights on the Battle ground the second night an Indian named We-sheet mounted a hill about a mile off & was distinctly heard giving commands. We hope to catch them soon & finish this disagreeable business.

"I see that the young men of St. Louis have raised companies of Volunteers after their services were required but could not afford it before or at that time--poor Set.

"I shall write you more at length soon. I only want to get one trophy first notwithstanding

* The "children" of the Superintendant of Indians Affairs, were, of course, the Indians.

2d Lt. Meriwether Lewis Clark,
Aide de Camp to Atkinson

Genl Scott has positively prohibited scalping &c* yet if I bring a Red Rascal I think Ill manage to have his head off before he dies, which will not be mutilating him you know and Ill have to cut off his head to kill him & having his noddle I can take his scalp with impunity. Give my love to all

"Your affect Son Lewis

"(In great haste & on my knee I write.)"[5]

Dr. Addison Philleo also participated in this busy morning of letter writing, as the following item from *The Galenian* newspaper shows: "July 27.--we received a letter today from the editor, dated Blue Mound, 25th July, from which we learn that Gen. Atkinson's army of regulars, together with Gen. Alexander's brigade, arrived at that place on the previous evening; and was to take up a line of march for Helena on the following day. Gen. Posey was then at Helena, and Gen's Henry and Dodge were expected there on that day, (the 26th.)"[6]

Not everyone, however, was writing letters. Esau Johnson had this to report:

"General Dodge...sent a Captain [William N.] Dobbins from Clay County [actually Marion County] Illinoise to our Fourt [at the Blue Mounds] with his [spy] company [of

---

* Brigadier General Winfield Scott was appointed in June by President Andrew Jackson to take supreme command of the Black Hawk war from Henry Atkinson (who seemed to be taking too long to get nowhere). Asiatic cholera prevented Scott from reaching the theater of war, but one of Scott's general orders to his troops included the following item: "12. The General commanding, owes an apology to the brave men whom will be his pride to conduct to battle, when he positively prohibits, under the highest penalties of the law, as he does, all mutilating and scalping of prisoners, or the bodies of the enemy who may be killed in action. But as [a?] few inconsiderate or worthless individuals might, if not warned and checked, bring odium on the whole army, those barbarian practices are denounced in advance."[4]

Posey's First Brigade], and Stationed them there with us. He had a company that thought they were a little smarter than any other company that belonged to the whole brigade, and they said they had a man in their company that could lift or could throw a heavy weight further than any other man that belonged to the whole army.

"One day after the battle with the Indians at the Wisconsin River when there was over three thousand of us together, he, Mr. Myers [Daniel Myres], began to brag, and said, "I can out lift or can throw a heavy weight further than any other man that belongs to the Regiment."

"I asked, 'What kind of weight would you throw?"

"He said, 'I do not care so it is heavy.'

"I said, 'How will you throw it?'

"He said, 'Take it up on one hand on the shoulder, make a mark, stand with both toes to that scribe or mark, and throw...and where it strikes, that is the distance you have throwed it.'

"I pointed to a pig of Lead. I said, 'There is a pig of Lead. How will that do?'

"He said, 'That is the very thing.'

"I said, 'Make your mark and throw. I want to beat you.'

"He made his mark, stood with both his toes to the mark, throwed the pig of Lead. He throwed it fourteen feet.

"He said, 'I thought it was going further than that!'

"I picked the pig of Lead up, throwed it four Inches over where he had throwed it.

"He picked it up again, throwed four inches over where I had throwed it.

"I took it, throwed it two Inches over his throw.

"He, Mr. Myers [Myres] throwed it four or five times, but could not throw it as far as he had throwed the second time he throwed.

"I then said, 'I have not been throwing yet.'

"I picked up the pig of Lead, stepped into his tracks, throwed it four feet over where I had throwed it before"[7]

This morning General Atkinson reported to General Winfield Scott, who was still in Chicago with his cholera-afflicted troops, and to Alexander Macomb, Commanding General of the Army in Washington. The letter to Scott, a copy of which Atkinson enclosed in his note to General Macomb, was addressed to Macomb even though it was directed to Scott:

"Genl: Atkinson To Genl Macomb

"Head Qrs: of the division of the North West Army west of Rock river,

"Blue Mounds Michigan Territory 25th July 1932.

"Sir, I have the honor to report to you that General Henry with his Brigade accompanied by Genl Dodge with a Battalion of Michigan [Territory] volunteers, who were as I informed you by letter on the 21st. Inst. detached in pursuit of the enemy, succeeded by forced marches in coming up with him on the banks of the Ouisconsin opposite this place on the evening of the 21st Inst: and immediately made an attack upon him which resulted in his defeat with a loss of Thirty five men Killed and it is presumed a much larger number wounded, as he was seen during the action bearing them off--our loss amounts to: but one man Killed & seven wounded night coming on our Troops were called back and the enemey saved from entire destruction, and he passed over to an Island where he had, and was in the act, of sending Women and Children. Henry and Dodge remained on the ground the succeeding day & night and part of the next day but were unable to renew the attack in consequence of the entire absence [of] boats, canoes, or the means of constru[c]ting rafts to cross to the Island. They

fell back to this place on the evening of the 23rd. for a supply of Provisions, where I Joined them last evening with the regular Troops and part of Alexander's Brigade after a forced march of three days from Cosconong

"I shall move this morning with my whole force to a point on the Ouisconsin sixteen miles below where we shall endeavour to cross the [river] by Rafts or some other means and if possible overtake the enemy and subdue him, although we are worn down with fatigue and privation. He must be much crippled, and is suffering for subsistanc[e].

"The Troops under Henry & Dodge behaved with the greatest gallantry, resisting a charge of the enemy's Cavalry, and in turn charged him at every point with the greatest promptness and success to which may be attributed the very small loss they sustained.

"(Signed) H Atkinson Brigr. Genl U.S. Army"[8]

Atkinson then wrote a cover letter to General Alexander Macomb:

"Genl Atkinson--To Genl Macomb

"Head Quarters Division of the North West Army

"Blue Mounds, 25th. July 1832

"Sir, I have the honour to enclose herewith copies of my letters to Genl Scott of the 21st. & 25th Inst. [above, just written] copies of Henry's & Dodge's report to me of an affair with the enemy on the 21st. Inst: These will put you in possession of my operations and of my views as to future movements

"(Signed) H. Atkinson Brigr Genl U.S. Army"[9]

Major General Winfield Scott

Wisconsin Heights Battleground Marker

APPENDIX A

Eye-Witness Accounts

Eye-Witness Account by
Brigadier General James D. Henry,
Commanding Third Brigade,
Illinois Mounted Militia Volunteers.

"Camp on the Heights of the Ouisconsin, July 23, 1832.

"To Brigadier General Atkinson,

"Sir-- Part of the 3d Brigade, together with the squadron under the command of Gen. Dodge, moved from its encampment at the Four Lakes, on the 21st inst. at quick time. Having passed this defile, the brigade entered an open country thinly covered with over cup oak on the right bank of one of the four Lakes. About 10 o'clock A.M., a party of scouts from the squadron, discovered and killed the first Sac [Kickapoo?] warrior. Proceeding on the trail of the enemy a few miles further in advance at the head of our line, three other hostile Sacs were discovered, two of which were killed; the other made his escape. These circumstances raised the hopes of the Brigade to the belief that the wily Hawk and his desperate followers, could and would be overtaken: its movements consequently were greatly accelerated. In the mean while a chilling rain began to fall and continued until night, which rendered the time exceedingly unfavorable for the anticipated fight.

"Passing rapidly from this point, the enemy began to show itself from the heights on the right and left. The enemy threw back a party of mounted warriors to occupy a position on the left; this movement occasioned a temporary halt, and formation of the line of Battle. It was however, soon discovered to be a characteristic stratagem of the Sac leader, and the Brigade moved forward. The enemy occasionally shewing itself in front and flank until the advanced columns composed of General Dodge's squadron and Maj. Ewing's Battalion of spies halted. This step was taken in consequence of a scattering and skirmishing fire heard on the left. It was immediately discovered that the close pursuit and daring courage of the scouts from the squadron had brought the enemy at bay--at this point the Ouisconsin was in sight on the right, a succession of lofty peaks on the left, and less elevated heights on the right; the Brigade occupying an uneven plain; in front lay the second step of the river, thinly covered with low over-cup oak; on the left and between the position of the Brigade and the above-mentioned Sacs, runs a deep ravine from left to right, diagonally across the front and bounding the aforesaid step; before this lies a marsh covered with the most luxuriant growth of grass, which continues to the margin of the river, being interrupted only by one slight elevation of sandy ground.

"Thus was the situation of the country when it was discovered that the whole force of the enemy was advancing. The right and left columns of the advance under the command of Gen. Dodge, and the centre column under Maj. Ewing, were immediately formed in line of Battle, by their respective commanders; at this instant the enemy in its accustomed manner directed its attack against the front. These troops gallantly withstood the shock and drove back the survivers in confusion and dismay. The Brigade advancing from the right and left and centre, by heads of Regiments, the line of battle was immediately completed, under the command of Col. Jones, on the left, supported by Col. Collins, who, as soon as they were dismounted, commenced and maintained a well directed fire against the enemy.

"The right wing was commanded by Col. Fry, who advanced on the right with the first battalion and occupied a position on the high ground above the marsh, and drove back the enemy in its attempt to flank to the right of us.

"The enemy being driven back at all points, took possession of strong positions on the sides of the heights to the left, and in the ravine at their base. Thus posted they threw a number of shot against the front and left wing, without the possibility of being reached by ours; at this juncture, I ordered the left wing under Col. Jones, (whose horse was shot under him at this time) and Collins to advance at a charge and take possession of the enemy's position, and cover the heights; and Maj. James, of the 2d Battalion 2d Regt., with two companies of said Battalion, was ordered to charge on the right. By request of Gen. Dodge and Maj. Ewing, they were ordered to charge the enemy at point of bayonet, lying covered in the ravine. These movements were effected with the greatest promptitude, and in the most gallant style. In a few minutes the battle became general, and the enemy was driven from the heights, fleeing down the precipitous declivities, and took refuge in the swamps, thick woods and high grass in the bottom of the Ouisconsin.

"Col. Fry, with the first battalion of his (2d) Regiment having completely routed the enemy on our right, was withdrawn from the position he then occupied in the battle, and was ordered to guard the horses and baggage until the issue of the conflict was determined. This important duty was confided to the charge of Lt. Col. Smith, while Col. Fry was engaged on the lines. Major Wood, of the 3d and Major Miller of the 4th regiments, commanded and sustained the left of their respective regiments, while engaged with the enemy, on the charge, and acquitted themselves in a manner worthy of their characters as officers and men.

"Having no information of the probably position of the residue of the enemy, and the situation of the ground, and because of the approach of night, I withdrew the troops, and about eight o'clock went into the encampment on the grounds where the attack was first made by the enemy.

"In all these movements I received efficient aid from Col. McConnel, who in the absence of my first aid-de-camp [Alexander Pope Field, who was furloughed July 10], performed the duties of that station with coolness, promptness, and to my entire satisfaction. Assisted by Mr. Johnson [Nelson H. Johnston] and others, he communicated to the officers of the line all orders directed to be given, and accompanied Col. Fry in his charge upon the enemy upon the right.

"In short, it is with much pleasure that I have it in my power to say to you, that the officers and men under my command, without a single exception, demand and have my sincere thanks, and deserve well of their country, for the prompt obedience of orders, and unyielding bravery upon this occasion.

"At an early hour this morning the whole army was marched on foot (except the 4th Regt. left to guard camp under the command of Col. Collins) through the swamps to the bank of the river, where we expected to find the residue of the enemy's force--but they had escaped. By means of bark canoes they were enabled to pass the river during the night, leaving behind the principal part of their effects.

"We had one man killed, and eight wounded, none mortally. The number of the enemy killed and wounded is unknown, as the dead are scattered over a large tract of country covered with thick woods and high grass. Between thirty and forty have been found, and others are continually being discovered by our scouts. From appearances, the wounded, and many of the dead were removed during the night succeeding the battle.

"The name of the person killed, is J. T. [Thomas Jefferson] Short, of Randolph County, Ill.

"Signed, &c [J. D. Henry]

"Names of the wounded in the 3d Regt. 3d Brigade.

"Meredith S. M'Millen [McMillion], from Washington co. James Thompson, do. [ditto] Joseph Wells, Perry, Armstead Jones, Randolph.

"Four more were wounded in the Squadron."[1]

Colonel Henry Dodge

Eye-Witness Account by
Colonel Henry Dodge,
Commanding Michigan Territory
Mounted Militia Volunteers.

"Camp on the Wisconsin Thirty miles below Fort Winnebago July 22d. 1832 Brigadier General Atkinson

"Dear Sir In my last communication to you, I stated my intention to follow the hostile Sacks with General Henry. We crossed the Mud lake fork of Rock [actually the Crawfish] river at about 2 Oclk P M on the 19th. where the Sacks had encamped in a body.

"On the 20th. we made a forced march & reached the head of the 4 lakes, and on the 21st. we overtook the enemy at this place, our advanced spies killed two Sacks before we met with a body of the enemy--they showed themselves freequently on the surrounding hills to divert our attention, our spies met with three & pursued them within a mile of their camp, our men were pursued in turn by the enemy on horseback. believing the main body of the enemy near us, I dismounted my squadron of horse, which formed the right & left columns of the advanced guard, the centre column was composed of the spies commanded by Colo. Ewing, I ordered my squadron to advance in front, and fortunately met with a good position, a natural elevation of ground which covered my men who were ordered to squat down, the Enemy raised the Yell and galloped up within thirty yards of us, we fired on them and killed one and wounded one or two others, when they retreated.

"General Henry arrived with his Brigade dismounted & formed in order of battle, the enemy rallied and commenced a fire on the left flank, his object was evidently to outflank us. the prompt movement of one of General Henrys Regiments defeated the object he had in view.

"The Indians occupied a height which enabled them to kill one of Genl Henrys men & wounded one of mine.

"after consulting Genl Henry we determined to charge the enemy, my squadron, with the spies commanded by Colo. Ewing, & the regiment of Colo Jones charged the enemy in good order, with part of Col Collins Regiment.

"we dislodge him from his position & drove him down the height into the high grass in the swamp. our fire was so heavy he soon gave way, I thought from the movement of the enemy he might aim at turning the right flank. I advanced briskly at the head of Clarks & Camps Companies to watch his movements, supported by two Companies ordered by Genl. Henry to the right flank. The enemy then gave way in every direction retreating to the river.

"The Winnebagoes scalped eleven Indians killed by the whites, and the whites took thirteen scalps last night--eight were found today and three were killed in the chase. The enemy were seen to carry a number from the field during the action, so that the numbers killed cannot fall short of forty (perhaps more) many were wounded but the number not known.

"We lost one killed & seven wounded, one of our men was wounded before the battle, on our march.

"When the battle was over it was 7 Oclk. our men had made a forced march of forty miles many of them on foot, and exposed about six hours in the rain their arms wet and out of order. Knowing they had retreated to the river and that they had chosen their position and that we could not reach them before dark, after consulting with Genl. Henry it was agreed to defer a further attack on the enemy untill the next morning.

"We marched from our position to the river early in the day, and found he had crossed the river, he had left his camp in much hurry & confusion, from the appearance of the trees, bark canoes had been prepared for the purpose of crossing the Wisconsin when they might arrive there with the main body

"The conduct of the officers & men composing my Squadron was brave & cool, they advanced to the charge with a quick pace and even front, they all behaved well, and it would be difficult for me to driscriminate between them, they deserve the confidence of their country. The officers & men of Genl. Henry Brigade have met the high expectations formed of them. They have done honor to their state & themselves. I would always unite with great confidence with such brave & gallent men

"I am with sentiments of great respect Your obedient Servant

"H Dodge Col. Commanding Michigan [Territory] Mounted Volunteers"[2]

Captain David M. Parkinson,
Michigan Territory Mounted Militia

Eye-Witness Account by
Captain Daniel M. Parkinson,
Michigan Territory Mounted Militia,
Colonel Henry Dodge Commanding.

"The next morning—the memorable 21st of July—we were upon their trail by sunrise, with every expectation of overtaking them soon. The march or pursuit was consequently rapid. On the bank of the Third Lake, near where the Lake House in Madison now stands, our advance guard killed an Indian, who...was sitting upon the grave of his wife, who had perhaps died of fatigue, hunger and exhaustion, and her disconsolate companion had resolved to await the advancing foe, and die there also; and he boldly bared his naked breast, and presented a full front, as a willing target for the balls of the scouts. He but too soon met the death he coveted. This may be thought to have been cruel on the part of the scouts; but it will be recollected that our motto was, '*no quarter;*' and besides, in such an exciting pursuit, there was little time to deliberate as to their course of action in such a case, even had they then been aware of the attending circumstances.

"In our pursuit, we passed an encampment on what is now called Pheasant Branch, at the head of Fourth Lake, where was a freshly made Indian grave, where a squaw was buried, supposed to have died the night before. About five miles from this place, our scouts killed an Indian, who said he was a Winnebago; and when in the act of falling, he fired his rifle, wounding one of the volunteers of Capt. Clark's company. From this point, our scouts were continually chasing the Indians, and being in turn chased by them. Consequently the march became almost a flight in pursuit of the enemy. Upon one occasion, we were thrown into order of battle, but the enemy immediately receded, and a running fire was then kept up almost constantly by our scouts and the rear guard of the Indians, until the main battle was fought. It was brought about by the chasing of our scouts, who were commanded by Capt. Joseph Dickson, now of Grant county, by a large body of the enemy who had been secreted in the low bottom of the Wisconsin River. While they were pursuing the scouts up a long slope, the advance portion of our men were rapidly ascending from the opposite side, and, as a consequence we met near the top.

"Here we had barely time to form ourselves into battle order. Col. Dodge's command, of which my command formed a part, and Col. Wm. L. D. Ewing's formed the front, and were barely faced about, when the enemy commenced firing upon us. We returned the fire with great rapidity, and with deadly aim, as it was ascertained that forty-eight of the enemy were killed in this charge. My orderly sergeant, John McNair, was wounded in this onset, by a shot in the thigh, but was not conscious of it until the firing ceased, and the enemy had fled. By this time, the remainder of Gen. Henry's command, except the command of Col. Fry, a part of whom were dragoons, was brought into line of battle, and which was within ten minutes after the firing commenced.

"As an act of justice to Gen. Henry and his command, I would here remark, that Gen. Smith's historical narrative of the march after we left the Four Lakes, and of the battle, is not altogether correct. The General says: 'The advance was commanded by Col. Wm. L. D. Ewing, but Col. Dodge's command becoming dissatisfied with what they considered a tardy march, broke off to the right and left, and took the front;' and, furthermore: 'The position of Col. Dodge was maintained under a constant fire from the Indians for fully an hour before the line of battle was formed by the arrival of Gen. Henry with the rest of his brigade.' Now, according to my recollection, and which I am confident is correct in this particular, the facts are, that Col. Dodge's command marched in front *all that day,* as well as on all the previous days of the pursuit; that Gen. Henry's entire command kept close in our rear and were there when the engagement commenced, and were in line of battle, in ten minutes at most after the first firing. But it is true, that Colonels Dodge and Ewing's commands alone received the fire of the first charge of the enemy.

"After the line of battle was now fully formed, which was upon a high eminence, and in open ground, considerable firing was kept up by the Indians, who had taken shelter in some underbrush upon the brink of the opposite declivity, by which seven of our brave volunteers were wounded, and one killed—two of the wounded belonged to Capt. Clark's company, and the others to Colonels Jones and Collins' regiments; and the man who was killed, was named Short, and belonged to Col. Jones' command. It was Col. Jones who had his horse shot from under him, and not Col. Collins as stated in Gen. Smith's History. Seeing that our men were suffering more in this firing than perhaps the enemy were, though we were not idle, I stepped to Col. Dodge, and suggested the propriety of a charge; and he immediately suggested it to Gen. Henry, when the charge was at once ordered. The enemy were at once dislodged from their hiding place, and in their flight, twenty more of them were slain and scalped, making in all sixty-eight of the enemy killed in the battle. This is my recollection of the matter, and which is corroborated, I believe, by Gen. Atkinson's report to the War Department. We pursued them to the bottom of the Wisconsin, where we reached the tall grass, which was wet, it having rained nearly the entire afternoon of that day, and it being now nearly dark, the pursuit was continued no farther.

"We returned to camp, and just after supper, we were cheered by the arrival of Adjutant Woodbridge and Adjutant Merriman, who, it will be recollected, had been sent from the

Rapids of Rock River, as an express to Gen. Atkinson, on Bark River. With them came Capt. James B. Estes, who claims to have been in the battle, but was, according to my recollection, about two hours too late. Our interpreter, Mr. Poquette, and our Indian spies who had accompanied us from Fort Winnebago, left us immediately after the battle."[3]

Eye-Witness Account by

2d Lt. James J. Justice,

Colonel Gabriel Jones's Third Regiment

Brigadier General James D. Henry's Third Brigade

"the next morning which was the 21st of July we took up our horses which we had allowed to Run at large thro the night (not withstanding we were not far distant from the Indians) and commenced our march passing through the narrows of the four lakes where the spis come on two Indians and killed them one only of which I saw which was the first man I ever saw that had been killed   we followed on In pursuit passing on by the lakes which would have afforded a delightful vew to the traveler who was exploring the country but we had only time to take a passing vew of the Romantic beauties of the willderness and pass on from the beautiful sandy shores of the lakes into the Broken and Barrony woods where from the top of one stupendious hill we could vew nothing but the savage wilds of high hills and narrow Vales untill the afternoon when our spies could discover when they were on one of those high stony hills the Indians on another   meantime we were pushing on hard after them and some of our men who had broken down their horses kept the march on foot while those that were mounted went on in a full trot The after part of the day was Rainy and the utmost care was necessary to keepe the armes dry and notwithstanding in spite of all that could be done there were a number of guns which was incapable of use in the evening we approached the hights of the Ousconsin where the Indians having chosen their ground were Ready for Battle there was no time to spend in counsel we were ordered to form two companies had been detailed as Rear guards Browns and Banksons The others formed and the Indians made a feint charge (in which one or two were killed) and then Retreated into the high weedes in the hollow in which they at first formed our men soon made a charge and Routed them out of their coverts and continued to charge repeatedly none of which the Indians disputed with any Kind of obstinacy the Battle continued about an hour and a half & the Indians retreated across a swamp to the margin of the Ouisconsin and it being then dark the troops were called off the pursuit and encamped on the ground where we first formed and posted a strong guard expecting the Indians to give us another Battle But they kept at a proper distance The next morning we perraded and marched down to the River But the Indians had got across the River"[4]

Lt. Charles Bracken,
Aide de Camp to Dodge,
Adjutant with Michigan Territory Militia

Eye-Witness Account by

Lt. Charles Bracken,

Aide de Camp to Colonel Henry Dodge,

Adjutant with Michigan Territory Militia.

"Early the next morning the pursuit was renewed. An Indian who was sick and unable to travel, was shot the moment the eye of Capt. Fred. Dickson [Dixon], of Capt. Jo. Dickson's company of spies, fell on him, he not being aware that the Indian was sick. This Indian was killed on the bank of Third Lake, within less than one half mile of where the Capitol now stands. Another sick or disabled Indian who begged for quarter was shot by Dr. Philleo during the pursuit. In falling, the Indian discharged his gun, and wounded a young man of Clark's company, of Dodge's command.

"The advance, from the time we left Rock River, preceeded by Capt. Jo Dickson's spies, was led by Col. W. L. D. Ewing's battalion of Henry's brigade, the order of march being in two columns. Dodge's command becoming dissatisfied with the slow gait at which Ewing's battalion led the pursuit, reasoned among themselves that it was safer to dash ahead, overtake the enemy, and fight them on *terra firma,* than to suffer them to reach the islands of the

Wisconsin, where if we advanced on them, we would be without cover and liable to be shot in the water. They therefore insisted on Gen. Dodge's taking the lead and engaging the enemy with his command. For this purpose the heads of our columns, striking off at a brisk trot, were inclined to the right and left of Ewing's battalion. On seeing this movement, that officer urged his men forward with blows and curses, and suceeded in keeping up with us, and held a position in our centre. In this order we advanced rapidly, halting and forming once or twice to meet the enemy, who appeared in some numbers in our front, until we arrived near the Wisconsin bottom, where the horse guard was told off, and the men dismounted. This had scarcely been effected, when Capt. Dickson and his spies came galloping over a ridge a little in advance of us, pursued by a number of the enemy. The columns immediately advanced, Ewing's battalion formed the centre, to the top of the ridge, and formed in line by wheeling the heads of columns to the right. One fire from our line caused the Indians to retreat as rapidly as they had advanced. We occupied this position until the arrival of General Henry with Collins', Jones' and Fry's regiments, who, owing to our rapid advance, had been left far to the rear. During this delay, the enemy were concentrating their forces on a hill that commanded our position, about two hundred yards in advance of us, and kept up a constant fire on our line for fully one hour before Henry arrived and arrangements were made to charge them. When the line of battle was formed, Dodge's command, including Ewing's battalion, formed the right wing; Fry's regiment was ordered to occupy a position on our right, to prevent the Indians from out-flanking us when we charged, consequently this regiment was not in action. As I before remarked, owing to the delay of General Henry in coming up, the main body of the enemy had concentrated in front of Dodge's command. I have no doubt but that the Indian commander, who occupied a high mound which overlooked our position, was deceived by the movement of Fry's regiment to our right. He reasonably supposed that movement was to cut him off from his women and children at the river. He was distinctly heard giving an order to his warriors in a loud voice, who immediately retreated. That the Indian commander fell into this error, is confirmed by the fact, that just previous to the charge, the hill fronting the right wing was covered with Indians, and although our advance was over open ground and in full view of the enemy, yet we had none killed and but one man wounded, in reaching the position occupied by them. The action lasted but a short time after the charge. In front of Dodge's command the principal part of the Indians were killed. The greater part of the Winnebago Indians who accompanied us from the fort, hid in sink holes or sheltered behind trees, except the White Pawnee and the son of White Crow, who together with Poquette fell into our ranks, and fought uncovered like white men. All the Indians, together with Poquette, started for Fort Winnebago immediately after the action."[5]

Surgeon's Mate John A. Wakefield,
Spy Battalion, Third Brigade
Illinois Mounted Militia

Eye-Witness Account by

Surgeon's Mate John A. Wakefield,

Major William Lee D. Ewing's Spy Battalion,

Brigadier General James D. Henry's Third Brigade.

"July 21st. At the break of the day the bugle sounded, and all were soon up, and in a few minutes had breakfast ready; and after taking a little food, we mounted our horses, and again commenced the pursuit.

"We soon found that the pilot had told us no lies for we found the country that the enemy was leading us into, to be worse if possible, than what he told us. We could turn neither to the right nor left, but were compelled to follow the trail the Indians had made; and that too, for a great distance at the edge of the water of the lake.

"Here it may not be uninteresting to the reader, to give a small outline of those lakes. From a description of the country, a person would very naturally suppose that these lakes were as little pleasing to the eye of the traveler, as the country is. But not so. I think they are the most beautiful bodies of water I ever saw. The first one that we came to, was about ten miles in circumference, and the water was as clear as crystal. The earth sloped back in a gradual rise; the bottom of the lake appeared to be entirely covered with white pebbles, and no appearance of its being the least swampy. The second one we came to, appeared to be much larger. It must have been twenty miles in circumference. The ground rose very high all around;—and the heaviest kind of timber grew close to the water's edge. If those lakes were anywhere else, except in the country they are, they would be considered among the wonders of the world. But the country they are situated in is not fit for any civilized nation of people to inhabit. It appears that the Almight intended it for the children of the forest. The other two lakes we did not get close enough to for me to give a complete description of them; but those who saw them, stated that they were very much like the other. I am digressing and leaving my subject too long; so I will go back and pursue our march.

"We had not marched more than five miles, before Doctor Philleo came back, meeting us, with the scalp of an Indian. He had been on ahead with the front scouts, and came on this Indian, who had been left as a rear guard to watch our movements. There were several shots fired at him about the same time, and I suppose all hit him, from the number of bullet holes that were in him; but Doctor Philleo scalped him; so he was called Philleo's Indian; which reminds me of the hunters: He who draws the first blood is entitled to the skin, and the remainder to the carcase, if there are several in the chase; which was the case at this time.

"But I am not done with Doctor Philleo yet. I will show you that he is a good soldier, and something of an Indian fighter. The signs now began to get very fresh, and we mended our pace very much. We had not proceeded more than ten or fifteen miles further, before our fighting Doctor run afoul of two more Indians; he showed his bravery in assisting to kill him. I suppose he killed one, and Mr. Sample Journey the other; so there was a scalp for each. But one of those miserable wretches sold his life as dear as possible. He, in the act of falling after he was shot, fired, and shot three balls into a gentleman who was himself in the act of shooting at him. The balls were all small; one went through his thigh, one through his leg, and the other through his foot. I am sorry that I have forgotten the gentleman's name; he belonged to General Dodge's squadron.

"We now doubled our speed, all were anxious to press forward, and as our horses were nearly worn out, we carried nothing, only what was actually necessary for us to eat; camp kettles, and many such articles, were thrown away.

"The trail was now literally, in many places, strewed with Indian trinkets, such as mats, kettles, &c.; which plainly told us that they knew we were in pursuit. We too, saw from the face of the country that we were drawing close to the Wisconsin river, and our object was to overtake them before they reached it; so we now went as fast as our horses were able to carry us;—but this was too severe for our poor horses; they began to give out; but even this did not stop a man. Whenever a horse gave out, the rider would dismount, throw off his saddle and bridle, and pursue on foot, in a run, without a murmur. I think the number of horses left this day, was about forty. The rear guard of the enemy began by this time (about three o'clock P.M.) to make feint stands; and as the timber stood thick, we did not know but that the whole army of Black Hawk was forming for action; in consequence of which, we got down and formed as often as twice, before we found out that their object was to keep us back until they could gain some strong position to fight from. Our front scouts now were determined not to be deceived any more; but the next they came to, they stopped not for their feigned manoeuvre, but pursued them to the main body of the enemy. They returned to us in great haste, and informed General Henry that the Indians were forming for action.

"We all dismounted in an instant. The line of battle was then formed in the same order that it had been laid off the preceeding day: General Dodge's corps and Major Ewing's spy battalion still in front. The horses were left, and every fourth man detailed to hold them; which gave seven horses to each man to hold.

"We had scarcely time to form on foot, before the Indians raised the war-whoop, screaming and yelling hideously, and rushed forward, meeting us with a heavy charge. General Dodge and Major Ewing met them also with a charge, which produced a halt on the part of the enemy. Our men then opened a tremendous volley of musquetry upon them, and accompanied it with the most terrific yells that ever came from the head of mortals, except from the savages themselves. They could not stand this. They now tried their well-known practice of flanking: but here they were headed again by the brave Colonel Jones and his regiment who were on our left, where he met them in the most fearless manner, and opened a heavy fire upon them. Colonel Fry was placed on the extreme right. They tried his line, but were soon repulsed. Their strong position was on the left, or near the centre, where Colonels Jones, Dodge, and Ewing, kept up a constant fire upon them for something like half an hour.

"The enemy here had a strong position. They had taken shelter in some very high grass, where they could lie down and load, and be entirely out of sight. After fighting them in this position for at least thirty minutes, during which time Colonel Jones had his horse shot from under him, and one of his men killed, and several wounded, Colonels Dodge, Ewing and Jones, all requested General Henry to let them charge upon them at the point of the bayonet, which General Henry readily assented to, and gave the order, 'charge!' which was obeyed by both men and officers in a most fearless manner. All were intent upon the charge. We had to charge up a rising piece of ground. When we got on the top, we then fired perfectly abreast. They could not stand this. They had to quit their hiding place, and made good their retreat. When they commenced retreating, we killed a great number.

"Their commander, who, it was said, was Na-pope, was on a white poney on the top of a mountain in the rear of his Indians; who certainly had one of the best voices for command I ever heard. He kept up a constant yell, until his men began to retreat; when he was heard no more. Colonel Collins was kept during this engagement, in the rear, as a reserve, and to keep the enemy from flanking, and coming in upon us in the rear, which was a very good arrangement of General Henry.

"It was now nearly sun down, and still raining as it had been all the evening; but so slow that we made shift to keep our guns dry. The enemy retreated toward the river with considerable speed. The ground they were retreating to, appeared to be low and swampy; and on the bank of the river there appeared to be a heavy body of timber, which the enemy could reach before we could bring them to another stand. So General Henry concluded not to pursue them any further that night, but remain on the battle ground until next morning; and then he would not be in danger of losing so many of his men; knowing that, in the dark, he would have to lose a number; for the Indians would have the timber to fight from, while we would have to stand in the open prairie."[6]

Wisconsin Heights Historical Marker

Black Sparrow Hawk
Engraving from his *Autobiography*.

Eye-Witness Account by Makataimeshekiakiak [Black Hawk], "British Band", Sauk & Fox Tribes

"During our encampment at the Four Lakes, we were hard put to, to obtain enough to eat to support nature. Situate in a swampy, marshy country, (which had been selected in consequence of the great difficulty required to gain access thereto,) there was but little game of any sort to be found--and fish were equally scarce. The great distance to any settlement, and the impossibility of bringing supplies therefrom, if any could have been obtained, deterred our young men from making further attempts. We were forced to dig *roots* and *bark trees,* to obtain something to satisfy hunger and keep us alive! Several of our old people became so much reduced, as actually to *die with hunger!* And, finding that the army had commenced moving, and fearing that they might come upon and surround our encampment, I concluded to remove my women and children across the Mississippi, that they might return to the Sac nation again. Accordingly, on the next day, we commenced moving, with five Winnebagoes acting as our guides, intending to descend the Ouisconsin.

"Ne-a-pope, with a party of twenty, remained in our rear, to watch for the enemy whilst we were proceeding to the Ouisconsin, with our women and children. We arrived, and had commenced crossing them to an island, when we discovered a large body of the enemy coming towards us. We were now compelled to fight, or sacrifice our wives and children to the fury of the whites! I met them with fifty warriors, (having left the balance to assist our women and children in crossing,) about a mile from the river, when an attack immediately commenced.

"I was mounted on a fine horse, and was pleased to see my warriors so brave. I addressed them in a loud voice, telling them to stand their ground, and never yield it to the enemy. At this time I was on the rise of a hill, where I wished to form my warriors, that we might have some advantage over the whites. But the enemy succeeded in gaining this point, which compelled us to fall back into a deep ravine, from which we continued firing at them and they at us, until it began to grow dark.

"My horse having been wounded twice during this engagement, and fearing from his loss of blood, that he would soon give out--and finding that the enemy would not come near enough to receive our fire, in the dusk of the evening—and knowing that our women and children had had sufficient time to reach the island in the Ouisconsin, I ordered my warriors to return, in different routes, and meet me at the Ouisconsin--and were astonished to find that the enemy were not disposed to pursue us.

"In this skirmish, with fifty braves, I defended and accomplished my passage over the Ouisconsin, with a loss of only six men; though opposed by a host of mounted militia.

"I would not have fought there, but to gain time for my women and children to cross to an island. A warrior will duly appreciate the embarrassments I labored under--and whatever may be the sentiments of the *white people,* in relation to this battle, my nation, though fallen, will award to me the reputation of a great brave in conducting it.

"The loss of the enemy could not be ascertained by our party; but I am of opinion, that it was much greater, in proportion, than mine. We returned to the Ouisconsin, and crossed over to our people.

"Here some of my people left me, and descended the Ouisconsin, hoping to escape to the west side of the Mississippi, that they might return home. I had no objection to their leaving me, as my people were all in a desperate condition--being worn out with travelling, and starving from hunger. Our only hope to save ourselves, was to get across the Mississippi. But few of this party escaped. Unfortunately, a party of soldiers from Prairie du Chien, was stationed on the Ouisconsin, a short distance from its mouth, who fired upon our distressed people. Some were killed, others drowned, several taken prisoners, and the balance escaped to the woods and perished with hunger. Among this party were a great many women and children.

"I was astonished to find that Ne-a-pope and his party of *spies* had not yet come in--they having been left in my rear to bring the news, if the enemy were discovered. It appeared, however, that the whites had come in a different direction, and intercepted our trail but a short distance from the place where we first saw them--leaving our spies considerably in the rear. Ne-a-pope, and one other, retired to the Winnebago village*, and there remained during the war! The balance of his party, being *brave men,* and considering our interest as their own, returned, and joined our ranks.

"Myself and band having no means to descend the Ouisconsin, I started, over a rugged country, to go to the Mississippi, intending to cross it, and return to my nation. Many of our people were compelled to go on foot, for want of horses, which, in consequence of their having had nothing to eat for a long time, caused our march to be very slow. At length we arrived at the Mississippi**, having lost some of our old men and little children, who perished on the way with hunger."[7]

---

* Of White Crow, located on Carcajou Point on Lake Koshkonong near today's Fort Atkinson, Wisconsin.

** Where occurred, on August 1 and 2, 1832, (at today's Victory, Wisconsin) the massacre at Bad Axe.

APPENDIX B
Black Hawk's Trail

THE WISCONSIN ARCHEOLOGIST

Published Quarterly by The Wisconsin Archeological Society

VOL. 24 No. 4

MILWAUKEE, WIS., DECEMBER, 1943

New Series

BLACK HAWK RETREAT IN DANE COUNTY

A. O. Barton

Dane County Register of Deeds

The Black Hawk war should have been an Illinois war, but unfortunately most of it was fought in Wisconsin, and unfortunately to the disgrace of Wisconsin, where probably not a drop of blood need have been shed, since Black Hawk was retreating all the time, seeking only to return to the west side of the Mississippi and trying vainly at all times to arrange a peaceful understanding and a safe passage out for his warriors and his people.

His retreat covered the whole length of Dane County from east to west. This area was crossed probably between July 18 and 21, 1832, inclusive. After committing several massacres in Illinois notably that at Indian Creek and after several clashes with troops, Black Hawk had fled up the valley of the Rock River past Lake Koshkonong, Jefferson County, in the latter part of May and had gone into hiding in the lake region near the present site of Hustisford, Dodge County. During the month of June Gen. Atkinson, Col. Henry Dodge and others had been organizing militia and building forts and stockades in the lead mining area of southwestern Wisconsin. About the middle of July, Gen. Atkinson dispatched Col. Dodge, Gen. James D. Henry and a detachment of troops to go from Fort Koshkonong to Fort Winnebago (Portage) for supplies. When returning their scouts came upon traces of Black Hawk's departure and retreat in Jefferson County and immediately took up the persuit westward, sending their supplies to Gen. Atkinson, and not consulting him. Black Hawk and his followers had apparently descended the Rock River, following its course from Hustis Rapids to the neighborhood of Johnson's Creek, and then had turned westward and crossed the Crawfish River at Aztalan and headed toward Lake Ripley, near the site of the present village of Cambridge. At this point they entered Dane County, hiding in the swamps and deep grass, then traveling westward toward the Madison lakes. After passing over the present site of Madison between Lakes Monona and Mendota, they headed northward for the Wisconsin River, near the present site of Sauk City.

This took place on July 20, 1832. That night the Indians camped at the present site of the village of Pheasant Branch, at the head of Lake Mendota, now adjoining the village of Middleton. On the same night Col. Dodge and Gen. Henry and their rangers camped about a quarter of a mile northeast of Lake Monona. The next morning the Indians started for the Wisconsin River and the white soldiers followed in pursuit over the present site of Madison. In crossing the Yahara River near Lake Monona, they came upon an Indian warrior sitting dejectedly on the grave of his wife. To put him out of his misery and to be on the safe side, they ended his life with a bullet. So fast was the persuit that it said forty horses of the white troopers gave out before the rear guard of twenty Indians was encountered near the Wisconsin River. Black Hawk may have had about 300 warriors; but he also had many women, children, old people, and considerable baggage, as when he had crossed the Mississippi at Rock Island to occupy his old village on the Rock, he had taken his whole tribe en masse with him. Many had now been lost due to death, desertion and other causes.

Col. Dodge assigned every fourth man to hold the horses and with the others attacked the Indians. Black Hawk had started sending his women and children and baggage down a small stream, between the present townships of Roxbury and Mazomanie, to the Wisconsin River. His warriors he had posted on the high ground overlooking the river; hence the name "Battle of Wisconsin Heights." From here he directed their operations. The Indians sought to surround the white troops, but were driven back and sought refuge in the deep grass near the river. This was near evening and a rain was falling, so Gen. Henry and Col. Dodge returned to their horses and camped for the night. In the night Black Hawk succeeded in getting his whole band over the river and continued his flight westward. A few had been killed and wounded on each side, the Indians taking their wounded with them. So ended the battle of Wisconsin Heights. An Indian orator made a long harrangue in the night evidently intended for the white troops. It was believed he was making a defense of the Indians and a plea for a chance to return west. Also he may have done it to keep the whites on guard while the escape was in progress.

The next day the white soldiers went overland to the fort at Blue Mounds for supplies, and three weeks later Black Hawk's band was cut to pieces and largely exterminated at the Bad Axe massacre in Vernon County. Soon afterwards Black Hawk was taken prisoner, and after being confined for a time at Fort Crawford, taken by Col. Jefferson Davis down the Mississippi River to St. Louis. Writing near the end of his life, the one-time President of the southern confederacy said he had studied Black Hawk's generalship at the battle of Wisconsin Heights and that it was of a high order.

Surveyor notations of 110 years ago, found in the state Land Office at Madison, have lent new interest to the story of the famous Sauk chieftain who staged the last Indian war in Wisconsin. In the field notes of the surveyors made in 1832 and 1833 the flight of Black Hawk and his band from the four lakes at Madison to the Wisconsin River is shown by markings on the maps indicating where the pursued and pursuers crossed section lines on entering or leaving a township. Also the exact site of the battlefield is shown.

In the recent session of the Legislature, a bill was

introduced, sponsored by Speaker Vernon Thomson, making a study of the route of Black Hawk in Wisconsin and the erection of suitable markers at points. Appearing for the bill in committee were Theodore Herfurth, insurance man and Black Hawk authority, Dr. Edward P. Alexander, Superintendent of the State Historical Society and others.

The bill failed of passage, but in the meantime Albert O. Barton, Register of Deeds of Dane County, a member of the committee headed by Mr. Herfurth, made the discovery of the route taken by Black Hawk from the eastern boundary of Dane County at Cambridge to the northwest corner near Sauk City.

The following letter was addressed to Col. J. W. Jackson, as of February 23, 1943.

Col. J. W. Jackson,
Sec. Madison & Wis. Foundation

Dear Colonel:

I enclose herewith a small map showing roughly the route followed by Black Hawk and followers from Madison to the Wisconsin River in 1832 as gleaned from records in the state land office. The notations are taken from surveys and surveyor's notes set down in 1833, when the marks of the flight and the battle must have still been plainly visible. The surveyor was John Mullett. He and his party marked very plainly just where the battle of Wisconsin Heights took place near the Wisconsin River and also noted the points where the pursuing army crossed each township line. It was presumably at these points that the Indians also crossed. (Books of Towns 9 and 10).

From some tracings it would appear that Black Hawk after going over the upper campus (if the tablet there is correct) turned south at the University Farm instead of following the lake shore. There may have been a swamp between the University Farm and College Hills, as now, so they seem to have swung over to the old Sauk Road (present University Ave.). Also as there were women and children along they may have wanted to go around the "mountain" (Eagle Heights) instead of over it.

At the Black Hawk Country Club (the concrete bridge) they seemed to have turned north again to the lake, as relics have been found there near Merrill Springs. Then they followed the lake past Mendota Beach and on to Pheasant Branch.

At Pheasant Branch they camped over night in a grove, presumably the present Sakrison grove. They thus entered Middleton on Sec. 12, near junction of the old and new roads (Ph Branch). There was then no Middleton and probably no road west. From the grove they went west to Section 3 and entered Springfield in Section 34. Then they went northwest presumably over Sections 34, 28, 29, and 19. Here they entered Berry in the S.E. ¼ of Sec. 24. Then they went almost north through Sections 24, 14, 11, 2 and 3 into Roxbury, entering Roxbury at S.E. ¼ Sec. 34. From there they went through Sections 34, 28, 20 and 19, into Mazomanie in the middle of Sec. 24. Here the battle was fought right near the town lines (the later Taylor farm, I think).

From the battle they went through the deep grass to the river, crossing to the island opposite Sec. 24, or went west and crossed to island opposite Sec. 23. Some marks might indicate the latter. (In Springfield or Berry some kettles and other baggage were later ploughed up. If these fields could be located they would mark the exact route.)

In his field notes Surveyor Mullett left an exact description of the location of the battlefield, as follows:

'East Boundary Town 9 North, Range 6 East.
Marked on East Side Sec. 24.
40.00 (chains ½ miles) set oak post for qr. sec. corner. marked ¼ Sec. 24.
W(hite) oak 24 (diameter in inches S18°west 1.32 (links).

B (. . .) oak 9 N 4 W 2.32.
(These are called "witness trees").

Marked ¼ Sec. 24 B.T. (Bearing trees).
56.50 Stream 3C west (Battle Ground).' (Book 52, 1833).

Little is known as to just where the Indians entered Dane County from the east. It is said that they were hard up for food near Deerfield. Possibly they came over later Seminary Springs road, or even father north.

A. O. Barton

Two markers have been erected on the Black Hawk Trail in Dane County, one on the north side of the hill behind Bascom Hall at the University of Wisconsin, and one beside the road near the Wisconsin Heights battlefield. The latter marker is a small monument erected by the John Bell Chapter, Daughters of the American Revolution, and was dedicated on Labor Day, 1923. The famous chieftain is most strikingly perpetuated in the giant statue overlooking the Rock River near Oregon, Illinois, made by the distinguished sculptor Lorado Taft.

Settlement must have rapidly followed the close of the Black Hawk War. The exterior of the town of Mazomanie (the outline) was surveyed by John Mullett and party, and the "interior" (by sections) was finished in the third quarter of 1833. This shows the battlefield in the N. E. ¼ of Sec. 24, near the Roxbury line, by a small stream. (Field Book No. 52, 1833, in state land office, Madison.)

At the end of this note book the surveyor writes under the head of "Remarks:"

"On the northeast corner of Section 1 (this would be over the river in what is now Sauk County—A.O.B.) there is a town plat with several houses thereon called Prairie du Sac. On the east half of Section 12 there is another town plat known as "Lower Town," on which there is now building a splendid hotel; there are also several other dwellings now thereon. On the northeast quarter of Section 17 there is a corn cracker and a sawmill now building."

How far north the Indians went in Jefferson and Dodge Counties can perhaps be ascertained in those counties. They were above Watertown. They seemed to have retraced their route to the vicinity of Aztalan where they crossed the Crawfish River at the present site of Aztalan, then struck west through the present townships of Deerfield, Cottage Grove and Blooming Grove, crossing the Yahara River near its entrance into Lake Monona. Soldiers wrote afterwards that the woods and brush were so dense that they had to follow close to the lake shore (they don't say what lake, presumably Mendota.) I wonder if they really went over the University Hill near Main Hall, if they had to drag along women and children. They would be apt to follow the more level lake shore or avoid the hill by following the University ground.

At Pheasant Branch they may have camped in the Sakrison grove, or the higher wooded ground back of the Pheasant Branch School which could be better defended and would be near the famous Bellefontaine Spring with its high look out ground.

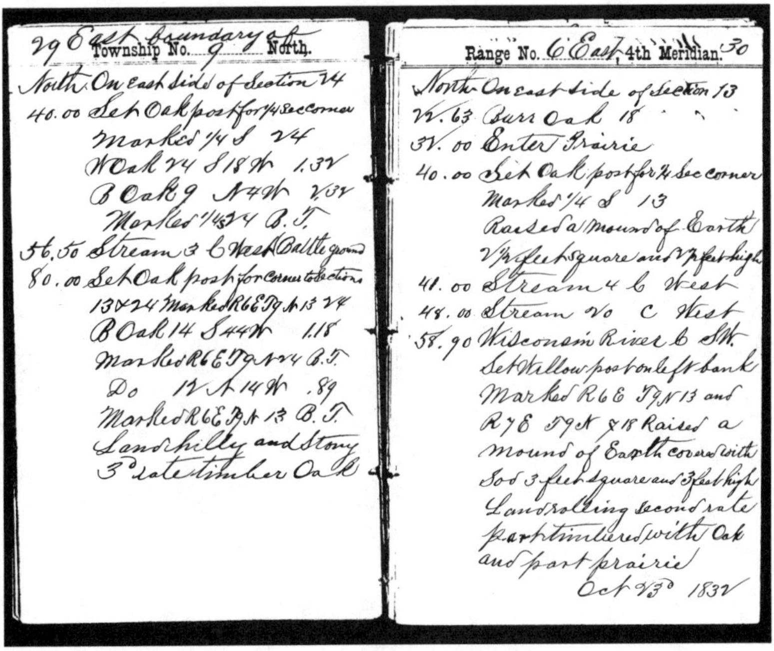

29 East boundary of Township No. 9 North.
North On east side of Section 24
40.00 Set Oak post for 1/4 Sec corner
Marked 1/4 S 24
W Oak 24 S 18 W 1.32
B Oak 9 N 4 W 2.38
Marked 1/4 S 24 B.T.
56.50 Stream 3 C West Battle ground
80.00 Set Oak post for Corner to Sections
13 & 24 Marked R6E T9 N 13 24
B Oak 14 S 44 W 1.18
Marked R6E T9 N 24 B.T.
Do 12 N 14 W .89
Marked R6E T9 N 13 B.T.
Land hilly and Stony
3d rate timber Oak

Range No. 6 East, 4th Meridian. 30
North On east side of Section 13
22.63 Burr Oak 18
32.00 Enter Prairie
40.00 Set Oak post for 1/4 Sec corner
Marked 1/4 S 13
Raised a mound of Earth
2 1/2 feet square and 2 1/2 feet high
41.00 Stream 4 C West
48.00 Stream 20 C West
58.90 Wisconsin River 6 SW.
Set Willow post on left bank
Marked R6E T9N 13 and
R7E T9N & 18 Raised a
mound of Earth covered with
Sod 3 feet square and 3 feet high
Land rolling second rate
part timbered with Oak
and part prairie
Oct 23d 1832

Pages from Surveyor's Field Notebook

EYE-WITNESS SOURCES

Tiny superscript numbers in the body copy refer to the source of the word, phrase, clause, sentence or paragraph cited. Those sources are listed here, chapter by chapter. The most readable sources, published as complete books, are Cooke, Kinzie, Wakefield, and, of course, Black Hawk's autobiography.

INTRODUCTION

1. Henry Atkinson to Roger Jones, November 19, 1832, in Whitney, Ellen M., *The Black Hawk War 1931-1832,* Volume II, "Letters and Papers" , Part II, June 24, 1832, through October 14, 1834, Illinois State Historical Library, Springfield, Illinois, 1975, p. 1204. Hereafter referred to as *BHW.*

2. *Ibid.,* Part I, April 30, 1831, through June 23, 1832, Illinois State Historical Library, Springfield, Illinois, 1973, p. 225.

3. *Ibid.,* p. 343. note 2.

4. *Ibid.,* p. 628, note 5.

5. *BHW.* II:1204-1212.

MONDAY, JULY 9, 1832

1. Cooke, Philip St. George, *Scenes and Adventures in the Army: Or Romance of Military Life.* Philadelphia: Lindsay & Blakiston, 1857, pp. 166-167.

2. Johnston, Albert Sidney, "April 1-August 2 Johnston Edited Journal", Tulane University Library, Howard Tilton Memorial Library, Mrs. Mason Barret Collection, New Orleans, Louisiana.

3. Russell, John, skeleton history, Russell Family Papers, Illinois State Historical Library, Springfield, Illinois.

4. Johnston, Albert Sidney, "June 12-August 16 Johnston Field Journal", Tulane University Library, Howard Tilton Memorial Library, Mrs. Mason Barret Collection, New Orleans, Louisiana.

5. John H. Kinzie to George B. Porter, July 12, 1832, in Whitney, Ellen M., *The Black Hawk War 1831-1832,* Volume II, "Letters and Papers", Part II, June 24, 1832, through October 14, 1834, Illinois State Historical Library, Springfield, Illinois, 1975, p. 775. Hereafter referred to as *BHW.*

6. Henry Atkinson to Roger Jones, November 19, 1832, *BHW* II: 1210.

7. Henry Atkinson: Orders, July 9, 1832, *BHW* II:754.

TUESDAY, JULY 10, 1832

1. Wisconsin, State Historical Society of. *Collections of the State Historical Society of Wisconsin.* [Hereafter referred to as *WHC.*] Volume II (1856), Bracken, Charles, "Further Strictures on Ford's Black Hawk War", p. 405.

2. Henry Atkinson: Orders, July 10, 1832, in Whitney, Ellen M., *The Black Hawk War, 1831-1832,* Volume II, "Letters and Papers", Part II, June 24, 1832, through October 14, 1834, Illinois State Historical Library, Springfield, Illinois, 1975, p. 757. Hereafter referred to as *BHW.*

3. Albert S. Johnston to Joseph Plympton, July 10, 1832, *BHW* II:760.

4. John Ryan to H. J. Wrigglesworth, no date, manuscript owned by Evelyn A. Weiskircher of Shullsburg, Wisconsin. A photostat copy is in the Hoard Museum Black Hawk War Collection of the Fort Atkinson, Wisconsin, Historical Society.

5. Henry Atkinson: Orders, July 10, 1832, *BHW* II:758.

6. James M. Strode to Henry Atkinson, June 30, 1832, *BHW* II:722-724, including notes.

7. Parish, John Carl. *George Wallace Jones.* Iowa Biographical Series. Iowa City: State Historical Society of Iowa, 1912, p.149.

8. Justice, James J., "Journal" in *BHW* II:1323.

9. Henry Dodge to Henry Atkinson, July 14, 1832, *BHW* II:791

10. Bracken, *WHC* II:405

11. James D. Henry to Henry Atkinson, July 14, 1832, *BHW* II:793.

12. Shaw, Ninevah, "Shaw's Journal", Shaw Family Papers, Illinois State Historical Library, Springfield, Illinois, *BHW* II:1334.

WEDNESDAY, JULY 11, 1832

1. Henry Dodge to Henry Atkinson, July 18, 1832, in Whitney, Ellen M., *The Black Hawk War 1831-1832,* Volume II, "Letters and Papers", Part II, June 24, 1832, through October 14, 1834, Illinois State Historical Library, Springfield, Illinois, 1975, p. 820. Hereafter referred to as *BHW.*

2. Wisconsin, State Historical Society of. *Collections of the State Historical Society of Wisconsin.* Volume II (1856), Bracken, Charles, "Further Strictures on Ford's Black Hawk War", p. 405.

3. Henry Dodge to Henry Atkinson, July 14, 1832, *BHW* II:791.

4. "Diary of the Weather", Fort Winnebago, Portage, Wisconsin, for July 11, 1832, in State Historical Society of Wisconsin, Madison, Wisconsin, filed "Wis. MSS 3 CL Fort Winnebago".

5. Shaw, Ninevah, "Shaw's Journal", Shaw Family Papers, Illinois State Historical Library, Springfield, Illinois, *BHW* II:1334.

6. *Ibid.*

7. *BHW,* Volume I, "Illinois Volunteers", Illinois State Historical Library, Springfield, Illinois, 1970, p. 357.

8. *Ibid.,* p. 409.

9. *Ibid.*

10. *Ibid.,* p. 410.

11. *Ibid.,* p. 409.

THURSDAY, JULY 12, 1832

1. Justice, James J., "Journal" [Hereafter referred to as Justice.] in Whitney, Ellen M., *The Black Hawk War 1831-1832,* Volume II, "Letters and Papers", Part II, June 24, 1832, through October 14, 1834, Illinois State Historical Library, Springfield, Illinois, 1975, p. 1323. Hereafter referred to as *BHW.*

2. William Lee D. Ewing to Henry Atkinson, *ca.* July 14, 1832, *BHW* II:792.

3. *BHW*, Volume I, "Illinois Volunteers", Illinois State Historical Library, Springfield, Illinois, 1970, p.416.

4. *Ibid.*, p. 417

5. *Ibid.*, p. 323.

6. Affidavit, Crawford County, January 6, 1851, in Highsmith Family Papers, Fort Atkinson, Wisconsin, and copies filed in Black Hawk War Papers, Hoard Museum, Fort Atkinson, Wisconsin. See also January 14, 1851, affidavit.

7. Kinzie, Juliette, *Wau-Bun, The "Early Day" in the Northwest,* edited by Louise Phelps Kellogg, 1968, The National Society of Colonial Dames in Wisconsin, Menasha, Wisconsin, pp. 260-261. Hereafter referred to as Kinzie.

8. *Ibid.*, p. 261

9. Shaw, Ninevah, "Shaw's Journal", Shaw Family Papers, Illinois State Historical Library, Springfield, Illinois, *BHW* II:1334. Hereafter referred to as Shaw, although the journal is in three different handwritings, one of which is Ninevah Shaw's.

10. Kinzie, pp. 59-60.

11. Wisconsin, State Historical Society of. *Collections of the* State Historical Society of Wisconsin. [Hereafter referred to as *WHC*.] Volume XII (1892), Paquette, Moses, "The Wisconsin Winnebagoes: An Interview with Moses Pauquette", pp. 399-400.

12. Kinzie, p. 323.

13. *Ibid.*, p. 324.

14. *Ibid.*, pp. 324-325.

15. *Ibid.*, p. 320.

16. De La Ronde, John T., "Personal Narrative", *WHC,* Volume VII (1876), p. 350.

17. Justice, *BHW* II;1323.

18. Henry Dodge to Henry Atkinson, July 14, 1832, *BHW* II:791.

19. Decorah, Spoon, "Narrative of Spoon Decorah", *WHC,* Volume XIII (1895), pp. 450-452.

20. James D. Henry to Henry Atkinson, July 14, 1832, *BHW* II:793.

21. National Archives, Washington, D.C., Record Group 94, Adjutant General's Office, August 31, 1832, Muster Roll for Company D, Fifth Regiment, United States Army Infantry.

22. "Diary of the Weather", Fort Winnebago, Portage, Wisconsin, for July 12, 1832, in State Historical Society of Wisconsin, Madison, Wisconsin, filed "Wis. MSS 3 CL Fort Winnebago".

23. "Reminiscences of Wisconsin", *WHC,* Volume X (1888), p. 233, reprint from *Madison Democrat,* July 1, 1871.

24. Dodge, *BHW* II:791.

25. Bracken, Charles, "Further Strictures on Ford's Black Hawk War", *WHC,* Volume II (1856), p. 405.

26. Decorah, *WHC* XIII:452.

27. Clark, Satterlee, "Early Times at Fort Winnebago and Black Hawk War Reminiscences", *WHC,* Volume VIII (1879), pp. 316-317. Hereafter referred to as Clark.

28. Merrell, Henry, "Pioneer Life in Wisconsin", *WHC* VII: 382-383.

29. *Ibid.*, p. 391.

30. Wakefield, John Allen, *History of the War between the United States and the Sac and Fox Nations of Indians,* Calvin Goudy, Jacksonville, Illinois, 1834. Because this is a rare book, all citations refer to a reprint edited by Frank Everett Stevens. Chicago: Caxton Club, 1908. Hereafter referred to as Wakefield. This quote is from p. 85.

31. Bracken, *WHC* II:405.

32. Dodge, *BHW* II:791.

33. Decorah, *WHC* XIII:453.

34. John H. Kinzie to George B. Porter, July 12, 1832, *BHW* II:774-775.

35. Justice, *BHW* II:1323.

36. Shaw, *BHW* II:1334.

37. *Ibid.*

38. Henry, *BHW* II:793.

39. Ewing, *BHW* II:792.

40. Wakefield, pp. 85-86.

41. Justice, *BHW* II:1323.

42. Clark, *WHC* VIII:314.

43. Reynolds, John, *Reynolds' History of Illinois: My Own Times; Embracing Also the History of My Life.* 1855; Chicago: Chicago Historical Society; Fergus Printing Co., 1879, pp. 399-401.

44. *BHW* I:318.

45. *Ibid.*, p. 352.

46. *Ibid.*, p. 353, note 10.

47. *Ibid.*, p. 420.

48. *Ibid.*

49. "Diary of the Weather" for July 15, 1832.

50. Clark, *WHC* VIII:315.

FRIDAY, JULY 13, 1832

1. Shaw, Ninevah, "Shaw's Journals", Shaw Family Papers, Illinois State Historical Library, Springfield, Illinois, [Hereafter referred to as Shaw.] in Whitney, Ellen M., *The Black Hawk War 1831-1832,* Volume II, "Letters and Papers", Part II, June 24, 1832, through October 14, 1834, Illinois State Historical Library, Springfield, Illinois, 1975, p. 1335. Hereafter referred to as *BHW.*

2. Wakefield, John Allen, *History of the War between the United States and the Sac and Fox Nations of Indians,* Calvin Goudy, Jacksonville, Illinois, 1834. Because this is a rare book, all citations refer to a reprint edited by Frank Everett Stevens. Chicago: Caxton Club, 1908. Hereafter referred to as Wakefield. This quote is from p. 86.

3. Shaw, *BHW* II:1335.

4. *BHW,* Volume I, "Illinois Volunteers", Illinois State Historical Library, Springfield, 1970, p. 393.

5. *Ibid.*

6. William Lee D. Ewing to Henry Atkinson, *ca.* July 14, 1832, *BHW* II:792.

7. Henry Dodge to Henry Atkinson, July 14, 1832, *BHW* II:791.

8. Wisconsin, State Historical Society of. *Collections of the State Historical Society of Wisconsin.* [Hereafter referred to as *WHC.*] Volume II (1856), Parkinson, Daniel M., "Pioneer Life in Wisconsin", p. 354.

9. Bracken, Charles, "Further Strictures on Ford's Black Hawk War", *WHC* II:405-406.

10. Parkinson, Peter, Jr., "Strictures upon Ford's Black Hawk War", *WHC* II:394.

11. Wakefield, p. 102.

12. Bracken, *WHC* II:406.

13. Parkinson, Peter, Jr., *WHC* II:393-394.

14. Smith, William R., *The History of Wisconsin. In Three Parts, Historical, Documentary, and Descriptive,* Madison, Wi., Beriah Brown, 1854, Volume I, Historical, pp. 278-279.

15. Dodge, *BHW* II:791.

16. Parkinson, Daniel M., *WHC* II:354.

17. Bracken, *WHC* II:406.

18. Parkinson, Daniel M., *WHC* II:354.

19. Henry Atkinson: Orders, Order 51, July 9, 1832, *BHW* II:754 and Order 55, July 10, 1832, *BHW* II:758.

20. Parkinson, Daniel M., *WHC* II:354-355.

21. Wakefield, p. 102.

22. *The Galenian* newspaper, Volume 1, Number 12, Wednesday, July 18, 1832, Galena, Illinois.

23. *BHW* II:746, Note 2.

24. Dodge, *BHW* II:791.

SATURDAY, JULY 14, 1832

1. Lewis Cass to Winfield Scott, June 15, 1832, in Whitney, Ellen M., *The Black Hawk War 1831-1832,* Volume II, "Letters and Papers", Part I, April 30, 1831, through June 23, 1832, Illinois State Historical Library, Springfield, Illinois, 1973, p. 590. Hereafter referred to as *BHW.*

2. Henry Dodge to Henry Atkinson, July 14, 1832, *BHW* II, Part II, June 24, 1832, through October 14, 1834, Illinois State Historical Library, Springfield, Illinois, 1975, p. 791. Hereafter referred to as *BHW.*

3. James D. Henry to Henry Atkinson, July 14, 1832, *BHW* II:793

4. *BHW,* Volume I, "Illinois Volunteers", Illinois State Historical Library, Springfield, Illinois, 1970, p. 421.

5. William Lee D. Ewing to Henry Atkinson *ca.* July 14, 1832, *BHW* II:792.

6. Henry Dodge to Henry Atkinson, July 18, 1832, *BHW* II:820.

7. John H. Kinzie to George B. Porter, July 14, 1832, *BHW* II:796.

8. *The Galenian* newspaper, Volume I, Number 13, Wednesday, July 25, 1832, Galena, Illinois.

9. Reynolds, John, *Reynolds' History of Illinois: My Own Times; Embracing Also the History of My Life.* Philadelphia: Lindsay & Blakiston, 1857, p. 402. Hereafter referred to as Reynolds.

10. Wisconsin, State Historical Society of. *Collections of the State Historical Society of Wisconsin.* [Hereafter referred to as *WHC.*] Volume II (1856), Bracken, Charles, "Further Strictures on Ford's Black Hawk War", p. 406.

11. *The Galenian* newspaper, Volume 1, Number 14, Wednesday, August 1, 1832, Galena, Illinois.

12. Parkinson, Peter, Jr., "Strictures upon Ford's Black Hawk War", *WHC* II:394.

13. *Ibid.*

14. Reynolds, pp. 402-404.

15. Parkinson, Daniel M., "Pioneer Life in Wisconsin", *WHC* II:355.

16. Bracken, p. 406.

17. H.S. Townsend, speech, *Vernon County Censor* newspaper, August 10, 1898, Viroqua, Wisconsin.

18. Wakefield, John Allen, *History of the War between the United States and the Sac and Fox Nations of Indians,* Calvin Goudy, Jacksonville, Illinois, 1834. Because this is a rare book, all citations in this book refer to a reprint edited by Frank Everett Stevens. Chicago: Caxton Club, 1908, p. 102.

19. Bracken, *WHC* II:406.

20. Dodge, *BHW* II:820.

SUNDAY, JULY 15, 1832

1. William Lee D. Ewing to Henry Atkinson, *ca.* July 14, 1832, in Whitney, Ellen M., *The Black Hawk War 1831-1832,* Volume II, "Letters and Papers", Part II, June 24, 1832, through October 14, 1834, Illinois State Historical Library, Springfield, Illinois, 1975, p. 792. Hereafter referred to as *BHW.*

2. *BHW,* Volume I, "Illinois Volunteers", Illinois State Historical Library, Springfield, Illinois, 1970, p. 351.

3. *Ibid.*, p. 353.

4. *Ibid.*, p. 351.

5. *Ibid.*, p. 353.

6. *Ibid.*, p. 336.

7. *Ibid.*, p. 379.

8. *Ibid.*, p. 374.

9. *Ibid.*, p. 375.

10. *Ibid.*, p. 389.

11. *Ibid.*, p. 402.

12. *Ibid.*, p. 391.

13. *Ibid.*, p. 397.

14. *Ibid.*, p. 399.

15. *Ibid.*, p. 402.

16. *Ibid.*, p. 412.

17. *Ibid.*, p. 421.

18. *Ibid.*, pp. 574-575.

19. James D. Henry to Henry Atkinson, July 14, 1832, *BHW* II:793.

20. Henry Atkinson: Orders, July 18, 1832, *BHW* II:819.

21. William Lee D. Ewing to Henry Atkinson, *ca.* July 14, 1832, *BHW* II:792.

22. *BHW* I:374-375 and Henry Atkinson: Orders, July 19, 1832, *BHW* II:823.

23. *BHW* I:390-391 and Henry Atkinson: Orders, July 19, 1832, *BHW* II:823.

24. *BHW* I:396.

25. *Ibid.*, p. 396 and Henry Atkinson: Orders, July 19, 1832, *BHW* II:823.

26. *BHW* I:404 and Henry Atkinson: Orders, July 19, 1832, *BHW* II:823.

27. *BHW* I:423-424.

28. *Ibid.*, p. 403.

29. *Ibid.*, p. 396.

30. "Diary of the Weather", Fort Winnebago, Portage, Wisconsin, in State Historical Society of Wisconsin, Madison, Wisconsin, filed "Wis. MSS 3CL Fort Winnebago".

31. Justice, James J., "Journal", *BHW* II:1323.

32. Wakefield, John Allen, *History of the War between the United States and the Sac and Fox Nations of Indians,* Calvin Goudy, Jacksonville, Illinois, 1834. Because this is a rare book, all citations refer to a reprint edited by Frank Everett Stevens. Chicago: Caxton Club, 1908. Hereafter referred to as Wakefield. This quotation is from page 86.

33. Gratiot, Henry, "Journal", *BHW* II:1304.

34. Shaw, Ninevah, "Shaw's Journal", Shaw Family Papers, Illinois State Historical Library, Springfield, Illinois, *BHW* II:1335.

35. Reynolds, John, *Reynolds' History of Illinois: My Own Times; Embracing Also the History of My Life.* Philadelphia: Lindsay & Blakiston, 1857, p. 404.

36. Wisconsin, State Historical Society of. *Collections of the State Historical Society of Wisconsin.* [Hereafter referred to as *WHC.*] Volume VIII (1879), Clark, Satterlee, "Early Times at Fort Winnebago and Black Hawk War Reminiscences", p. 315.

37. Parkinson, Daniel M., "Pioneer Life in Wisconsin", *WHC*, Volume II (1856), p. 355.

38. Paquette, Moses, "The Wisconsin Winnebagoes: An Interview with Moses Pauquette", *WHC*, Volume XII (1892), p. 431.

39. De La Ronde, John T., "Personal Narrative", *WHC*, Volume VII (1876), p. 350.

40. Wakefield, pp. 102-103.

41. Bracken, Charles, "Further Strictures on Ford's Black Hawk War", *WHC* II:406.

42. Justice, *BHW* II:1323.

43. Kinzie, Juliette, *Wau-Bun, The "Early Day" in the Northwest,* edited by Louise Phelps Kellog, 1968, The National Society of Colonial Dames in Wisconsin, Menasha, Wisconsin, p. 358.

44. *BHW* I:420 and Henry Atkinson: Orders, July 19, 1832, *BHW* II:823.

MONDAY, JULY 16, 1832

1. Shaw, Ninevah, "Shaw's Journal", Shaw Family Papers, Illinois State Historical Library, Springfield, Illinois, in Whitney, Ellen M., *The Black Hawk War 1831-1832,* Volume II, "Letters and Papers", Part II, June 24, 1832, through October 14, 1834, Illinois State Historical Library, Springfield, Illinois, 1975, p. 1335. Hereafter referred to as *BHW.*

2. *BHW*, Volume I, "Illinois Volunteers", Illinois State Historical Library, Springfield, Illinois, 1970, p. 389.

3. *Ibid.*

4. *Ibid.*, p. 379.

5. *Ibid.*

6. *Ibid.*, p. 420.

7. [Black Hawk], *Black Hawk: An Autobiography,* First Edition, 1833, edited by Donald Jackson, University of Illinois Press, Urbana, Illinois, 1964, p. 133.

8. Reynolds, John, *Reynolds' History of Illinois: My Own Times; Embracing Also the History of My Life,* 1855; Chicago: Chicago Historical Society; Fergus Printing Co., 1879, p. 404.

9. Wakefield, John Allen, *History of the War between the United States and the Sac and Fox Nations of Indians,* Calvin Goudy, Jacksonville, Illinois, 1834. Because this is a rare book, all citations refer to a reprint edited by Frank Everett Stevens. Chicago: Caxton Club, 1908. This quote is from p. 103.

10. Justice, James J., "Journal", *BHW* II:1323.

11. *BHW* II:1030

TUESDAY, JULY 17, 1832

1. Shaw, Ninevah, "Shaw's Journal", Shaw Family Papers, Illinois State Historical Library, Springfield, Illinois, in Whitney, Ellen M., *The Black Hawk War 1831-1832,* Volume II, "Letters and Papers", Part II, June 24, 1832, through October 14, 1834, Illinois State Historical Library, Springfield, Illinois, 1975, p. 1335. Hereafter referred to as *BHW.*

2. *Ibid.*

3. Justice, James J., "Journal", *BHW* II:1323.

4. Henry Dodge to Henry Atkinson, July 18, 1832, *BHW* II:820.

5. *The Galenian* newspaper, Volume 1, Number 12, Wednesday, July 25, 1832, Galena, Illinois.

6. *BHW,* Volume, I, "Illinois Volunteers", Illinois State Historical Library, Springfield, Illinois, 1970, p. 531.

7. *The Galenian* newspaper, Volume 1, Number 12, Wednesday, July 25, 1832, Galena, Illinois.

8. *BHW* I:406.

WEDNESDAY, JULY 18, 1832

1. Wakefield, John Allen, *History of the War between the United States and the Sac and Fox Nations of Indians,* Calvin Goudy, Jacksonville, Illinois, 1834. Because this is a rare book, all citations refer to a reprint edited by Frank Everett Stevens. Chicago: Caxton Club, 1908. This quote is from p. 103.

2. Wisconsin, State Historical Society of. *Collection State Historical Society of Wisconsin.* [Hereafter referred to as *WHC.*] Volume II (1856), Bracken, Charles, "Further Strictures on Ford's Black Hawk War", p. 406.

3. Parkinson, Daniel M., "Pioneer Life in Wisconsin", *WHC* II:355.

4. Justice, James J., "Journal", *BHW* II:1323-1324.

5. Wakefield, pp. 103-104.

6. Justice *BHW* II:1324.

7. Wakefield, p. 104.

8. *Ibid.*

9. Henry Dodge to Henry Atkinson, July 18, 1832, *BHW* II:820.

10. *BHW* II:794 Note.

11. Wakefield, p. 105.

12. Parkinson, Daniel M., *WHC* II:355.

13. Henry Dodge to Henry Atkinson, July 19, 1832, *BHW* II:825.

14. Justice, *BHW* II:1324.

15. Parkinson, Daniel M., *WHC* II:355.

16. Bracken, *WHC* II:407.

17. Parkinson, *BHW* II:355.

18. Wakefield, pp. 105-106.

19. Reynolds, John, *Reynolds' History of Illinois: My Own Times; Embracing Also the History of My Life.* 1855; Chicago: Chicago Historical Society; Fergus Printing Co., 1879, p. 406.

20. Bracken, *WHC* II:407.

21. *Ibid.,* footnote by Lyman C. Draper.

THURSDAY, JULY 19, 1832

1. Wakefield, John Allen, *History of the War between the United States and the Sac and Fox Nations of Indians,* Calvin Goudy, Jacksonville, Illinois, 1834. Because this is a rare book, all citations refer to a reprint edited by Frank Everett Stevens. Chicago: Caxton Club, 1908. Hereafter referred to as Wakefield. This quote is from p. 106.

2. Whitney, Ellen M., *The Black Hawk War 1831-1832,* Volume I, "Illinois Volunteers", Illinois State Historical Library, Springfield, Illinois, 1970, pp. 354-355.

3. Henry Dodge to Henry Atkinson, July 19, 1932, *BHW* II, "Letters and Papers", Part II, June 24, 1832, through October 14, 1834, Illinois State Historical Library, Springfield, Illinois, 1975, p. 826.

4. Justice, James J., "Journal", *BHW* II:1324.

5. *Ibid.*

6. Dodge, *BHW* II:825-826.

7. James D. Henry to Henry Atkinson, July 19, 1832, *BHW* II:826.

8. Wisconsin, State Historical Society of. *Collections of the State Historical Society of Wisconsin.* [Hereafter referred to as *WHC.*] Volume II (1856), Bracken, Charles, "Further Strictures on Ford's Black Hawk War", p. 408.

9. Parkinson, Daniel M., "Pioneer Life in Wisconsin", *WHC* II:355.

10. Wakefield, p. 106.

11. Justice, *BHW* II:1324.

12. Reynolds, John, *Reynolds' History of Illinois: My Own Times; Embracing Also the History of My Life.* 1855; Chicago: Chicago Historical Society; Fergus Printing Co., 1879, p. 404.

13. Wakefield, p. 106.

14. Justice, *BHW* II:1324.

15. Wakefield, p. 106.

16. Justice, *BHW* II:1324.

17. Parkinson, *WHC* II:355.

18. *WHC,* Volume IV (1859), Chapman, C.B., "Early Events in the Four Lake Country", p. 345.

19. Dodge, *BHW* II:842.

FRIDAY, JULY 20, 1832

1. Justice, James J., "Journal", in Whitney, Ellen M., *The Black Hawk War 1831-1832,* Volume II, "Letters and Papers", Part II, June 24, 1832, through October 14, 1834, Illinois State Historical Library, Springfield, Illinois, 1975, p. 1324. Hereafter referred to as *BHW.*

2. H. S. Townsend speech in *Vernon County Censor* newspaper, August 10, 1898, Viroqua, Wisconsin.

3. Wakefield, John Allen, *History of the War between the United States and the Sac and Fox Nations of Indians,* Calvin Goudy, Jacksonville, Illinois, 1834. Because this is a rare book, all citations refer to a reprint edited by Frank Everett Stevens. Chicago: Caxton Club, 1908. Hereafter referred to as Wakefield. This quote is from pp. 106-107.

4. Justice, *BHW* II:1324.

5. Wakefield, pp. 107-108.

6. Wisconsin, State Historical Society of. *Collections of the State Historical Society of Wisconsin.* [Hereafter referred to as *WHC.*] Volume II (1856), Bracken, Charles, "Further Strictures on Ford's Black Hawk War", p. 408.

7. Wakefield, p. 108.

8. Bracken, *WHC* II:408.

9. Wakefield, p. 108

10. *WHC,* Volume X (1888), Parkinson, Peter, Jr., "Notes on the Black Hawk War", pp. 207-208.

11. Parkinson, Daniel M., "Pioneer Life in Wisconsin", *WHC* II:355-356.

12. Justice, *BHW* II:1324.

13. Wakefield, p. 108.

14. Parkinson, Daniel M., *WHC* II:356.

15. Justice, *BHW* II:1324.

SATURDAY, JULY 21, 1832

1. Wisconsin, State Historical Society of. *Collections of the State Historical Society of Wisconsin* [Hereafter referred to as *WHC.*] Volume II (1856), Bracken, Charles, "Further Strictures on Ford's Black Hawk War", p. 408.

2. Wakefield, John Allen, *History of the War between the United States and the Sac and Fox Nations of Indians,* Calvin Goudy, Jacksonville, Illinois, 1834. Because this is a rare book, all citations refer to a reprint edited by Frank Everett Stevens. Chicago: Caxton Club, 1908. Hereafter referred to as Wakefield. This quote is from p. 108.

3. Magoon, Richard H., "Memoires" in *History of Grant County, Wisconsin . . .* Edited by C. W. Butterfield. Chicago: Western Historical Co., 1881, p. 431. Hereafter referred to as Magoon.

4. Parkinson, Daniel M., "Pioneer Life in Wisconsin", *WHC* II:356.

5. Wakefield, p. 108.

6. Justice, James J., "Journal" in Whitney, Ellen M., *The Black Hawk War 1831-1832,* Volume II, "Letters and Papers", Part II, June 24, 1832, through October 14, 1834, Illinois State Historical Library, Springfield, Illinois, 1975, p. 1324. Hereafter referred to as *BHW.*

7. James D. Henry to Henry Atkinson, July 23, 1832, *BHW* II:858.

8. Bracken, *WHC* II:408.

9. Smith, William R., *The History of Wisconsin. In Three Parts, Historical, Documentary, and Descriptive,* Madison, Wis.: Beriah Brown, 1854, Volume 3, Documentary History, p. 220, quoting Charles Bracken. Hereafter referred to as Smith, *Doc. Hist.*

10. Fonda, John H., "Early Wisconsin", *WHC,* Volume V (1868), p. 260.

11. Parkinson, Peter, Jr., "Notes on the Black Hawk War", *WHC,* Volume X (1888), p. 208.

12. Butler, James D., "Tay-cho-pe-rah—The Four Lakes Country—First White Foot-Prints There", *WHC* X:77.

13. Parkinson, Daniel, M., *WHC* II:356.

14. Parkinson, Peter, Jr., *WHC* X:207.

15. Bracken in Smith, *Doc. Hist.,* p. 220.

16. Wakefield, p. 108.

17. Magoon, p. 431.

18. Henry, *BHW* II:858

19. Parkinson, Peter, Jr., "Strictures upon Ford's Black Hawk War", *WHC* II:395.

20. Parkinson, Peter, Jr., *WHC* X:208.

21. Bracken, *WHC* II:408.

22. Butler, *WHC* X:77.

23. Chapman, C. B., "Early Events in the Four Lake Country", *WHC,* Volume IV (1859), p. 345.

24. Parkinson, Daniel M., *WHC* II:356.

25. Magoon, p. 431.

26. Wakefield, p. 109.

27. *Ibid.*, pp. 109-110.

28. *Ibid.*, p. 109.

29. Justice, *BHW* II:1324.

30. Chapman, *WHC* IV:345.

31. *Ibid.*, pp. 345-346.

32. *Ibid.*, p. 346.

33. Parkinson, Peter, Jr., *WHC* X:208.

34. Henry *BHW* II:858.

35. Bracken in Smith, *Doc. Hist.,* p.220.

36. Magoon, p. 431.

37. Parkinson, Daniel M., *WHC* II:356-357.

38. Wakefield, p. 110.

39. Magoon, p. 431.

40. Justice, *BHW* II:1324.

41. Bracken in Smith, *Doc. Hist.,* p. 220.

42. Meriwether L. Clark to William Clark, July 25, 1832, *BHW* II:877.

43. Henry, *BHW* II:858.

44. Wakefield, p. 110.

45. Bracken, *WHC* II:408.

46. *The Galenian* newspaper, Volume I, Number 14, Wednesday, August 1, 1832, Galena, Illinois.

47. Magoon, p. 431.

48. *The Galenian* newspaper, Volume I, Number 14, Wednesday, August 1, 1832, Galena, Illinois.

49. Magoon, p. 431.

50. *The Galenian* newspaper, Volume I, Number 14, Wednesday, August 1, 1832, Galena, Illinois.

51. Bracken, *WHC* II:408.

52. Wakefield, p. 110

53. Parkinson, Peter, Jr., *WHC* X:208.

54. Magoon, p. 431.

55. Townsend, H. S., *Vernon County Censor* newspaper, August 10, 1898, Viroqua, Wisconsin.

56. Parkinson, Daniel M., *WHC* II:357.

57. Chapman, *WHC* IV:346.

58. *BHW,* Volume I, "Illinois Volunteers", Illinois State Historical Library, Springfield, Illinois, 1970, p. 532.

59. Magoon, p. 431.

60. Rouse, May Belle, *Galena's Old Stockade,* Galena, Illinois, p. 49.

61. Magoon, p. 431.

62. Chapman, *WHC* IV:346.

63. Rouse, p. 49.

64. Eby, Cecil, *"That Disgraceful Affair", the Black Hawk War,* W. W. Norton & Company, Inc., New York, 1973, p. 234.

65. *The Galenian* newspaper, Volume I, Number 14, Wednesday, August 1, 1832, Galena, Illinois.

66. Henry, *BHW* II:858.

67. Parkinson, Daniel M., *WHC* II:357.

68. Butler, *BHW* X:77.

69. Henry, *BHW* II:858.

70. Justice, *BHW* II:1325.

71. Parkinson, Daniel M., *WHC* II:358.

72. Bracken in Smith, *Doc. Hist.,* p. 220.

73. Bracken, *WHC* II:408.

74. Wakefield, p. 110.

75. *Ibid.*

76. *BHW* I:380.

77. *Ibid.*, p. 381.

78. *Ibid.*, p. 393.

79. *Ibid.*

80. Justice, *BHW* II:1325.

81. *Ibid.,* pp.1324-1325.

82. Bracken in Smith, *Doc. Hist., p. 220.*

83. Henry, BHW II:858.

84. Magoon, p. 431.

85. Henry Dodge to Henry Atkinson, July 22, 1832, *BHW* II:842.

86. Bracken, *WHC* II:409.

87. Parkinson, Daniel M., *WHC* II:357.

88. Wakefield, pp. 110-111.

89. Henry, *BHW* II:858.

90. Wakefield, p. 111.

91. Magoon, p. 431.

92. Estes, James B. in Smith, *Doc. Hist.,* p. 228.

93. Magoon, p. 431.

94. Clark, Satterlee, "Early Times at Fort Winnebago, and Black Hawk Reminiscences", *WHC,* Volume VIII (1879), p. 315.

95. Justice, *BHW* II:1325.

96. Henry, *BHW* II:859.

97. Joseph M. Street to William Clark, July 24, 1832, *BHW* II:871.

98. Philleo, Addison, *The Galenian* newspaper, Volume I, Number 14, Wednesday, August 1, 1832, Galena, Illinois.

99. Meriwether L. Clark to William Clark, July 25, 1832, *BHW* II:877.

100. Fonda, *WHC* V:260.

101. Henry, *BHW* II:858.

102. Dodge, *BHW* II:842.

103. Magoon, p. 432.

104. Parkinson, Daniel M., *WHC* II:357.

105. Bracken in Smith, *Doc. Hist.,* p. 220.

106. Dickson, Joseph, "Personal Narrative of Black Hawk War", *WHC* V:316.

107. Wakefield, p. 111.

108. Magoon, p. 431.

109. Henry, *BHW* II:858.

110. Clark, Meriwether L., *BHW* II:877.

111. Bracken in Smith, *Doc. Hist.,* p. 220.

112. Townsend, H. S., *Vernon County Censor* newspaper, August 10, 1898, Viroqua, Wisconsin.

113. Dodge, *BHW* II:842.

114. Smith, *The History of Wisconsin,* Volume 3-Historical, p. 287.

115. Henry, *BHW* II:859.

116. Dodge, *BHW* II:842-843.

117. Bracken in Smith, *Doc. Hist.,* pp. 220-221.

118. Parkinson, Daniel M., *WHC* II:357.

119. Bracken, *WHC* II:409.

120. Parkinson, Daniel M., *WHC* II:362.

121. Magoon, p. 432.

122. Townsend, H. S., *Vernon County Censor* newspaper, August 10, 1898, Viroqua, Wisconsin.

123. Henry, *BHW* II:859.

124. Philleo, Addison, *The Galenian* newspaper, Volume I, Number 14, Wednesday, August 1, 1832, Galena, Illinois.

125. Parkinson, Daniel M., *WHC* II:362.

126. Clark, Meriwether L., *BHW* II:877.

127. Wakefield, p. 111.

128. Dodge, *BHW* II:843.

129. Wakefield, p. 111

130. Parkinson, Peter, Jr., *WHC* II:395.

131. Clark, Meriwether L., *BHW* II:877.

132. Henry, *BHW* II:859.

133. Magoon, p. 432.

134. Bracken, *WHC* II:409.

135. Dodge, *BHW* II:843.

136. Parkinson, Daniel M., *WHC* II:362.

137. Bracken in Smith *Doc. Hist.,* p. 221.

138. Brown, Henry, *The History of Illinois, from Its First Discovery and Settlement, to the Present Time,* New York: J. Winchester, 1844, p. 368.

139. Magoon, p. 432.

140. Parkinson, Daniel M., *WHC* II:362.

141. Magoon, p. 432.

142. Parkinson, Daniel M., *WHC* II:358.

143. *Ibid.,* p. 357.

144. Bracken, *WHC* II:409.

145. Bracken in Smith, *Doc. Hist.,* p. 221.

146. Townsend, H. S., *Vernon County Censor* newspaper, August 10, 1898, Viroqua, Wisconsin.

147. *Ibid.*

148. Bracken, *WHC* II:410.

149. *The Galenian* newspaper, Volume I, Number 30, Wednesday, November 21, 1832, Galena, Illinois.

150. Winfield Scott and John Reynolds to William Clark, September 22, 1832, *BHW* II:1186.

151. Collins, James, July 25, 1832, *BHW* II:879.

152. Dodge, *BHW* II:843.

153. Justice, *BHW* II:1325.

154. Henry, *BHW* II:859.

155. *The Galenian* newspaper, Volume I, Number 14, Wednesday, August 1, 1832, Galena, Illinois.

156. Wakefield, p. 111.

157. Dodge, *BHW* II:843.

158. Henry, *BHW* II:859.

159. Wakefield, p. 111.

160. Justice, *BHW* II:1325.

161. *The Galenian* newspaper, Volume I, Number 14, Wednesday, August 1, 1832, Galena, Illinois.

162. Wakefield, pp. 111-112.

163. *The Galenian* newspaper, Volume I, Number 14, Wednesday, August 1, 1832, Galena, Illinois.

164. Henry, *BHW* II:859.

165. Collins, *BHW* II:879.

166. Dodge, *BHW* II:843.

167. Parkinson, Daniel M., *WHC* II:358.

168. Fonda, *WHC* V:260.

169. Chapman, *WHC* IV:346-347.

170. Bracken in Smith, *Doc. Hist.,* p. 221.

171. Chapman, *WHC* IV:346.

172. [Black Hawk], *Ma-ka-tai-me-she-kia-kiak, Black Hawk: An Autobiography,* Donald Jackson, Editor, 1st Edition, 1833; Urbana: University of Illinois Press, 1955, p. 134.

173. Wakefield, 112.

174. Parkinson, Daniel M., *WHC* II:358.

175. Dodge, *BHW* II:843.

176. Parkinson, Daniel M., *WHC* II:358.

177. Wakefield, p. 112.

178. Collins, *BHW* II:879.

179. Henry, *BHW* II:859.

180. *The Galenian* newspaper, Volume I, Number 14, Wednesday, August 1, 1832, Galena, Illinois.

181. Bracken in Smith, *Doc. Hist.,* p. 221.

182. Wakefield, p. 112.

183. Parkinson, Peter, Jr., *WHC* II:395-396.

184. Henry, *BHW* II:859.

185. Magoon, p. 432.

186. Dodge, *BHW* II:843.

187. Collins, *BHW* II:879.

188. Henry, *BHW* II:859.

189. Bracken, *BHW* II:409.

190. Bracken, in Smith, *Doc. Hist.,* p. 221-222.

191. Bracken, *WHC* II:409-410.

192. Justice, *BHW* II:1325.

193. Magoon, p. 432.

194. Dodge, *BHW* II:843.

195. Joseph M. Street to William Clark, July 24, 1832, *BHW* II:871-872.

196. Henry, *BHW* II:859.

197. Wakefield, P. 112.

198. Justice, *BHW* II:1325.

199. Henry, *BHW* II:859.

200. Townsend, H. S., *Vernon County Censor* newspaper, August 10, 1898, Viroqua, Wisconsin.

201. Wakefield, p. 112.

202. Magoon, p. 432.

203. Henry, *BHW* II:859.

204. Dodge, *BHW* II:843.

205. Wakefield, p. 112.

206. Black Hawk, p. 134.

207. Bracken, *WHC* II:410.

208. Dodge, *BHW* II:843.

209. Parkinson, Daniel M., *WHC* II:359.

210. Clark, Meriwether L., *BHW* II:877.

211. Justice, *BHW* II:1325.

212. Magoon, p. 432.

213. Street, *BHW* II:872.

214. Bracken in Smith, *Doc. Hist.,* p. 221.

215. Wakefield, p. 112.

216. Fonda, *WHC* V:260.

217. Clark, Satterlee, *WHC* VIII:315.

218. Dodge, *BHW* II:843.

219. Henry, *BHW* I:859.

220. Wakefield, p. 112.

221. Magoon, p. 432.

222. Parkinson, Daniel M., *WHC* II:359.

223. Clark, Meriwether L., *BHW* :877.

224. *Ibid.*

225. Dodge, *BHW* II:843.

226. Justice, *BHW* II:1325.

227. Street, *BHW* II:872.

228. De La Ronde, John T., "Personal Narrative", *WHC,* Volume VII (1876), p. 350.

229. Smith *Doc. Hist.,* p. 221.

230. Parkinson, Daniel M., *WHC* II:358.

231. Clark, Meriwether, *BHW* II:878 note.

232. Estes in Smith, *Doc. Hist.,* pp. 228-229.

233. Parkinson, Daniel M., *WHC* II:359

234. Wakefield, p. 117.

235. Parkinson, Daniel M. *WHC* II:359.

236. Estes in Smith, *Doc. Hist.,* p. 228.

237. Henry Atkinson to Winfield Scott, July 17, 1832, *BHW* II:815.

238. Wakefield, p. 117.

239. Henry Atkinson to James D. Henry and Henry Dodge, July 20, 1832, *BHW* II:832-833.

240. Minutes of an Examination of Prisoners, *BHW* II:1031.

241. *Ibid.,* p. 1028.

242. *Ibid.*

243. Black Hawk, p. 134.

244. Henry, *BHW* II:860.

245. Dodge, *BHW* II:843.

246. Wakefield, p. 121.

247. Collins, *BHW* II:879.

248. *The Galenian* newspaper, Volume I, Number 14, Wednesday, August 1, 1832, Galena, Illinois.

249. Black Hawk, p. 134.

250. Minutes of an Examination of Prisoners, *BHW* II:1032.

251. *Ibid.*

252. *Ibid.,* pp. 1055 and 1056.

253. *Ibid.,* p. 1056.

254. *Ibid.,* p. 1057.

255. *Ibid.,* pp. 1029 and 1030.

256. *Ibid.,* p. 1031.

257. *Ibid.,* p. 1033.

258. *Ibid.,* p. 1029.

259. *Ibid.,* p. 1028.

260. *Ibid.*

261 Street, *BHW* II:908.

262. Gustavus Loomis to Henry Atkinson, July 30, 1832, *BHW* II:907.

263. Wakefield, p. 113.

264. Henry Atkinson to Winfield Scott, July 25, 1832, *BHW* II:875.

265. Parkinson, Daniel M., *WHC* II:359.

266. Bracken, *WHC* II:410.

267. De La Ronde, *WHC* VII:350.

268. Decorah, Spoon, "Narrative of Spoon Decorah", *WHC,* Volume XIII (1895), p. 453.

269. Kinzie, Juliette, *Wau-Bun, The "Early Day" in the Northwest,* edited by Louise Phelps Kellogg, 1968, The National Society of Colonial Dames in Wisconsin, Menasha, Wisconsin, p. 348.

270. Draper, Lyman C., *WHC* II:411.

271. Bracken, *WHC* II:411.

272. Clark, Satterlee, *WHC* VIII:315.

273. *Ibid.*

274. Black Hawk, p. 134.

275. Minutes of an Examination of Prisoners, *BHW* II:1035.

276. Black Hawk, p. 136.

277. Minutes of an Examination of Prisoners, *BHW* II:1030.

278. *Ibid.,* p. 1035.

279. Black Hawk, p. 136.

280. *Ibid.,* p. 135.

281. *The Galenian* newspaper, Volume I, Number 13, Wednesday, July 25, 1832, Galena, Illinois.

282. *Ibid.,* Wednesday, August 8, 1832.

283. Minutes of an Examination of Prisoners, *BHW* II:1028.

284. *Ibid.*

285. Street, *BHW* II:908-909.

286. Minutes of an Examination of Prisoners, *BHW* II:1032.

287. Black Hawk, p. 135.

288. Minutes of an Examination of Prisoners, *BHW* II:1036.

289. *Ibid.,* p. 1037.

290. *The Galenian* newspaper, Volume I, Number 15, Wednesday, August 8, 1832, Galena, Illinois.

291. Street, *BHW* II:1042 and 1043 note.

292. *The Galenian* newspaper, Volume I, Number 15, Wednesday, August 8, 1832, Galena, Illinois.

293. Street, *BHW* II:908-909.

294. Black Hawk, p. 135.

295. Minutes of an Examination of Prisoners, *BHW* II:1033.

296. *Ibid.,* p. 1029.

297. Black Hawk, p. 136.

298. Street, *BHW* II:909.

299. *The Galenian* newspaper, Volume I, Number 15, Wednesday, August 8, 1832, Galena, Illinois.

300. Loomis, *BHW* II;907.

301. Street, *BHW* II:908.

302. Minutes of an Examination of Prisoners, *BHW* II:1028.

303. *Ibid.*, pp. 1028-1029.

304. *Ibid.*, pp. 1032-1033.

305. *Ibid.*, p. 1030.

306. *Ibid.*, p. 1055.

307. *Ibid.*, p. 1030.

308. Samuel C. Stambaugh to George Boyd, August 28, 1832, *BHW* II:1075.

309. Minutes of an Examination of Prisoners, *BHW* II:1036.

310. Loomis, *BHW* II:907.

311. *Ibid.*, p. 906.

312. *The Galenian* newspaper, Volume I, Number 15, Wednesday, August 8, 1832, Galena, Illinois.

313. Black Hawk, p. 135.

SUNDAY, JULY 22, 1832

1. Wakefield, John Allen, *History of the War between the United States and the Sac and Fox Nations of Indians,* Calvin Goudy, Jacksonville, Illinois, 1834. Because this is a rare book, all citations refer to a reprint edition edited by Frank Everett Stevens. Chicago: Caxton Club, 1908. Hereafter referred to as Wakefield. This quote is from p. 113.

2. Justice, James J., "Journal", in Whitney, Ellen M., *The Black Hawk War 1831-1832,* Volume II, "Letters and Papers", Part II, June 24, 1832, through October 14, 1834, Illinois State Historical Library, Springfield, Illinois, 1975, p. 1325. Hereafter referred to as *BHW.*

3. Wakefield, p. 113.

4. Justice, *BHW* II:1325.

5. Smith, William R., *The History of Wisconsin. In Three Parts, Historical, Documentary, and Descriptive...* Madison, Wisconsin: Beriah Brown, 1854. (Volumes 1 and 3 only printed.) Volume 3, Documentary History, p. 222, quoting Charles Bracken. Hereafter referred to as Smith.

6. Henry Dodge to Henry Atkinson, July 22, 1832, *BHW* II:843.

7. *The Galenian* newspaper, Volume 1, Number 14, Wednesday, August 1, 1832, Galena, Illinois.

8. *History of Grant County, Wisconsin* . . .Edited by C. W. Butterfield. Chicago: Western Historical Co., 1881, quoting Richard H. Magoon's memoires, p. 432.

9. Wakefield, p. 113.

10. Henry Atkinson to Winfield Scott, July 25, 1832, *BHW* II:875.

11. Justice, *BHW* II:1325.

12. Wakefield, p. 113.

13. *BHW,* Volume I, "Illinois Volunteers", Illinois State Historical Library, Springfield, Illinois, 1970, p. 406.

14. Wakefield, p. 114.

15. Wisconsin, State Historical Society of *Collections of the State Historical Society of Wisconsin.* [Hereafter referred to as *WHC.*] Volume II (1856), Parkinson, Daniel M., "Pioneer Life in Wisconsin", p. 360.

16. *BHW* I:404.

17. Wakefield, pp. 113-114.

18. Bracken in Smith, *Doc. Hist.,* pp. 222-223.

19. Parkinson, Daniel M., *WHC* II:360.

20. Estes, James B., in Smith, *Doc. Hist.,* p. 229.

21. Henry Dodge to Gustavus Loomis, July 22, 1832, *BHW* II:845.

22. James D. Henry to Henry Atkinson, July 23, 1832, *BHW* II:858-860.

23. Henry Dodge to Henry Atkinson, July 22, 1832, *BHW* II:842-843.

24. James D. Henry to Henry Atkinson, July 19, 1832, *BHW* II:826.

25. *The Galenian* newspaper, Volume 1, Number 14, Wednesday, August 1, 1832, Galena, Illinois.

26. Parkinson, Peter, Jr., "Strictures upon Ford's Black Hawk War", *WHC* II:399-400.

27. Wakefield, p. 113.

28. *Ibid.*, pp. 114-115.

29. Justice, *BHW* II:1325.

30. Wakefield, p. 115.

31. Justice, *BHW* II:1325.

MONDAY, JULY 23, 1832

1. *Sangamo Journal* newspaper, Saturday, August 25, 1832, Springfield, Illinois.

2. Wakefield, John Allen, *History of the War between the United States and the Sac and Fox Nations of Indians,* Calvin Goudy, Jacksonville, Illinois, 1834. Because this is a rare book, all citations refer to a reprint edited by Frank Everett Stevens. Chicago: Caxton Club, 1908. Hereafter referred to as Wakefield. This quote is from p. 115.

3. Justice, James J., "Journal", in Whitney, Ellen M., *The Black Hawk War 1831-1832,* Volume II, "Letters and Papers", Part II, June 24, 1832, through October 14, 1834, Illinois State Historical Library, Springfield, Illinois, 1975, p. 1325. Hereafter referred to as *BHW.*

4. Smith, William R., *The History of Wisconsin. In Three Parts, Historical, Documentary, and Descriptive. . .* Madison, Wisconsin: Beriah Brown, 1854. (Volumes 1 and 3 only printed.) Volume 3, Documentary History, p. 222, quoting Charles Bracken.

5. Wisconsin, State Historical Society of. *Collections of the* State Historical Society of Wisconsin. [Hereafter referred to as *WHC.*] Volume II (1856), Parkinson, Daniel M., "Pioneer Life in Wisconsin", p. 359. Hereafter referred to as Parkinson.

6. *BHW,* Volume I, "Illinois Volunteers", Illinois State Historical Library, Springfield, Illinois, 1970, p. 530.

7. Robert Anderson: Memoranda, [August 27, 1832], *BHW* II:1058.

8. Minutes of an Examination of Prisoners, [August 27, 1832], *BHW* II:1056.

9. *Ibid.,* p. 1058.

10. *History of Jo Daviess County, Illinois,* Chicago, H. F. Kett & Co., Times Building, 1878, p. 294.

11. *Ibid.*

12. Gratiot, Adele P., "Mrs. Adele P. Gratiot's Narrative", *WHC,* Volume X (1888), pp. 268-269.

13. Parkinson, *WHC* II:359-360.

14. Justice, *BHW* II:1325.

15. Wakefield, pp. 115-116.

16. Justice, *BHW* II:1325

17. *Sangamo Journal* newspaper, Saturday, August 25, 1832.

18. *History of Jo Daviess County,* p. 294.

19. *Sangamo Journal* newspaper, Saturday, August 25, 1832.

20. Wakefield, p. 134.

21. Parkinson, *WHC* II:360.

22. Smith, III:222, quoting Charles Bracken.

23. Townsend, H.S. in *Vernon County Censor,* August 10, 1898, Viroqua, Wisconsin.

24. Wakefield, p. 116.

25. *History of Jo Daviess County,* p. 294.

26. Justice, *BHW* II:1325.

27. *History of Grant County, Wisconsin . . .*Edited by C. W. Butterfield. Chicago: Western Historical Co., 1881, quoting Richard H. Magoon's memoires, p. 432.

28. Bracken, Charles, "Further Strictures on Ford's Black Hawk War", *WHC* II:411-412.

29. Wakefield, p. 118.

30. Justice, *BHW* II:1325.

31. *History of Grant County, Wisconsin,* p. 432., quoting Magoon.

32. Parkinson, *WHC* II:360.

33. Wakefield, p. 118.

34. Parkinson, *WHC* II:360-362.

35. *Ibid.,* p. 362.

36. Minutes of an Examination of Prisoners, *BHW* II:1028 & 1033, Note 3.

37. Esau Johnson Papers, State Historical Society of Wisconsin, Area Research Center, University of Wisconsin-Platteville, Platteville, Wisconsin.

38. *Ibid.*

39. Beouchard, Edward D., *"Beouchard's Vindication", WHC,* Volume VII (1876), pp. 293-294.

40. Wakefield, p. 118.

41. Henry Dodge to Henry Atkinson, July 24, 1832, *BHW* II:863.

42. Bracken, *WHC* II:412.

43. *History of Grant County, Wisconsin.* p. 432, quoting Magoon.

44. Parkinson, *WHC* II:363.

45. *BHW* I:421.

46. Justice, *BHW* II:1325.

47. Shaw, John, "Indian Chiefs and Pioneers of Northwest", *WHC* X (1888), p. 218.

TUESDAY, JULY 24, 1832

1. Henry Dodge to Henry Atkinson, July 24, 1832, in Whitney, Ellen M., *The Black Hawk War 1831-1832,* Volume II, "Letters and Papers, Part II, June 24, 1832, through October 14, 1834, Illinois State Historical Library, Springfield, Illinois, 1975, pp. 863-864. Hereafter referred to as *BHW.*

2. James D. Henry to Henry Atkinson, July 24, 1832, *BHW* II:866.

3. *BHW,* Volume I, "Illinois Volunteers", Illinois State Historical Library, Springfield, Illinois, 1970, p. 393.

4. *BHW* I:393-394.

5. *Ibid.*

6. *BHW* I:393.

7. *BHW* I:420.

8. Wisconsin, State Historical Society of. *Collections of the State Historical Society of Wisconsin.* [Hereafter referred to as *WHC.*] Volume II (1856), Parkinson, Daniel M., "Pioneer Life in Wisconsin", p. 362. Hereafter referred to as Parkinson.

9. *WHC,* Volume X (1888), "Reminiscences of Wisconsin in 1833", p. 232, (reprinted from the *Madison Democrat* newspaper, July 1, 1871).

10. Henry Dodge to James W. Stephenson, July 24, 1832, in *The Galenian* newspaper, Volume I, Number 14, Wednesday, August 1, 1832, Galena, Illinois.

11. *WHC* X:233.

12. Wakefield, John Allen, *History of the War between the United States and the Sac and Fox Nations of Indians,* Calvin Goudy, Jacksonville, Illinois, 1834. Because this is a rare book all citations refer to a reprint edited by Frank Everett Stevens. Chicago: Caxton Club, 1908. Hereafter referred to as Wakefield. This quote is from p. 119.

13. Cooke, Philip St. George, *Scenes and Adventures in the Army; Or Romance of Military Life,* Philadelphia, Lindsay & Blakiston, 1857, p. 170. Hereafter referred to as Cooke.

14. Parkinson, *WHC* II:363.

15. Wakefield, p. 119.

16. Smith, Henry, "Diary" extracts from newspaper article [Milwaukee Sentinel?, no date] in Notebook 501B in Fort Atkinson, Wisconsin, Historical Society, Hoard Museum.

17. Henry Atkinson to Roger Jones, November 19, 1832, *BHW* II:1210.

18. Meriwether L. Clark to William Clark, July 25, 1832, *BHW* II:877.

19. Wakefield, p. 119.

20. Henry Atkinson: Orders, July 9, 1832, *BHW* II:754.

21. Reynolds, John, *Reynolds' History of Illinois: My Own Times; Embracing Also the History of My Life.* 1855; Chicago: Chicago Historical Society; Fergus Printing Co., 1879, p. 412.

22. Cooke, pp. 170-171.

WEDNESDAY, JULY 25, 1832

1. William B. Archer to Jacob Harlan, July 25, 1832, in Whitney, Ellen M., *The Black Hawk War 1831-1832,* Volume II, "Letters and Papers", Part II, June 24, 1832, through October 14, 1834, Illinois State Historical Library, Springfield, Illinois, 1975, p. 874 note. Hereafter referred to as *BHW.*

2. *Ibid.,* p. 873.

3. James Collins Extract, July 25, 1832, *BHW* II:879.

4. Winfield Scott: Orders, July 3, 1832, *BHW* II:736.

5. Meriwether L. Clark to William Clark, July 25, 1832, *BHW* II:877-878.

6. *The Galenian* newspaper, Volume I, Number 14, Wednesday, August 1, 1832, Galena, Illinois.

7. Esau Johnson Papers, State Historical Society of Wisconsin, Area Research Center, University of Wisconsin-Platteville, Platteville, Wisconsin.

8. Henry Atkinson to Winfield Scott, July 25, 1832, *BHW* II:874-875.

9. Henry Atkinson to Alexander Macomb, July 25, 1832, *BHW* II:874.

APPENDIX A

1. James D. Henry to Henry Atkinson, July 23, 1832, in Whitney, Ellen M., *The Black Hawk War 1831-1832,* Volume II, "Letters and Papers". Part II, June 24, 1832. through October 14, 1834, Illinois State Historical Library, Springfield, Illinois, 1975, pp. 858-860. Hereafter referred to as *BHW.*

2. Henry Dodge to Henry Atkinson, July 22, 1832, *BHW* II: 842-843.

3. Wisconsin, State Historical Society of. *Collections of the State Historical Society of Wisconsin,* Volume II (1856), Parkinson, Daniel M., "Pioneer Life in Wisconsin", pp. 356-359. Hereafter referred to as *WHC.*

4. Justice, James J., "Journal", *BHW* II: 1324-1325.

5. Bracken, Charles, "Further Strictures on Ford's Black Hawk War", *WHC* II:408-410.

6. Wakefield, John Allen, *History of the War between the United States* and the Sac and Fox Nations of Indians, Calvin Goudy, Jacksonville, Illinois, 1834. Because this is a rare book, all citations refer to a reprint edited by Frank Everett Stevens. Chicago: Caxton Club, 1908. This quote is from pp. 108-112.

7. [Black Hawk], *Ma-ka-tai-me-she-kia-kiak, Black Hawk: An Autobiography,* Donald Jackson, Editor, 1st Edition, 1833; Urbana, University of Illinois Press, 1955, pp. 132-136.

BIBLIOGRAPHY

only of Eye-Witness Sources used in this book. For a more complete bibliography, see Ellen M. Whitney's The Black Hawk War 1831-1832, *Volume II, Part III, "Appendices and Index", Illinois State Historical Library, Springfield, 1978.*

Barret, Mrs. Mason, Collection, Howard Tilton Memorial Library, New Orleans, Louisiana.

[Black Hawk] *Ma-ka-tai-me-she-kia-kiak, Black Hawk: An Autobiography.* Ed. Donald Jackson. 1st ed., 1833; Urbana: University of Illinois Press, 1955.

Black Hawk War Collection, Hoard Museum, Fort Atkinson Historical Society, Fort Atkinson, Wisconsin.

Black Hawk War Collection, Illinois State Historical Library, Springfield.

Brown, Henry, *The History of Illinois, from Its First Discovery and Settlement, to the Present Time,* New York: J. Winchester, 1844.

Cooke, Philip St. George. *Scenes and Adventures in the Army: Or Romance of Military Life.* Philadelphia: Lindsay & Blakiston, 1857.

Eby, Cecil, *"That Disgraceful Affair," the Black Hawk War,* W. W. Norton & Company, Inc., New York, 1973.

Galenian, The, newspaper, Volume 1, Numbers 10-13, July, 1832, Galena, Illinois.

Hagan, William Thomas. "Black Hawk's Route through Wisconsin." Mimeo. Madison: State Historical Society of Wisconsin, 1949.

.... "The Dodge-Henry Controversy", *Collections of the Illinois State Historical Library,* Volume 50 (1957), Illinois State Historical Library, Springfield, 1957, pp. 377-384.

Highsmith Affidavit, Crawford County, January 6, 1851, Highsmith Family Papers, Fort Atkinson, Wisconsin, and copies filed in Black Hawk War Papers, Hoard Museum, Fort Atkinson, Wisconsin.

History of Grant County, Wisconsin. . . Edited by C. W. Butterfield, Chicago: Western Historical Co., 1881.

History of Jo Daviess County, Illinois. . . Chicago: H. F. Kett & Co., Times Building, 1878.

Johnson, Esau, Esau Johnson Papers, State Historical Society of Wisconsin, Area Research Center, University of Wisconsin-Platteville, Platteville, Wisconsin.

Johnston, Albert Sidney. "April 1-August 2 Johnston Edited Journal". Tulane University Library, Howard Tilton Memorial Library, Mrs. Mason Barret Collection, New Orleans, Louisiana.

.... "June 12-August 16 Johnston Field Journal", Tulane University Library, Howard Tilton Memorial Library, Mrs. Mason Barret Collection, New Orleans, Louisiana.

.... "April 1-August 2 Johnston Public Journal", Tulane University Library, Howard Tilton Memorial Library, Mrs. Mason Barret Collection, New Orleans, Louisiana.

.... "April 1-August 2 Johnston Public Journal", Illinois State Historical Library, Springfield, Illinois.

Kinzie, Juliette M. *Wau-Bun, The "Early Day" in the Northwest.* Ed. Louise Phelps Kellogg. The National Society of Colonial Dames in Wisconsin, Menasha, 1968, Wisconsin.

National Archives, Washington, D.C.

Record Group 75, Bureau of Indian Affairs, Letters Received, Prairie du Chien.

Record Group 94, Adjutant General's Office, Returns from U.S. Military Posts.

Military Service Records.

Parish, John Carl. *George Wallace Jones*. Iowa Biographical Series. Iowa City: State Historical Society of Iowa, 1912.

Reynolds, John. *Reynolds' History of Illinois: My Own Times: Embracing Also the History of My Life,* 1855; Chicago: Chicago Historical Society: Fergus Printing Co., 1879.

Rouse, May Belle, *Galena's Old Stockade,* Galena, Illinois.

Russell, John, skeleton history, Russell Family Papers, Illinois State Historical Library, Springfield, Illinois.

Ryan, John. Letter. Evelyn Weiskircher, Shullsburg, Wisconsin, and Fort Atkinson Historical Society, Fort Atkinson, Wisconsin.

Smith, Henry. Diary, extracts from newspaper article in Notebook 501B. Fort Atkinson Historical Society. Hoard Museum, Fort Atkinson, Wisconsin.

.... *The Expedition against the Sauk and Fox Indians, 1832. The Following Narrative of the Expedition against the Sauk and Fox Indians, Last Year, Has Been Kindly Furnished to the Military and Naval Magazine by an Officer Who Served in General Atkinson's Brigade.* New York: n.p., 1914.

Smith, William R. *The History of Wisconsin. In Three Parts, Historical, Documentary, and Descriptive...* Madison, Wis.: Beriah Brown, 1854. (Volumes 1 and 3 only printed.)

Townsend, H. S., *Vernon County Censor,* August 10, 1898, Viroqua, Wisconsin.

United States Congress. *American State Papers: Indian Affairs,* Volume I, Washington: Gales & Seaton, 1832.

.... Congressional Documents (Serial Set 233). 22nd Congress, 2d Session.

Wakefield, John Allen. *History of the War between the United States and the Sac and Fox Nations of Indians.* Calvin Goudy. Jacksonville, Illinois, 1834.

.... *Wakefield's History of the Black Hawk War: A Reprint of the 1st Edition by John A. Wakefield, Esquire, from the Press of Calvin Goudy, Jacksonville, Illinois, 1834....* Ed. Frank Everett Stevens. Chicago: Caxton Club, 1908.

"Weather, Diary of the", Fort Winnebago, Portage, Wisconsin, in the State Historical Society of Wisconsin, Manuscript Archives, Filed "Wis. MSS 3 CL Fort Winnebago", Madison, Wisconsin.

Whitney, Ellen M. *The Black Hawk War 1831-1832.* Volume I, "Illinois Volunteers". Illinois State Historical Library, Springfield, 1970. Published as Volume XXXV of *Collections of the Illinois State Historical Library.*

.... *The Black Hawk War 1831-1832.* Volume II, "Letters and Papers", Part I, April 30, 1831, through June 23, 1832. Illinois State Historical Library, Springfield, 1973. Published as Volume XXXVI of *Collections of the Illinois State Historical Library.*

.... *The Black Hawk War 1831-1832.* Volume II, "Letters and Papers", Part II, June 24, 1832, through October 14, 1834. Illinois State Historical Library, Springfield, 1975. Published as Volume XXXVII of *Collections of the Illinois State Historical Library.*

.... *The Black Hawk War 1831-1832.* Volume II, "Letters and Papers", Part III, Appendices and Index. Illinois State Historical Library, Springfield, 1978. Published as Volume XXXVIII of *Collections of the Illinois State Historical Library.*

Wisconsin, State Historical Society of. *Collections of the State Historical Society of Wisconsin,* Madison, Wisconsin.

Volume 2 (1856)

Parkinson, Daniel M., "Pioneer Life in Wisconsin", pp. 326-364.

Parkinson, Peter, Jr., "Strictures upon Ford's Black Hawk War", pp. 393-401.

Bracken, Charles, "Further Strictures on Ford's Black Hawk War", pp. 402-414.

Volume 4 (1859)

Chapman, C. B., "Early Events in the Four Lake Country", pp. 343-349.

Volume 5 (1868)

Fonda, John H., "Early Wisconsin", pp. 205-284.

Dickson, Joseph, "Personal Narrative of the Black Hawk War", pp. 315-317.

Volume 7 (1876)

[Beouchard, Edward D.], "Edward D. Beouchard's Vindication", pp. 289-296.

De La Ronde, John T., "Personal Narrative, pp. 345-365.

Merrell, Henry, "Pioneer Life in Wisconsin", pp. 366-402.

Volume 8 (1879)

Clark, Satterlee, "Early Times at Fort Winnebago, and Black Hawk War Reminiscences", pp. 309-321.

Volume 10 (1888)

Butler, James D., "Tay-cho-pe-rah—The Four Lakes Country—First White Foot-Prints There", pp. 64-78.

Smith, Henry, "Indian Campaign of 1832", pp. 150-166.

Anderson, Robert, "Reminiscences of the Black Hawk War", pp. 167-176.

Parkinson, Peter, Jr., "Notes on the Black Hawk War", pp. 184-212.

"Reminiscences of Wisconsin in 1833", pp. 231-234.

[Gratiot, Adele P.], "Mrs. Adele P. Gratiot's Narrative", pp. 261-275.

Volume 12 (1892)

[Paquette, Moses], "The Wisconsin Winnebagoes: An Interview with Moses Paquette...", pp. 399-433.

Volume 13 (1895)

[Decorah, Spoon], "Narrative of Spoon Decorah", pp. 448-462.

INDEX

INDEX

A

B

C

D

E

F

G

H

I

J

K

L

M

N

O

P

R

S

T

U

V

W

Y

PROFILE OF THE EDITOR

Crawford B. Thayer

PROFILE OF THE EDITOR

No one in Wisconsin has a firmer grasp on the day-today details of the Black Hawk war of 1832 than Crawford B. Thayer of Fort Atkinson.

Black Hawk is commemorated by several markers throughout southern Wisconsin, but the significance of his exploits and his spirit might have been largely lost if not for the efforts of Crawford Thayer.

In fact, Thayer finds the lore of the Black Hawk war so interesting that he took early retirement as advertising manager of the Jamesway Division of Butler Manufacturing Company to write about it.

Thayer describes his series of books as "an eye-witness account" of Black Hawk's flight up Rock river and across Wisconsin to the Mississippi river, where his band of some 1200 men, women, children, including about 500 warriors, was wiped out at the massacre at Bad Axe river.

"Almost every word in these books is by an active participant in the war, an eye-witness," he said. "In fact, if a person was not actually involved, his remarks do not get into my books."

Thayer said, "I told a friend that there's scarcely a word of mine in the entire eye-witness series, and he said, 'Good!'."

The Black Hawk war series was born in Thayer's mind in 1971 when he became the first director of the popular Fort Atkinson "Black Hawk" pageant, a post he held during its first five formative years. So intrigued was he by the historical content of the pageant—written by Bill Starke, local history buff—and by the reception of the enthusiastic audiences that Thayer felt impelled to research the Black Hawk war thoroughly and to compile, edit, and publish his own books.

"I began to read everything I could find on the war and never stopped," Thayer said.

That's an understatement, for Thayer made the Black Hawk war a third career.

A native of Haverhill, Massachusetts, he earned a Bachelor of Arts degree with excellence in English at Bowdoin College in Brunswick, Maine, where he was also honored as recipient of the Henry Wadsworth Longfellow Graduate Scholarship.

From the University of Iowa at Iowa City, Thayer received a Master of Arts degree in Creative Writing. Here he was named to *Who's Who Among Students in Universities and Colleges*. For three years, he taught at the University, first as Instructor in English, and later, in the School of Journalism.

Thayer received his Master of Arts degree in English Literature from Yale University, where he served as Instructor in English for two years. In New Haven he also served as Director of Public Relations at today's Quinnipiak College.

Thayer came to Wisconsin in 1949 to serve as Director of Publications (and Instructor in English and Journalism) at the University of Wisconsin-Whitewater.

His second career began in 1951 when Thayer joined the advertising department of James Mfg. Co., where he served for 30 years before his early retirement.

Thayer ponders how to stage the 1972 "Black Hawk" pageant with Rock River flooding the stockade replica.

"Ever since I first directed the pageant, I have been gathering Black Hawk war data," he said. "I remember the day I filed my first note. It was dated June 3, 1832. Now I have 17 loose-leaf binders crammed full of words by people who were actually in the Black Hawk war," he said.

His quest for primary source material took Thayer to Springfield, Illinois, where he found original orders and letters written by Brigadier General Henry Atkinson...to the State Historical Society of Wisconsin archives in Madison, Wisconsin, where reminiscences of early settlers who fought or suffered in the war are stored...to the National Archives in Washington, D. C., where much valuable information is buried, waiting to be unearthed. Et cetera...et cetera...et cetera.

"What really made my books possible was Ellen M. Whitney's brilliant editing and publishing of all of the Black Hawk war manuscripts in the archives of the Illinois State Historical Library," Thayer said. In fact, Thayer dedicated his first book to her in appreciation of her outstanding achievement.

"What I've learned from research is that today's trash is tomorrow's treasure," Thayer added.

Thayer's first book, *Hunting A Shadow: The Search for Black Hawk* (1981), details the Black Hawk war as it moves through today's Rock and Jefferson counties, Wisconsin, during the hot, wet Summer of 1832. It reports events experienced both by the Illinois militia, including 23-year-old Abraham Lincoln, and by the regular U. S. Army Infantry units under then-Colonel Zachary Taylor.

Thayer's second book, *The Battle of Wisconsin Heights* (1982), follows the movements of the Illinois and Michigan Territory (Wisconsin) mounted militia volunteers through today's Dane and Dodge counties, Wisconsin. Under the commands of James D. Henry and Henry Dodge, they "disobey" the orders of Brigadier General Henry Atkinson and so "win" the encounter with Black Hawk and his starving band.

Thayer's third book, *Massacre at Bad Axe* (1983), provides an eye-witness account of the pursuit of Black Hawk and his starving people across the Ocooch Mountains to the Mississippi river through today's Sauk, Richland, Vernon, and Crawford counties, Wisconsin. The military and defensive moves of the August 2, 1832, battle on the Mississippi just below Bad Axe river show how an unnecessary massacre decimates Black Hawk's band and brings the four-month-long Black Hawk war to a close...or does it?

Thayer's fourth book, *Menominees in the Black Hawk War* (1984)....

HOW many books?

"My intention," said Thayer, "is to publish eye-witness

accounts of the war annually until the series is completed or my career is, whichever comes first."

Thayer publishes his own books and is thus able to sell at a price considerably less than a publishing house would have to charge. In fact, by being his own publisher, Thayer is able to sell each book for just about half of what it would cost if published through a commercial source.

"I'm not trying to make money," Thayer said. "As soon as I get my investment back, then I put that same money into the publication of the next book. If any one book should fail to sell out, I'd be dead in the water. I'd have to take up senior citizen golf."

Look how ferocious Thayer gets when he gives a speech... and this speech was about the importance of *love*!

Since he is publishing his books independently, Thayer must do his own publicity for selling them. He has a natural flair for public speaking. His animated speeches and wry sense of humor have made him much in demand as a speaker before school groups, youth and senior citizen groups, church groups, service clubs, historical societies, civic groups, and on radio and television talk shows.

Thayer is very happy to share his newly found knowledge about the Black Hawk war by word of mouth as well as by the written word. He averages about 42 speeches per year—most, but not all, about the Black Hawk war. He jokes that he can't afford to pay to speak on his favorite subject, but he'll come for travel expenses only, no fee.

Elementary school youngsters are among Thayer's favorite audiences, but one time a group of fourth graders beat him to the punch-line of one of his quips. He had asked them what the message was on the Black Hawk's bumper sticker as he retreated from Illinois into Wisconsin.

"Escape to Wisconsin," they chorused, quoting the well-known tourist bureau slogan.*

---

* This **Profile of the Editor** makes extensive use of wording from feature articles written and published by Bob Brown in the *Janesville Gazette,* Chris Blumer and Chris Wanie in the *Daily Jefferson County Union,* Bob Mullen in the *LaCrosse Tribune,* Jim Jewell in *The Dodgeville Chronicle,* Lonni Nidy and Pat Peckham in *The Sauk Prairie Star,* Marshall Cook in *Directions,* and John O. Holzhueter in the *Wisconsin Magazine of History.*

Thayer takes a break under his map of Black Hawk's trail through Wisconsin in the Summer of 1832.

BACK COVER:

Black Hawk by George Catlin (1796-1872) on the back cover is reproduced through the courtesy of the National Portrait Gallery, Smithsonian Institution, Washington, D.C. 20560.

Catlin painted this 29″ x 24″ oil on canvas portrait of Black Hawk when Black Hawk was imprisoned at Jefferson Barracks, Missouri, ten miles south of St. Louis, during the winter of 1832-1833, following the Black Hawk war.

Catlin remembered the situation as follows:

"When I painted Black Hawk he was dressed in a plain suit of buckskin, with strings of wampum in his ears and around his neck. He held his medicine-bag, which was the skin of a black hawk from which he had taken his name, and the tail of which made him a fan, which he was almost constantly using."

When Catlin's wild west show went bankrupt in Europe, he lost possession of his *Gallery unique* containing more than 500 paintings of Indians which he had personally painted from life. To make up for the loss, Catlin made copies of his paintings, either from sketches in his notebooks or from memory. The back cover of *Hunting A Shadow: The Search for Black Hawk* shows one such copy. The painting here, however, is the original for which Black Hawk himself posed. Here's how it was saved:

Among Catlin's creditors was Joseph Harrison, owner of the Harrison Boiler Works in Philadelphia, "largest builders of locomotives in the world". Harrison had just completed building and outfitting the railroad from St. Petersburg to Moscow. With $40,000 he stood off Catlin's other creditors in the bankruptcy, then crated and shipped the *Gallery unique* back to Philadelphia, where it was stored on the grounds of the Harrison Boiler Works.

In May, 1879 (fourteen years after the Smithsonian fire which destroyed most of Charles Bird King's Indian portraits), Mrs. Joseph Harrison, widow of Catlin's creditor, turned over the *Gallery unique* to the Smithsonian Institution, as an heirloom for the nation. During the thirty years it was stored on the grounds of the Harrison Boiler Works, there had been a number of fires. In each fire it had been smoked, or doused by the fire companies trying to save it. The costumes, robes, teepees, and other things vulnerable to such care were ruined. Yet 80 percent of the 507 paintings listed in Catlin's catalog for his opening in London were saved ... including this famous painting.

Black Hawk by George Catlin, courtesy of the National Portrait Gallery, Smithsonian Institution, Washington, D.C.

"I would not have fought there, but to gain time for my women and children to cross to an island. A warrior will duly appreciate the embarrassments I labored under—and whatever may be the sentiments of the *white people*, in rela

wil

con